M000274764

THE
SECRETS OF
ABU GHRAIB
REVEALED

RELATED TITLES FROM POTOMAC BOOKS

Getting Away with Torture:
Secret Government, War Crimes, and the Rule of Law
by Christopher H. Pyle

Overcoming the Bush Legacy in Iraq and Afghanistan
by Deepak Tripathi

America's Covert Warriors:
Inside the World of Private Military Contractors
by Shawn Engbrecht

Losing the Golden Hour:
An Insider's View of Iraq's Reconstruction
by James Stephenson

Through Veterans' Eyes:
The Iraq and Afghanistan Experience
by Larry Minear

Wanting War:
Why the Bush Administration Invaded Iraq
by Jeffrey Record

Iraq in Transition:
The Legacy of Dictatorship and the Prospects for Democracy
by Peter J. Munson

THE
SECRETS OF
ABU GHRAIB
REVEALED

American Soldiers on Trial

Christopher Graveline and Michael Clemens

POTOMAC BOOKS, INC.
WASHINGTON, D.C.

Copyright © 2010 by Christopher Graveline and Michael Clemens

Published in the United States by Potomac Books, Inc. All rights reserved. No part of this book may be reproduced in any manner whatsoever without written permission from the publisher, except in the case of brief quotations embodied in critical articles and reviews.

The views expressed in this book are those of the authors and do not represent the views of the U.S. Army, Army Judge Advocate General's Corps, U.S. Attorney's Office–Eastern District of Michigan, Executive Office of U.S. Attorneys, or the U.S. Department of Justice.

Some of the information contained in this book is confidential information that the Army could protect from disclosure pursuant to Army Rules of Professional Conduct for Lawyers, Rule 1.13, Army as Client, and Rule 1.6, Confidentiality of Information. After careful consideration of the information contained in the manuscript, the Army expressly consented to inclusion of this information.

The views expressed in the book by Michael Clemens are those of the author and are not endorsed by his employer, an agency of the federal government.

Library of Congress Cataloging-in-Publication Data
Graveline, Christopher.
    The secrets of Abu Ghraib revealed : American soldiers on trial / Christopher Graveline and Michael Clemens.— 1st ed.
        p. cm.
    Includes bibliographical references and index.
    ISBN 978-1-59797-441-7 (alk. paper)
    1. Courts-martial and courts of inquiry—United States. 2. Prisoners of war—Crimes against—Iraq. 3. Military prisons—Officials and employees—Legal status, laws, etc.—United States. 4. United States—Armed forces—Military police. 5. Abu Ghraib Prison. 6. England, Lynndie—Trials, litigation, etc. 7. Iraq War, 2003– I. Clemens, Michael. II. Title.
    KF7641.G73 2010
    343.73'0143—dc22

                                                                2009053974

Printed in the United States of America on acid-free paper that meets the American National Standards Institute Z39-48 Standard.

Potomac Books, Inc.
22841 Quicksilver Drive
Dulles, Virginia 20166

First Edition

10 9 8 7 6 5 4 3 2 1

Dedicated to:
Staff Sergeant Stephen Martin,
Staff Sergeant Charles Kiser,
Staff Sergeant Darren Cunningham, and
all of the fallen heroes who bravely fought and served in Iraq

Contents

Preface

On April 28, 2004, CBS's *60 Minutes II* gave Americans and the world the first glimpse of the images that would shake our country's undertaking in Iraq, our allies' trust, and many of our countrymen's faith in the military. Longtime CBS News anchor Dan Rather began the segment by warning his audience that the "pictures are difficult to look at."

For months, the photographs were displayed on a daily basis. We saw the American soldiers' smiling faces positioned around stripped Iraqi prisoners. Everyone remembers the thumbs-up photos that depicted soldiers mugging for the camera. No one can forget the iconic photos of the hooded Iraqi standing on a box with wires affixed to his fingers or the prisoner at the end of a leash held by Lynndie England. These images are, unfortunately, seared into our nation's collective memory.

The very words *Abu Ghraib* still evoke intense emotion. Even now, debate rages over the best way to handle allegations of detainee abuse. In spite of numerous investigations conducted by the Department of Defense and the prosecution of eleven enlisted soldiers, questions linger in the public's mind: Why weren't officers prosecuted? Who gave the orders to abuse Iraqi prisoners? Did President George W. Bush and Secretary of Defense Donald Rumsfeld know about or order the torture? Who cares if anyone tortured Iraqi terrorists? Is the U.S. government hiding something about what happened at Abu Ghraib?

This book is intended to bring clarity to these questions. A very small group of people, the Army's prosecution team for these abuses committed at Abu

Ghraib, was privy to all of the evidence, interviews, and trials. As a former major and a master sergeant who both lived the investigation and prosecution of every American soldier involved, we have come forward to relate the facts to you in *The Secrets of Abu Ghraib Revealed: American Soldiers on Trial.*

We have taken our roles in this investigation very seriously. When we saw the photos of naked detainees, we were offended—not only as American citizens, but as citizens of the world. We were offended that soldiers in our Army could have perpetrated these crimes. Mike, in particular, was offended that military policemen and women (MPs) were involved in the abuses. These soldiers were members of his MP Corps. But, despite our initial reactions, we strove to conduct an impartial investigation with one focus—to get to the truth and to bring the individuals who were criminally responsible to justice.

Our only purpose in writing this book is to set the record straight on what occurred at Abu Ghraib during the latter half of 2003. We have endeavored, however imperfectly, to remove our opinions and present the events through the words and memories of the individuals who were firsthand witnesses. All quotes during the in-court proceedings are the exact sworn testimony of each witness. We have no particular partisan agenda of our own and, in fact, are split in our own political loyalties.

We believe that historians, policymakers, and informed readers are best armed with the truth.

U.S. Army Rank Abbreviations

OFFICERS

General (four-star)	GEN
Lieutenant General (three-star)	LTG
Major General (two-star)	MG
Brigadier General (one-star)	BG
Colonel	COL
Lieutenant Colonel	LTC
Major	MAJ
Captain	CPT
First Lieutenant	1LT
Second Lieutenant	2LT
Chief Warrant Officer	CWO

ENLISTED SOLDIERS

Sergeant Major	SGM
Master Sergeant	MSG
First Sergeant	1SG
Sergeant First Class	SFC
Staff Sergeant	SSG
Sergeant	SGT
Corporal	CPL
Specialist	SPC
Private First Class	PFC
Private (E2)	PV2
Private (E1)	PVT

1

SIXTY MINUTES CHANGES EVERYTHING

Seven men stood silently shaking in the narrow prison hallway, unsure what lay in store for them. Clad in a mix of ragged clothing and jumpsuits, their hands were secured with plastic zipcuffs and green burlap sandbags covering their heads. Like their situation, their surroundings were unknown to them. Instead of the tents and plywood floors they knew from the sprawling Camp Ganci compound of the Baghdad Central Confinement Facility (BCCF), Abu Ghraib, they bumped into cinder block walls and felt cool concrete under their feet. The change in environment added to their apprehension.

Earlier that afternoon, on November 7, 2003, a riot over food had broken out among dozens of the detainees at Camp Ganci. One of two outdoor detention facilities consisting of rows of tents surrounded by barbed wire, Camp Ganci primarily housed common criminals alleged to have committed Iraqi-on-Iraqi crimes, such as theft, robbery, and assault. The riot had been ignited by a couple of the detainees and had quickly escalated to dozens pushing, shoving, and yelling as they threw bricks and rocks and pulled up their tent posts. Reportedly, one of them had hit a female military police (MP) soldier in the face with a brick.

The MPs quickly brought the crowd under control and identified seven prisoners as the instigators. To restore order to the camp, the guards relocated the seven men to the "hard-site"—the massive indoor prison standing a few hundred yards from Camp Ganci—where they were to be segregated for ten days as punishment.

Segregated, not interrogated.

Hiadar Sabar Abed Miktub Al-Aboudi, Nori Samir Gunbar Al-Yasseri, Hussein Mohssein Mata Al-Zayiadi, Hazem Khanger Gharib Al-Xa'hari, Ahmed Atya Kata, Mastfa Saleh Mahdi, and Hashim Muhsin Lazim Toby Al-Shuwali were in Abu Ghraib as a result of a variety of charges ranging from burglary to car theft to rape, all awaiting their court dates in the newly configured Iraqi justice system. None were accused of crimes against coalition soldiers or were suspected of having any intelligence value.

SSG Ivan Frederick stood in the 372d MP Company headquarters (HQ) area idly chatting with SPC Jeremy Sivits, one of the company's generator mechanics, when a call came over his handheld radio telling him the seven instigators were being brought into the hard-site. Frederick was not happy. As the hard-site's noncommissioned officer in charge (NCOIC) during the night shift, he did not know where he was going to find enough cells for these men. The minimal resources and the utter lack of input he had received over the movement of detainees always frustrated him. Simmering with a mix of annoyance and anger, he arranged to pick the prisoners up.

"You want some help?" Sivits asked when the call ended.

Even though the young generator mechanic had no MP training, Frederick knew that he could probably use the help, and he liked talking with Sivits, a very affable, young soldier.

"Sure, why don't you come along."

Frederick and Sivits arrived at the hard-site to find the seven detainees already in a large, eight-man holding cell adjacent to Frederick's office in Tier 4. The plan was to move the detainees down into Tier 1, in-process them, and assign them individual cells in Tier 1B. Normally in the hard-site, this movement required one MP per detainee, yet only four soldiers were there to handle the task: Frederick, Sivits, SSG Robert Elliot, and SPC Matthew Wisdom. The soldiers led the hooded, subdued men down into Tier 1A.

Once there, the MPs shoved the detainees into a pile in the middle of the floor. Several other MPs were waiting in the tier, including CPL Charles Graner, the NCOIC of Tier 1A; SFC Shannon Snider; SGT Javal Davis; SPC Sabrina Harman; and SPC Megan Ambuhl. Joining the crew was Graner's girlfriend, SPC Lynndie England, a file clerk in the MP headquarters platoon. England always seemed to be down in the tiers at night. Not being an MP, and according to normal procedure, England was not allowed to handle prisoners. Protocol, however, was not in order that night.

Three of the soldiers quickly left the tier. Snider, the highest-ranking soldier, and Ambuhl went up to the office on the second floor. Elliot, with other duties to attend to, made his way out of the tier and back down the main hallway. It is unlikely that any of the remaining soldiers knew that what was to happen over the next hour would become the source of international scandal and open censure, altering American public support for the military mission in Iraq in the process.

"Heh-dee!" The word (Arabic for "quiet") echoed down the double-tiered hallway. Using his booming drill instructor–like voice, Graner intended to frighten and disorient the detainees. The large, well-built prison guard, standing at slightly less than six feet tall and weighing around two hundred pounds, had already decided that it was time to teach these men a lesson—don't riot in my house.

Harman, a very young soldier with little military experience prior to Iraq, had already retrieved the seven detainees' face sheets that listed their names, their detaining unit, location of detention, and reason for being held. As she scanned the pieces of paper, she noticed that one of the men, Nori Samir Gunbar Al-Yasseri, was detained for rape. Harman separated him from the others and re-cruited Graner's assistance.

Approaching the man from behind, Graner ripped the prisoner's jumpsuit at the waist. Harman pulled out a black permanent marker and scrawled "I'm a rapeist" on his buttocks and upper thigh. The others laughed at Harman's misspelled label.

Inspired by Graner and Harman, Davis and England joined the act. Circling the pile, they began stomping on the detainees' bare hands and feet with their combat boots. The hooded prisoners groaned loudly and recoiled in pain as the two soldiers lifted their boots six inches off the ground and brought their weight down. At six-foot-two and weighing 220 pounds, Davis stepped back a few feet and threw himself atop the pile, landing heavily on the unsuspecting prisoners. After a second leap, he resumed punishment with his boots.

Suddenly, a loud voice rang out.

"Knock it off!" shouted Snider from the top tier, looking down as he made a slashing motion across his throat. The strong, authoritative voice startled all of the soldiers below. Sivits whirled around, shocked to find that it had come from Snider, a relatively diminutive man. Davis, not immediately seeing Snider above him, scanned the hallway trying to figure out who had barked the order. His gaze stopped on Specialist Wisdom who was standing on the bottom tier a few feet away.

Wisdom, a twenty-year-old MP, took advantage of the pause in Davis' beating to ask, "Sergeant Davis, what if you break one of their toes or something?"

"Were you the one telling me to stop?" retorted Davis.

"No, it was Sergeant Snider," Wisdom said, pointing to the top tier. Snider, however, had already stepped out of view. Irritated, Davis stormed out of the tier, leaving Frederick, Graner, England, Sivits, Wisdom, and Harman with the anguished detainees in the pile.

After the brief break in the action, Graner took the lead. A seasoned correctional officer, Graner had eight years of experience as a prison guard in the Pennsylvania correctional system and three years of prior service as a Marine MP during Operation Desert Storm. The other soldiers naturally deferred to him because of his experience and commanding personality. Prompting Harman and England to pull out their cameras, he started posing for pictures with the human pile. Harman snapped two quick photos of Graner grinning against his "props" with his thumbs up, and England took two more of Graner flexing his biceps on top of the pile.

Warming to the camera, Graner pulled one of the hooded detainees up by the neck, cradled the prisoner's head between his elbow and upper arm, and posed with his fist cocked back as if ready to deliver a blow. Sivits, Frederick, and Harman flashed away. Graner dropped the man back to the ground without hitting him. By this point, all of the soldiers were laughing—all except Wisdom. As Graner dropped the first detainee back on the pile, he lifted another detainee up by the hood and slammed his fist into the man's temple. The zipcuffed detainee slumped to the floor.

Sivits hurried over to the man and lifted his hood. The prisoner's eyes had rolled back in his head, and he was unconscious.

"Damn, that hurt," Graner said, laughing, as he strode away, shaking his hand in the air.

Frederick walked over to Hussein Mohssein Mata Al-Zayiadi, who he believed threw the brick at the female MP during the riot.

"Watch this," Frederick told the others as he traced an *X* on Al-Zayiadi's chest with his finger. Pulling his fist all the way back, he punched the unsuspecting man squarely in the chest. The blow propelled Al-Zayiadi backward, dropping him to his knees as he struggled for breath.

The blow caught the other soldiers by surprise. England and Sivits hurried to check on Al-Zayiadi, both worried that he was seriously hurt. After cutting the zipcuffs off the detainee, Sivits lifted his hood and motioned to him to take deep breaths. England asked if he wanted water by gesturing with her hands. They called for an asthma inhaler, and Ambuhl, who had been upstairs in the office between Tier 1A and 1B, brought it down after calling for a medic.

Wisdom had seen enough. He left the tier and headed to find his team leader, SGT Robert Jones. Although he had just returned from two weeks of R&R in the United States, Wisdom had been with the 372d since the beginning of its deployment. He had never seen anything like the scene that was unfolding in the hard-site, and it disgusted him.

Jones, a soldier with many years of police and combat experience, including six years of active duty in the Marine Corps, three additional years in the Army Reserve, and a civilian career as a City of Baltimore police officer, was on duty in Guard Tower 5. Wisdom related what he had seen, beginning with Davis stomping on hands and toes and ending with Graner's and Frederick's assaults.

"Go back to work and I'll handle it," Jones assured him. He believed Wisdom had probably witnessed a justified use of force against aggressive detainees but had misinterpreted it due to his age and inexperience. In Jones' experience, it was always best to give your fellow soldiers and police officers the benefit of the doubt when it came to the use of force.

Back in Tier 1A, the "fun" was only beginning. Undeterred by the scare with Al-Zayiadi, Graner and Frederick began performing strip searches, a common practice in any correctional setting when receiving new detainees. Sivits helped cut the zipcuffs from the men's wrists; then Graner stripped them naked and began to position the nude detainees against the wall without actually searching them. Instead, he paired the men: one on his knees facing the wall and the second squatting on the back of the first. The men were completely naked but for the hoods over their heads.

England and Harman resumed the photo sessions. Harman snapped pictures as England pointed derisively at one of the men's genitals with one hand while giving a thumbs-up with her other hand. The two female soldiers laughed at the men who had become the objects of their sexual taunts.

Graner dragged the hooded men to where England and Harman stood. He moved Al-Yasseri, already marked with "I'm a rapeist," in front of the other naked men who were still kneeling and squatting against the wall. England leaned in for another picture, smiling broadly as she pointed to the ridicule written on the prisoner's buttocks. Harman snapped a quick picture and took some short video segments with her digital camera.

After the men were stripped and freed from their zipcuffs, Graner dragged them to the middle of the floor. He positioned the first three on their hands and knees and then guided two of the others to kneel on top as he began to form a makeshift pyramid. Initially uncertain of what Graner was doing, his fellow soldiers soon found the scene hilarious. The remaining hooded detainees cowered against the wall, unaware of what was happening. With the pyramid complete and all seven prisoners stacked in the pile, Harman and Frederick snapped more photos. Frederick took a picture of the front of the pyramid, capturing Harman with her camera in the background as she prepared to take a photo from the back. The soldiers could hardly resist this prop. Frederick captured Harman hugging the pile with Graner posing behind her, his thumbs up, and broad grins across both of their faces. Harman took a picture of Graner and England embracing and smiling beside the pyramid. Their laughter echoed throughout the concrete tier. After about ten minutes, the prisoners began slipping from the pile, and the fun was momentarily over.

Shortly after midnight, Frederick and Graner picked up the prisoners and lined them up against the wall. Frederick lifted the sandbag from one of the detainee's heads and, taking the man's hand, gestured for him to masturbate by moving the detainee's hand up and down his penis. The prisoner continued the movement after Frederick let go. Frederick laughed, surprised that the man continued. Graner forced other detainees to do the same. Soon an entire line of hooded, naked men stood against the wall moving their hands in a forced act of masturbation.

Graner smiled and turned to Lynndie England: "Here's your birthday present."

Graner grabbed his camera while England posed in front of the men with a cigarette hanging out of her cockeyed smile, flashing her now infamous double thumbs-up. At midnight, she had turned twenty-one.

By this point, Sivits and Harman began to feel uneasy about the situation. Sivits tried to retreat into one of the cells and stay out of the main hallway to ensure that he did not end up in one of the masturbation photos. It finally dawned on him that Graner, Frederick, and England had crossed the line.

As some of the hooded detainees continued to masturbate, Frederick, Graner, and England decided to reposition the others. They brought two of the prisoners into the center of the hallway, placing one man on his knees and the second man directly in front of him, giving the appearance that the men were engaged in oral sex. The MPs quickly guided two more into a similar pose. This scene, of course, provided another perfect "photo op." Al-Zayiadi, the man punched earlier by Frederick, was one of the prisoners placed above his fellow prisoner. Deeply humiliated, he could not believe what was happening. All he could think was, *How can I possibly face my family, friends, and relatives after such an act?*

Wisdom returned to the hard-site to look for Sergeant Elliot regarding another duty. He had calmed down and was convinced that Jones would handle things appropriately within the chain of command. As he walked past Tier 1A, he looked down the hallway and witnessed what was happening to the detainees. The only soldier he saw in the tier was Frederick, who walked toward Wisdom and shouted, "Look what these animals will do if you leave them alone for two minutes!" Wisdom heard England shout excitedly, "He's getting hard!"

Disgusted yet again, Wisdom went directly to Jones at the guard tower. This time, Jones knew that whatever the young MP had witnessed had nothing to do with unruly prisoners or a justified use of force.

"You stay here," Jones told Wisdom as he went to find Frederick.

Meanwhile, Sivits looked for any opportunity to leave the tier. Although Harman had gone upstairs to the second-floor office, Sivits still hung back in one of the cells. Harman and Ambuhl returned to ask Frederick for permission to use the phones and computers at the Morale, Welfare & Recreation facility. When Frederick granted them permission, Sivits saw his chance to slip out as well.

As Sivits reached the gate to leave Tier 1A, Frederick yelled after him.

"You didn't see shit!"

Sivits nodded nervously and left, relieved to escape the depraved scene. With the group dispersing and the fun coming to an end, Frederick retrieved some jumpsuits, and Graner brought the prisoners down to Tier 1B and put them in segregation cells.

Jones finally caught up to Frederick to confront the NCOIC about Wisdom's reports. Nose to nose with Frederick, he aggressively pressed the staff sergeant for answers.

"What is going on down there? How can you jeopardize Wisdom's safety and career like that? If this is true . . . ," Jones paused looking at Frederick for a denial. "Is it true? Is it true?!?"

Frederick looked at Jones stone-faced. "What do you want?"

Since their deployment began, Jones had taken Wisdom under his wing, trying to protect him from the corrupting influence of some of the older sergeants in the 372d who Jones viewed as unprofessional. "Sergeant, I never want Wisdom to come down here and work with you again."

Unfazed, Frederick coolly replied, "Fine. Wisdom can work with you."

Unsatisfied with this conversation, Jones found Staff Sergeant Elliot, Frederick's second-in-charge, to report Wisdom's account of prisoner abuse. Elliot looked incredulously at Jones, seeming unwilling to believe Wisdom.

"Show me proof," Elliot told Jones.

Not having anything but Wisdom's word, Jones walked away. Still, he had Frederick's concession that Wisdom could now work with him; that problem had been solved. It was over.

✦

April 28, 2004. CBS's *60 Minutes II* gave Americans, and the world, the first glimpse of the images that would shake our country's undertaking in Iraq, our allies' trust, and many of our countrymen's faith in the military. Longtime CBS News anchor Dan Rather began the segment by warning his audience that the "pictures are difficult to look at."

Even with that warning, few were prepared for what followed: A young, female soldier holding a naked Iraqi man on the end of a leash. The same female soldier with a cigarette hanging out of her mouth, giving a thumbs-up and pointing at naked Iraqi men as they masturbated. A hooded man standing on a box with wires hanging from his hands. Naked men stacked in a pyramid with uniformed American soldiers smiling in the background.

As the photos flashed across the screen, Rather explained that with the revelation of these photos the U.S. Army had started an investigation, six soldiers now faced courts-martial charges, and their chain of command possibly faced the end of their military careers. In an attempt to provide context, the seasoned reporter interviewed BG Mark Kimmitt, a spokesman for the coalition forces in Iraq, and Staff Sergeant Frederick, one of the soldiers charged with the abuses. Their statements could not have been more opposed.

"Frankly, I think all of us are disappointed at the actions of a few," Kimmitt stated emphatically. "What would I tell the people of Iraq? This is wrong. This is reprehensible, but this is not representative of the 150,000 soldiers that are over here. I'd say the same thing to the American people. Don't judge your Army based on the actions of a few."

Frederick saw things quite differently. "We had no support, no training whatsoever. And I kept asking my chain of command for certain things, like rules and regulations, and it just . . . it just wasn't happening."

Rather read from Frederick's letters and e-mails that supported the prison guard's claims that he was helping U.S. interrogators. "Military intelligence has encouraged and told us, 'Great job.' They usually don't allow others to watch them interrogate, but since they like the way I run the prison, they've made an exception. We help getting them to talk with the way we handle them. We've had a very high rate with our style of getting them to break. They usually end up breaking within hours."

In the days that followed, outrage swept the world, leaving the top echelons of the U.S. government and military backpedaling. The editorial pages of American newspapers became clarion calls for immediate action. "RUMSFELD MUST GO." "THE NEW IRAQ CRISIS; DONALD RUMSFELD SHOULD GO." The international reaction was equally vehement. "THE LIBERATORS ARE WORSE THAN THE DICTATORS." "THIS IS THE STRAW THAT BROKE THE CAMEL'S BACK FOR AMERICA."

America struggled for answers. When pressed to address the photos, President George W. Bush quickly condemned them as "abhorrent" and vowed during interviews with the Arab press that "there will be a full investigation . . . we will find the truth . . . the world will see the investigation and justice will be served."

✦

With camera shutters clicking wildly, five men took their seats behind a long, rectangular table. The two civilians and three uniformed men were top officials in the Department of Defense (DoD): Secretary of Defense (SECDEF) Donald Rumsfeld; Chairman of the Joint Chiefs GEN Richard Myers; Secretary of the Army Les Brownlee; Chief of Staff of the Army GEN Peter Schoomaker; and the deputy commander of the U.S. Central Command (CENTCOM), LTG Lance Smith. They came before the U.S. Senate on May 7, 2004, to testify about the photos. The mood in the hearing room was solemn. Everyone wanted answers. The world was watching.

The senior senators from both parties expressed their dismay. Chairman of the committee and former secretary of the Navy, senator John Warner (R-VA) started, speaking slowly. "I have had the privilege of being associated with and, more importantly, learning from the men and women of the armed forces for close to sixty years of my life, and I can say that the facts that I now have from a number of sources represent to me as serious an issue of military misconduct as I have ever observed. These reports could also seriously affect this country's relationships with other nations, the conduct of the war against terrorism, and place in jeopardy the men and women of the armed forces wherever they are serving in the world."

The senior minority senator, Senator Carl Levin (D-MI), took the chain of command to task. "As we seek to bring stability and democracy to Iraq and to fight terrorism globally, our greatest asset as a nation is the moral values that we stand for. Those values have been compromised. To begin the process of restoring them, the people involved who carried out or who authorized or suggested that we should, quote, 'loosen prisoners up' or, quote, 'make sure they get the treatment' must be held accountable. In other words, those abusive actions do not appear to be aberrant conduct by individuals, but part of a conscious method of extracting information. If true, the planners of this process are at least as guilty as those who carried out the abuses.

"It is essential that our nation at the highest levels apologize directly to the victims and to the Iraqi people as a whole for these actions. But words alone are not sufficient. Prompt and decisive action, which establishes responsibility and holds people accountable, is essential here. It will also, hopefully, convince the world that our free and open society does not condone and will not tolerate this depraved behavior."

After these dramatic opening salvos, Secretary Rumsfeld addressed the panel of senators. "Mr. Chairman, members of the committee, in recent days there has been a good deal of discussion about who bears responsibility for the terrible activities that took place at Abu Ghraib. These events occurred on my watch. As secretary of defense, I am accountable for them and I take full responsibility. To those Iraqis who were mistreated by members of the U.S. armed forces, I offer my deepest apology. It was inconsistent with the values of our nation. It was inconsistent with the teachings of the military, to the men and women of the armed forces. And it was certainly fundamentally un-American.

"Mr. Chairman, that's why this hearing today is important. It's why the actions we take in the days and weeks ahead are so important."

2

GOOD LUCK IN IRAQ

While it is often said that a picture is worth a thousand words, these pictures instead posed a thousand questions. Who were these soldiers? Who were these Arab men in the photos? Why did anyone take these pictures? Who was in charge here? Was this really a means of obtaining intelligence as the soldiers claimed?

All of these questions flashed through CPT Chris Graveline's mind as he watched the *60 Minutes II* segment in his Heidelberg, Germany, apartment. A lawyer in the U.S. Army's Judge Advocate General's (JAG) Corps, Graveline was the V Corps' senior trial counsel (or prosecutor). He and his family had been stationed in Heidelberg for about a year. They had grown accustomed to watching their favorite American television shows on the Armed Forces Network a day or two after they aired in the States. While neither Graveline nor his wife, Colleen, were regular viewers of *60 Minutes II*, there was already considerable buzz throughout the military channels that this particular show was going to have significant implications for the military. Yet, nothing prepared them for what they saw.

Maybe the defense counsel interviewed on 60 Minutes II *was right,* Graveline thought. *Maybe these photos were some bizarre military intelligence [MI] techniques I have never heard of—why else would any normal soldier pose in these types of photos?*

At the end of the segment, Graveline turned to Colleen and said, "I don't know what to make of those pictures, but I pity the trial counsel who's going to have to prosecute this case. What a mess that's going to be!"

✦

The sun shone brightly on a picturesque early summer day in Charlottesville, Virginia. Having just completed their specialized mid-career training, or "grad course," sixty-five newly minted majors of the U.S. Army's JAG Corps sat in rows wearing dark green dress uniforms adorned with brass and ribbons, ready to embark on their new assignments. Some were heading to jobs in Europe or Korea, while others were moving to units that were preparing to deploy to the combat zones of Afghanistan and Iraq. MAJ Michael Holley looked forward to his new assignment as an instructor at the Judge Advocate General's Legal Center and School in Charlottesville, teaching other military lawyers on the sprawling University of Virginia campus. After coming off fast-paced assignments with the XVIII Airborne Corps at Fort Bragg, North Carolina, and being a defense counsel in Korea, he was ready for a more normal, less hectic schedule that would allow him more time to spend with his family.

As part of the ceremony, each graduate walked across the stage, received a diploma, and shook hands with The Judge Advocate General of the Army (TJAG), MG Thomas Romig. In turn, Holley collected his diploma and headed toward the smiling general.

"Holley, I understand that you are going to Iraq," Romig said as he reached out his hand to the larger man.

Holley did a double take. "Sir, not to my knowledge."

Romig appeared somewhat confused. Apparently, Romig thought that Holley already knew about his new temporary assignment as the lead prosecutor of the Abu Ghraib abuse cases.

Standing next to Romig was BG Scott Black, who quickly sized up the awkward situation between the two-star general and the young major. "We're sending you to work on some prosecutions. It should only take about ninety days."

Holley stammered that he would love to be involved and help in any way. But before he could learn anything more about his surprise assignment, he was nudged along by the other graduates filing onto the stage.

The ceremony continued with Holley's mind racing as he stared blankly at the stage. *Iraq? What cases could they be sending me to work on? How are Renee and the kids going to take this?*

As the ceremony wrapped up, Holley moved to the front of the stage and approached LTC Jim Garrett, the chair of the criminal law department at the

JAG school, the man Holley expected to be his next boss. Garrett, a balding man with an athletic build, had an apprehensive look on his face. "Please tell me that TJAG didn't just tell you that you were going to Iraq."

"Yes, sir, he did," responded Holley.

Sighing deeply, Garrett said that the decision had been made to put him on the Abu Ghraib cases, but the plan had been to inform him later that day. Holley started peppering Garrett with questions about what exactly his mission would entail, when he would be leaving, and how long he would be in Iraq. Garrett stated that Holley would be taking over as the lead prosecutor of the Abu Ghraib cases. The tasking was for ninety days and was to begin within days, but Garrett anticipated it would take much longer.

This announcement caught Holley entirely off guard. "Should I tell my wife anything at this point?"

Garrett laughed. "Yes, I think you should since she's standing right behind you."

✦

It had been weeks since Graveline sat in his living room watching the *60 Minutes II* segment on Abu Ghraib. Since then, he had read a few press accounts and editorials concerning the abuse scandal but had not given the cases any serious thought. Now, the morning of May 19, Graveline stood in the daily 6:30 a.m. formation with his fellow soldiers in the headquarters company. The unit assembled five days a week at this time to put out the day's announcements and conduct physical training. The group had already done some stretching and light calisthenics, but Wednesday morning meant that the main exercise would be a four-mile run through the local German community.

As the formation broke up to begin the run, Graveline's supervisor, MAJ Brad Huestis, caught up with him and gave his usual cheerful morning greeting. Huestis and Graveline ran together for at least part of the route on most days, discussing upcoming cases or the sports scene back in the States. Their conversation would be very different this day.

"Chris, how would you feel about deploying down to Iraq to help out on these Abu Ghraib cases?"

Graveline stopped short. "Seriously? I would love it." No sooner had those words come out of his mouth than questions rushed into his head. *What will my role be? What stages are the investigation and cases in? How many cases are there? What are the problems with the cases?* Adding another twist, he and Colleen had just found out that she was pregnant with their second child. *When would I leave? How long would I be gone? What will this mean for Colleen?* Huestis seemed to sense his young friend's unspoken concerns. Unfortunately, he did not have many answers.

The official notice came later that evening from V Corps' deputy staff judge advocate, LTC Richard Gross. "They want you down there as soon as possible," Gross stated. "Right now, they are saying that it's going to be a quick temporary duty, so you should be home by Labor Day or the end of September at the latest. Definitely let us know what we can do for Colleen." He paused, measuring up his young officer. "Don't worry. We'll be sure to give her whatever help she may need."

After a frenetic week maneuvering through military bureaucracy and packing the needed gear, Graveline, Colleen, and their fifteen-month-old son drove to the Rhein-Main Air Base in Frankfurt, where he was to catch a flight to Iraq. It was May 25, 2004, the young couple's second wedding anniversary. The plane to Balad, Iraq, was scheduled to take off in the mid-afternoon, but, as is usually the case with U.S. Air Force flights, the trip was delayed several times. The couple celebrated their anniversary while waiting in the stripped-down military airport and feeding their young toddler dinner out of the vending machine: a feast of M&M's, Skittles, and Diet Coke.

After waiting for several hours and through multiple flight cancellations and postponements, Colleen and their son left for home, still unclear when her husband would actually fly out. As his wife and son drove away, Graveline lay down on the floor with his duffel bag under his head. *Might as well get some sleep,* he thought.

Yet, his thoughts came back to the cases. Nothing he had seen or read so far had convinced him that these photos were not part of intelligence gathering gone wrong. *How far up the chain of command does this go?* Graveline wondered.

An announcement over the muffled PA system shook him out of his thoughts. His flight was ready to board. It was 4:00 a.m.

✦

"You need to leave immediately."

Holley kept replaying the conversation with Lieutenant Colonel Garrett over in his head. While the deployment had come as a shock to him, Holley was no stranger to the sometimes chaotic life a soldier leads. At age thirty-three, he had been in the Army for more than eleven years, starting his career as an MP officer in the 1st Cavalry Division, Fort Hood, Texas, and transitioning into the JAG Corps after attending law school at Texas Tech University.

Although he had deployed once as an MP to Panama for four months, this would be the first time the Texan deployed to a war zone. He knew it would not be easy to brace his kids for a sudden and indefinite absence. That weekend was the three-day Memorial Day weekend, and Holley tried to spend as much time as possible with his family. However, before he headed off to Iraq, he knew he needed to dig deeper into Abu Ghraib—and the known facts were at Fort Bragg.

Fort Bragg is the second largest Army post in the United States and home of the 16th MP Brigade. The Sixteenth had deployed to Iraq in January 2004 and had become the higher headquarters for the 372d MP Company, the company to which the accused soldiers belonged. Consequently, the 16th MP Brigade was responsible for the soldiers implicated in the abuse: finding them temporary duties, housing them, and taking care of their needs. When PFC Lynndie England, the most infamous of the soldiers, discovered she was pregnant, the Sixteenth sent her back to Fort Bragg to the remnants of their unit left behind.[*] With England at Fort Bragg, the legal office there began to compile and review the investigations related to her case.

Even though Fort Bragg was slightly over a four-hour drive from Charlottesville, Holley decided to make the drive in order to obtain his own copy of the preliminary Criminal Investigation Division (CID) investigation into the abuse. Wanting to spend more time with his oldest son to help ease the deployment news, Holley brought him along for the ride. The two left the day after Memorial Day, June 1, 2004.

When they arrived, Holley discovered that CID had already amassed more than a thousand pages in documentary evidence and witness statements. LTC Bob Cotell, the military justice chief of XVIII Airborne Corps, handed Holley

---

[*] Lynndie England had been demoted from specialist to private first class for a military discipline infraction, failure to obey a lawful order.

a binder of papers ten inches thick. Their office had just charged England, but they still had much reading and investigating to do.

These cases aren't going to be over anytime soon, Holley realized. He began to wonder how long it would be before he saw his wife and kids again.

✦

Graveline arrived at Victory Base, Baghdad, at approximately 11:00 p.m. on May 27. Landing at such a late hour, he hitched a ride from the Baghdad International Airport in the back of an open-air Humvee and made his way to the visitors' trailers on North Victory Base. Inside the trailer, there were two beds, two wall lockers, and a nightstand between the beds. He piled his bags into a trailer and hit the bed for his first good sleep in three days.

The next morning, Graveline awoke to the realization that he had no idea where to find the JAG office. Communications with the legal team in Iraq had been sporadic at best and virtually nonexistent the last few days. All Graveline knew was that he had to find the legal office for Multi-National Corps–Iraq (MNC-I). He hoped that if he started walking toward the center of the base someone could point him in the right direction; he did not realize that Victory Base is one of the largest and most expansive U.S. military bases in Iraq and houses thousands of U.S. and other coalition soldiers. Sitting a few kilometers north of Baghdad, it encompasses Saddam Hussein's Al Faw Palace complex and sits next to the Baghdad International Airport—a maze of dirt and paved roads connecting a number of post exchanges (PX), gyms, laundries, dining facilities, and even a Burger King.

Graveline threw his loaded backpack around his shoulders, grabbed his two duffel bags, and started lugging them down the sandy gravel road. As he began his trek, a young soldier stopped him.

"Sir, where you heading?"

"I'm looking for the MNC-I headquarters and JAG office. Do you happen to know where I can find them?"

"Sure, sir. Jump in." The soldier pointed to the Humvee that he was climbing into. "I think they're over at the palace."

The Al Faw Palace sits at the heart of Victory Base. Surrounded by a large man-made lake and Romanesque villas, the three-story palace once served as a hunting and fishing lodge for Hussein and his sons. As Graveline walked through the twenty-foot-high main doors into the circular foyer at the center of the palace, he was amazed by what he saw. Gold leaf adorned the top of the marble walls, which glittered by the light of an enormous glass chandelier, easily sixty feet wide. White marble staircases spiraled opposite one another in the foyer, and dozens of soldiers, dressed in desert camouflage uniforms, moved quickly along its polished marble floors. A six-foot-wide wooden throne embossed with gold was tucked up against one side of the foyer, and Arabic engravings in marble and granite bordered the thirty-foot-tall hallways that radiated from it. Hussein and his sons had had this opulent palace constructed just a few miles away from the decaying streets of Baghdad, and the palace—built on the backs of his poor subjects—demonstrated how much Saddam Hussein took from his people to indulge his extravagant tastes. Ironically, the palace was dedicated to the battle for a southern town that Hussein had recaptured from the Iranians, namely to "commemorate" the more than thirty thousand soldiers who had lost their lives to secure his domain.

Tucked away in the rear of the palace, the MNC-I JAG office occupied a large room featuring a vaulted, ornately decorated, concave ceiling; wall-length windows covering three-quarters of the room; and two stone verandas stretching out of either side that offered expansive views of the lake to the north and Baghdad to the south. The rumor among the soldiers in the palace was that this breathtaking room had been Hussein's bedroom.

Instead of Hussein's elaborate furniture, the room was now filled with blue foam-board walls that created small, individual cubicles for roughly forty attorneys and paralegals. Graveline's eyes surveyed the scene. *Surely Saddam could never have dreamed that U.S. military lawyers would someday occupy this space.* Located in the back corner was the one "office," two blue walls set up with no windows, reserved for the staff judge advocate, COL Karl Goetzke. A middle-aged man with graying hair and thick glasses, Goetzke was the principal legal adviser for the three-star general in charge of MNC-I, LTG Thomas Metz.

V Corps, the American unit based out of Heidelberg, Germany, under the command of LTG William Wallace and then LTG Ricardo Sanchez, directed the initial invasion and mission in Iraq. III Corps, Metz's unit, relieved V Corps in January 2004. However, in its efforts to meet the situation on the ground, the U.S. Army readjusted its structure in Iraq, keeping Sanchez and his staff as the lead command, Combined Joint Task Force 7 (CJTF-7), and supplementing them with Metz's staff and corps, MNC-I. While all the photos of the detainee abuse had been taken prior to their arrival, Metz and his staff were left to deal with the aftermath.

As Graveline walked into the main room, Goetzke was preparing to head out for a meeting. He welcomed Graveline and then passed the young attorney off to his deputy, LTC Barry Robinson. A reservist who worked as a civil litigator in the U.S. Attorney's Office in San Antonio, Texas, Robinson was a short man with a cheerful smile and circular glasses that accentuated his round features. "Let's go meet the rest of the crew," Robinson suggested.

Graveline still did not know what his exact role was going to be and did not want to be the outsider coming in to completely change or take over the prosecutions. He heard that another attorney was arriving as well, a MAJ Mike Holley, but he had no idea who he was or what his job was supposed to be either.

While most of the attorneys worked in the palace, the criminal lawyers, both the prosecutors and defense counsel, worked out of trailers about a half mile away. The JAGs had set up a courtroom in a small, circular stone building sitting off the main lake. It had previously served as a house for the imam who tended the mosque on the palace grounds. Robinson escorted Graveline into the third trailer. Graveline assessed the contents of the twelve-foot-wide trailer: two bookcases along the side walls overflowing with binders, books, and boxes full of crackers and candy; a foot locker; two desks facing the door; and two empty chairs facing the back wall. Behind the desks sat CPT Steven Charles "Chuck" Neill and CPT Kyson Johnson.

Neill, a baby-faced attorney with blond hair cut close to the scalp, was the chief of military justice for MNC-I. He had been a prosecutor at Fort Sam Houston in San Antonio, Texas, and a defense counsel for the 1st Cavalry Division at Fort Hood prior to becoming the senior prosecutor for III Corps before the deployment. Now, he was responsible for overseeing all of the pretrial and posttrial cases that fell to the MNC-I. A coffee lover, Neill always had a pot brewing, and the smell of gourmet coffee filled the tiny trailer.

Johnson was tall and thin, with angular features. He, like Robinson, was a reservist attorney who in his civilian practice was a prosecutor in Grayson County, Texas. Johnson had been activated for approximately twenty-two months at that point, having first served for more than a year at III Corps in Texas and then deploying with the corps in January 2004. Johnson had been one of the two prosecutors handling the Abu Ghraib cases but was preparing to redeploy and return to civilian life.

While Johnson and Neill were both very positive about the cases, they recognized that it was still going to be some time before the cases were wrapped up. The row of three-inch binders lining the bookcases, each full to capacity, told Graveline that he had a long road ahead of him in order to get up to speed.

Neill and Johnson explained that Colonel Goetzke was preparing to redeploy and was going to be replaced as the staff judge advocate by COL Clyde "Butch" Tate. Goetzke had been deployed in Kuwait for more than a year during 2003 and now had been in Iraq for five months. He had been selected for the U.S. Army senior staff college and would be leaving the first week of June. Tate was due to arrive within the next few days.

The two prosecutors who had been shepherding the cases from the beginning had been CPT John McCabe, the prosecutor for the 16th MP Brigade, and Johnson. While the Sixteenth was not due to return stateside until the end of the year, the JAG office at Fort Bragg had arranged prior to the deployment to rotate another attorney in for McCabe halfway through the deployment. Thus, both McCabe and Johnson were leaving within the next two weeks. MNC-I only had two other prosecutors currently on the ground, and neither were experienced enough to undertake the Abu Ghraib cases. While Neill did have the experience, he was actively engaged in numerous other cases. All of these circumstances had prompted Colonel Goetzke to ask for additional help: Major Holley was coming in to take over as the lead prosecutor, and Graveline was to fill Johnson's role as cocounsel.

The investigation had been opened on January 14, 2004, after a compact disc filled with pictures of prisoner abuse was slipped anonymously under CID's door at the BCCF, Abu Ghraib. In March, after the initial investigation, seven soldiers were brought up on a variety of charges to include conspiracy to maltreat, maltreatment of detainees, false official statement, and indecent acts. There were six soldiers in Iraq: SSG Ivan Frederick, SGT Javal Davis, CPL Charles Graner, SPC Jeremy Sivits, SPC Megan Ambuhl, and SPC Sabrina Harman. The remaining soldier, PFC Lynndie England, was charged at Fort Bragg. Three of the

Iraq six (Davis, Sivits, and Harman) had made incriminating statements to CID investigators, and Sivits had pleaded guilty and was willing to testify against the remaining five soldiers. All were represented by civilian attorneys located back in the States and military defense counsel spread throughout Iraq. Three of the cases (Graner, Davis, and Frederick) had a motion hearing scheduled for June 21, and Ambuhl's case was pending a forwarding decision by Lieutenant General Metz. Harman was still awaiting a pretrial probable cause determination, known as an Article 32 investigation in the military, akin to a preliminary hearing in civilian courts.

As their conversation continued, the door opened and SSG Corey Brann burst into the trailer.

"Is this the hired gun we've been hearing about?" Brann joked.

The NCOIC of military justice for III Corps, Brann assisted Neill in organizing the pending courts-martial; coordinated travel for the military judge, attorneys, and witnesses into and out of Iraq; and finalized the necessary posttrial paperwork. Brann was a big personality, proclaiming himself as "a person who makes things happen," and the consummate old-time politician, trading favors with his contacts in the other staff sections to get what was needed for the JAGs.

"We need to get you set up with a cot and a computer," he said. Just as quickly as he arrived, he was off on a mission.

"So, where should I start?" inquired Graveline. "How big is the CID case file?"

Johnson and Neill exchanged glances and chuckled. "A little over a thousand pages," replied Neill. "And there's also this administrative investigation done by Brigadier General [Antonio] Taguba that has over one hundred annexes. It's about three thousand pages. So, it's really up to you where you want to begin."

Despite his relative youth at thirty-one, Graveline knew that high-profile criminal prosecutions were an entirely different undertaking than most. During his law school years at Franklin Pierce Law Center in Concord, New Hampshire, Graveline interned at the federal prosecutor's office. He was hired to help two assistant U.S. attorneys—David Vicinanzo and Michael Connolly—prosecute six Boston men for numerous bank and armored car robberies that stretched up and down the East Coast. The trial lasted four months and drew significant regional attention since the men had murdered two armored car guards in cold blood. During this time, Graveline learned much about how to prepare, strategize, and present complex cases.

Moreover, he was no stranger to prosecuting cases with media interest in the military. Graveline had joined the Army JAG after law school, and only four months into his first assignment at the 101st Airborne Division, he had been placed on the team prosecuting two soldiers responsible for beating to death a homosexual soldier, PFC Barry Winchell. That case garnered national media attention; spawned investigative pieces by *60 Minutes* and *Rolling Stone*, among others; and prompted increased public debate of both homosexuals serving in the military and the status of hate crime legislation in the military.

Graveline knew these prosecutions were going to be scrutinized from every angle, and it would be imperative for the prosecutors to be well prepared, to know the facts better than the defense counsel, and to anticipate an issue before it was raised. Most importantly, though, in high-profile cases, prosecutors had to ensure that the process was exceedingly fair.

Don't prosecute in fear. You've got the facts. Give the defense everything it asks for and anything it doesn't ask for that you can think of. In the end, you'll win because you have the facts.

With a worldwide audience, the defense counsel would invariably put the "system" on trial—anything to keep the focus off their clients. The prosecutors' job was to guarantee that the process was fair, to give the defense any evidence that they needed, and to keep the trial directed on the one thing the defense did not want to talk about—their clients' conduct.

As Graveline read the various witness statements, he periodically asked Johnson questions about the witnesses and their background information. Johnson put the assorted characters into the context of the overall case and filled in details not found in the sworn statements, especially his opinions about various witnesses' believability. These sessions went on for the next several days. Graveline would start reading in the morning around 7:30 and stay late into the night. After a few days of this routine, Graveline looked up from a binder.

"What about the pictures? Where are those?"

Neill handed him a compact disc. "They're all on here."

"How many are there?"

"It's in the hundreds."

"How bad are they?"

Graveline had read the news accounts. Secretary of Defense Rumsfeld had warned that the worst pictures had yet to be seen by the public. Graveline wondered how much worse the abuse could be.

Neill and Johnson downplayed that notion. They both agreed that the photos being displayed in the media were representative of the remaining abuse photos. Both of the officers thought there had been a general misconception that the Army was hiding details of the entire investigation.

"CID started its investigation on January fourteenth when it got the photos," Neill stated. "It didn't take the command long to recognize how bad these pictures were. In fact, by the sixteenth Brigadier General Kimmitt, the command spokesman, announced at his daily news conference that we were investigating alleged detainee abuse at Abu Ghraib. And he announced the allegations again in March when we had preferred charges on these first six soldiers. The media just didn't pick up the story. It flew under the radar until the defense released the photos. It's the pictures that grabbed everybody's attention. People just assumed that the government was trying to keep it quiet. It wasn't that . . . we just were not about to start passing these photos around."

"If the government had released the photos, we would have been risking all of the prosecutions," Johnson chimed in. "We would have been accused of trying to turn public opinion and tainting the jury pool against the soldiers in the pictures."

Graveline agreed. "We're going to have a difficult enough time seating a jury that hasn't prejudged these soldiers. If we would have been the ones to release these pictures, it would be hard to make a straight-faced argument to the judge that it wasn't meant to prejudice the defendants and that the charges shouldn't just be dismissed."

The three JAGs agreed that seating a jury was only going to be the beginning of their problems. They were sure that the defense would seek to move these cases out of Iraq, citing a potentially hostile population and the continuing insurgency. They would have to figure out the feasibility of holding full-blown trials in the middle of Baghdad, as opposed to in Kuwait or back in the States. Although Lieutenant General Metz or the military judge would make the final determination as to the trials' location, they had to think through all of the contingencies.

Later that evening, Graveline went back to look at the photos. As he reviewed the images, he was more stunned than he anticipated. The disc's first folder contained numerous pictures of a naked or semi-clothed England posing alone in a sexually explicit manner. In a number of the photos, England was flashing the now infamous thumbs-up that had become the signature sign of the 372d MP soldiers. Graner had apparently taken dozens of these sexually explicit or crude shots of Lynndie England.

Thanks for warning me, Chuck, Graveline thought sarcastically. *These are not shy or prudish soldiers. For at least Graner and England, sexual conduct was blatant, open, and a primary way of joking.*

After spending an hour opening every picture in the first folder only to find more and more of the England and Graner sex photos, Graveline opened the next folder, which contained pictures of the human pyramid and naked detainees. Mixed in with these photos, Graveline found numerous pictures of one of the accused soldiers, Sabrina Harman, posing with a big smile and thumbs-up in front of a charred corpse and another corpse packed in ice. There were others of Harman posing with a cat's severed head, pretending to kiss it. *What was going through these soldiers' heads with these pictures?*

Despite having already seen many of the photos in the press, Graveline felt their impact much greater now. Studying their details and seeing the looks of horror on the victims' faces in several of the photos were particularly jarring. *How could U.S. soldiers have been so callous?*

✦

After getting the CID case file from Fort Bragg, Holley arranged to meet with Special Agents Paul Arthur, Warren Worth, and Manora Iem, the CID agents who were the initial investigators in Iraq. Both Arthur and Iem had been assigned at Abu Ghraib during January 2004. Although Worth had been assigned elsewhere in Baghdad, his assistance was requested as the number of suspects expanded. All of these CID agents had since redeployed out of Iraq—Arthur to Fort Hood; Worth to Fort Lee, Virginia; and Iem to Fort Riley, Kansas. Holley had already made plans to visit relatives in Texas, so they agreed to meet at Fort Hood. Holley was especially pleased to hear that CPT Kyson Johnson had returned to Texas from Iraq and would be sitting in on the meeting. Holley could not wait to pick his brain about these cases.

For several days during the week of June 7, the agents gave Holley a broad overview of the entire investigation. While the agents briefed him very professionally, Holley was not impressed. He sensed that the CID agents saw these cases as open and shut.

They've got the pictures and some incriminating statements. Slam dunk; case closed. We're going to have to dig deeper to prove our case. Holley was chomping at the bit to get to Baghdad and pick up where CID had left off. *There's no substitute for actually sitting across the table from prospective witnesses, judging their credibility, pressing them on the small details that are the glue to any successful case.*

Holley gleaned much more from Johnson's take on the cases. Holley found Johnson to be a highly intelligent and earnest prosecutor. Johnson obviously appreciated the enormity of these cases and had spent a great deal of time thinking through the various legal issues. However, something else struck Holley about Johnson.

Earlier that weekend, on June 4, former president Ronald Reagan had passed away. In remembrance, Fort Hood regularly fired a cannon every hour on the hour. Every time the cannon went off, Holley noticed Johnson dropped his pencil. Holley knew that Johnson had worked for a few months at Abu Ghraib in the detention operation section when the prison was subject to frequent mortar attacks. One night, a mortar had hit a gas truck near Johnson, causing a tremendous explosion. Mortar attacks were not part of the deployment Holley had spent much time dwelling on, and they certainly were not a part he wanted his family to consider. Watching Johnson's reaction left him wondering what impact the coming months would have on him.

3

MR. PRESIDENT, DON'T TOUCH
THAT PRISON

Monday, June 21, 2004. The air hung stagnant in the makeshift courtroom. *Can it get any hotter in here?* thought Graveline. Beads of sweat glistened
on his forehead and rolled down his back. *It has to be more than a hundred degrees
in here.* Graveline sat alone at the government table during this first round of
motion hearings.

Given the tremendous level of public and media interest in the cases, the
military command decided to hold the hearings at the Baghdad Convention
Center (already in use by the coalition forces as their media center) to accommodate as many spectators and journalists as possible. The convention center sits in
the Green Zone, a blocked-off section of downtown directly adjacent to the Al-
Rashid Hotel and containing many of the U.S., coalition, and Iraqi government
ministry buildings. The hearing room was on the first floor with movie theater–
style seating, rows of padded seats covered in purple fabric. The seats gently
sloped down toward the front of the conference room, where two long tables
faced the judge's "bench" and a witness chair, which were both perched a step
or two above the floor. An American flag stood to the right of the bench. Three
chairs stood behind the table on the left that was reserved for the defense, and
one chair sat behind the government's table on the right. Dark tinted panes of
glass, which allowed spectators to watch from three smaller, connected rooms,
made up the right wall.

More than fifty reporters from all over the world filled several rows in the
main room. Graveline recognized a few, and Neill pointed out journalists from

the *Washington Post,* the *New York Times,* and *Al-Jazeera.* The furor around the abuse photos had reached a fever pitch worldwide. Back in the United States, a number of senators, representatives, and political pundits were calling for the firing or resignation of Secretary of Defense Donald Rumsfeld. Both houses of Congress were bringing Secretary Rumsfeld and several generals in to testify about the photos. The press was interested in seeing what connections the defense counsel could make between the accused soldiers, the higher military chain of command in Iraq, and the Bush administration.

Holley had flown into Kuwait late the night before and would not be in Iraq until later that afternoon. He seemed to be the only person missing. Along with the throng of reporters, the five accused and their defense counsel sat in the front rows. There was also a platoon of MP soldiers providing security in and around the makeshift courtroom. Robinson, Neill, and two paralegals were there to handle all the behind-the-scenes logistical needs of the attorneys. There were also several representatives from the public affairs office, including CPT Roseanne Bleam, another JAG, brought along to act as the subject matter expert for the press. With all of the people in the room, Graveline could feel the temperature rise. It was only 8:00 a.m., but it seemed as if he was sitting in the midday heat.

Graveline was usually very calm in court; he had never had trouble with nerves before. *I wonder if everyone can see how much I'm sweating. Man, it's really hot in here.*

Fortunately for Graveline, the first words out of his mouth that day were the standard, scripted lines used to open a military court-martial.

"My name is Captain Christopher Graveline. I've been detailed to this court-martial by Captain S. Charles Neill, Chief of Military Justice, III Corps. I'm qualified and certified under the Uniform Code of Military Justice. . . ."

The first case on the docket was that of SGT Javal Davis. A tall, athletically built African American from New Jersey, twenty-six-year-old Davis had been a reserve MP soldier for more than six years. Despite having little police experience outside of the military (he had failed to complete the Baltimore, Maryland, police academy's program several years earlier), his military experience and prior deployments had allowed him to rise to the rank of sergeant. Graveline also gleaned from Davis' military file that his quick temper and anger issues had led to multiple run-ins with authority.

Davis, the father of two, was the least well known or recognizable of the accused soldiers since he did not appear in any of the abuse photos. Still, he was
charged with six offenses: one count of conspiracy to maltreat detainees on the
night of November 7, 2003; three counts of maltreatment and assault of detainees on that same night; one count of dereliction of duty for failing to protect
detainees from abuse in the months of November and December 2003; and one
count of giving a false official statement to a CID investigator at the beginning
of the investigation in January. Davis had two attorneys representing him, one
civilian and one military. The civilian, Paul Bergrin, from Newark, New Jersey, did not usually practice before military courts-martial. Yet, Bergrin was no
stranger to the military, having started his legal career with six years' active duty,
which included three years as a defense attorney at Fort Dix, New Jersey, and
risen to the rank of major in the Army Reserve JAG Corps.

A tan, muscular man with slicked-back, jet-black hair and mustache, Bergrin was an experienced and aggressive trial attorney. His speech was fast, me-
tered, and tinged with a slight New York accent. Always donning expensive
clothes, he was quick on his feet, confident in court, and seemed to be looking
for a fight.

Bergrin's military partner, CPT Scott Dunn, was the opposite of Bergrin
in almost every way. Dunn was rail thin, pale, tall, clean shaven, and quiet. He
preferred a more diplomatic approach to defense work, opting for congeniality
over pointed debate. Together, the two had filed several motions for this court
appearance. The first one, where the defense attempted to convince the military judge, COL James Pohl, to reopen the pretrial investigation, went nowhere.
However, the second issue that day, the classification review of documents previously classified as secret, found Pohl much more receptive to the defense's arguments. Pohl wanted the government to accelerate the process, and he was not
interested in bureaucratic excuses.

Sensing a shift in the tone of the hearing, Bergrin decided to press his mo-
mentum. "It's my position as I stand here before this court that we shouldn't have
to beg, plead, and specify every particular piece of discovery that we want. I'm
requesting, Your Honor, that this court order the government to search through
different Department of Justice memos, memos to Lieutenant General Sanchez,
memos to Major General Miller, and the other individuals who are involved intri-
cately in this particular case, and provide us with those particular pieces of evidence.

"For instance, Your Honor, there are memorandums by Ambassador Paul Bremer to which he outlines and asks for particular definitions and how to define interrogation as it pertains to specific detainees, al Qaeda, terrorists, and so on. There are Department of Justice memorandums that were asked for by Secretary of Defense Rumsfeld as well as Undersecretary to Intelligence [Stephen] Cambone, which specifically asked for definitions of interrogation of individuals, who could be interrogated in certain ways, and whether certain individuals fall under the applicability of the Geneva Convention. These are definitions. These are memorandums. These are pieces of evidence that I submit most firmly to this court will significantly impact on us seeking justice in this case, and that's all we're seeking in this case. We're trying to determine where the truth lies so that justice can be done, Your Honor."

Graveline had read about these memos in news accounts and editorials on the Internet but had not yet seen them. Nearly every day, he and Neill read articles online from the *New York Times* or CNN about some new legal opinion coming out of Washington concerning torture. If the stories were correct, then it seemed that government officials were doing some rather loose readings of the Geneva Conventions. While they were also interested in reading the memos Bergrin referenced, both Graveline and Neill failed to see any connection between these documents and the soldiers' actions at Abu Ghraib.

If the JAGs in Iraq had never seen these memos, how likely was it that the MPs at Abu Ghraib had seen or read them? Graveline thought as he listened to Bergrin. *If the guards had never read the documents, how could the defense argue that the memos had any influence over their clients?*

Despite Bergrin's impassioned plea, Pohl responded, "Mr. Bergrin, this case involves your client's actions in Abu Ghraib, and I understand the need for leeway as far as what the conditions at that prison were and who said what, who said it was okay. I have no problem with that theory. But I fail to see why a memorandum given to the secretary of defense would impact on your client's actions at the time, unless you're going to tell me he had access to that memorandum or somebody told him about it.

"Do you see what I'm saying? There's an attenuation argument here . . . you're entitled to any relevant evidence that shows [the] state of mind of your client. But I fail to see at this time the showing that you've made that the internal memorandum, or even external memorandum, at the highest levels of the United States government, somehow would impact on the accused's state of mind if he didn't know anything about them and nobody in the chain of command knew about them."

While he was denying the defense counsel's request for these high-level government memos now, Pohl ended by stating he would be open to revisiting the issue if they could show more relevance to each of their clients. Then, unprompted by the defense, he turned to Graveline.

"The court directs that the government make available for interviews by the defense team, if defense wishes to, General Sanchez, Lieutenant General Metz, and anybody below them, including lawyers who have relevant testimony in this case or could have. It seems to the court that until the defense has access to those witnesses, there's no way to make an informed command influence motion or any other type of motion."

Without hesitation, Bergrin was on his feet and requested a similar interview with GEN John Abizaid, the four-star commander of CENTCOM.

"Granted," Pohl declared.

Pohl clearly understood the military justice system's high sensitivity to any impression that the command influence or dictate the result of a court-martial. Given the high-level attention to these cases, he wanted to ensure that the defense had every opportunity to flesh out a potential issue. If ordering the interviews of several four-, three-, and two-star generals seemed bold, Pohl's next ruling would be the true headline grabber.

Bergrin rose and referenced a speech delivered days earlier by President Bush in which the commander in chief stated in deliberate terms, "With the approval of the Iraqi government, we will demolish the Abu Ghraib prison as a fitting symbol of Iraq's new beginning." The defense attorney asked Pohl to stop the demolition since the prison was a crime scene. As Bergrin put it, he wanted his team to be able to inspect the prison for themselves and the jury to "smell the fecal matter and the urine that service members, who worked inside that prison that are accused in this case, had to live with."

Pohl paused. "I think the smell today will be different than the smell tomorrow. But, that being said, it seems like a perfectly reasonable request under the circumstances."

Turning to Graveline, Pohl asked, "Do you have any objection to me issuing such an order?"

Graveline thought quickly. *I could really care less if the prison is kept or not. But the last thing we need is a judicial order coming out of here for the president of the United States.*

"The only objection that the government would have is that we be allowed to work through our own channels and that the court did not have to issue an order not to knock down the prison," Graveline responded.

Pohl was not impressed. "Well, Captain Graveline, what happens if you work through your channels, and they send the engineers out tomorrow and blow it up? Then what happens? Then you say, 'Well, there's no court order preventing that.' Why don't I just order it to be preserved, and then you don't have to worry about it."

Graveline slid back into his chair. *How am I going to explain to Colonel Tate that the judge just put a restraining order on the president?*

Within a span of fifteen minutes, Colonel Pohl had issued orders denying a number of defense motions and binding orders that applied to several senior officers and the president. This mix of rulings gave the attorneys and any observers a clear sense that Judge Pohl intended to have complete control of his courtroom.

Pohl—with slightly graying hair; a large, rectangular face; and a quick wit—enjoyed sparring verbally with the attorneys in court. He was an experienced criminal lawyer who insisted on fairness. He had been a prosecutor, defense counsel, and appellate criminal attorney, and now a military judge for more than four years. It was without question that Pohl had already decided that he was willing to grant the accused soldiers extraordinary access and a great deal of leeway in presenting their cases. However, he was not about to allow any of these trials to become a three-ring circus either.

✦

Next up would be CPL Charles Graner, an MP soldier coming from a middle-class working family from the suburbs of Pittsburgh, Pennsylvania. Other than Lynndie England, Graner was the most recognizable of the accused soldiers. He was the bespectacled, muscular guard photographed giving a thumbs-up and smiling broadly behind the human pyramid. Graner was also in a number of other photos with his arm cocked back, apparently ready to hit a hooded detainee.

Graveline looked over at the defense table. This was the first time he had been able to take a good look at Graner in person. *He looks different than he does in the photos,* Graveline thought. *He's put on a little weight and grown his hair out a bit.*

With his appearance in the photos and his name coming up throughout the other accused soldiers' sworn statements, it was becoming clear to Graveline that Graner had played a central role—if not the lead role—in the abuses at Abu Ghraib. Graner had been the NCOIC of Tier 1A during the night shift at Abu Ghraib. Graner had given two compact discs of abuse photos to SGT Joseph Darby, who then turned them over to CID. CID, in turn, found even more abuse photos on Graner's computer after seizing it as part of the investigation.

Moreover, Graner's personality and work history made him stand out as a leader. He had a reputation for being smart, charismatic, and outgoing and for possessing a dominant personality. While serving in the U.S. Marine Corps Reserve during Operation Desert Storm a decade earlier, Graner had assisted in guarding enemy prisoners of war (EPWs). Back in the States, he had numerous years of experience as a prison guard. However, there was a darker side to his personality. Graveline had read an article in the *Washington Post* that described allegations of physical abuse from Graner's past, both in his professional and personal life. Inmates at the Pennsylvania penitentiary where he worked complained of harassment from Graner, and his ex-wife had filed for three restraining orders for alleged physical abuse during a very contentious divorce.

Attention was also being heaped on Graner for his relationship with Lynndie England. England had quickly become the face of the scandal, her pixie-like features juxtaposed against shocking scenes. From the photos he had seen earlier, Graveline knew of the sexual relationship between the thirty-five-year-old prison guard and the twenty-year-old clerk. There were several shots of England exposing herself (either skinny-dipping at the beach or posing in a negligee) found on Graner's computer, and these predated their Iraq deployment. Many of them bore digital time stamps showing that they were taken while at Fort Lee, Virginia, as their unit prepared for Iraq. This relationship was apparently over now, but not before England became pregnant.

All of these elements had combined to establish Graner as an intriguing figure at the center of the scandal. Ringleader or not, Graner was facing the most jail time of all the guards. He was charged with two conspiracies to maltreat detainees, four counts of maltreatment of detainees, two counts of aggravated assault, two counts of assault and battery, dereliction of duty for failing to protect detainees from abuse, indecent acts, adultery, and obstruction of justice, fourteen counts in all. The maximum punishment for these alleged crimes was twenty-four and a half years of confinement and a dishonorable discharge.

Guy Womack joined Graner at the defense table. A retired Marine lieutenant colonel and JAG officer, Womack had opened his own law office specializing in federal and military defense in Houston, Texas. He possessed sharp facial features, with a jutting chin and nose, and still sported a Marine high and tight haircut. Womack seemed to believe in one strategy—straight ahead.

Womack's partner, CPT Jay Heath, was a JAG officer deployed to Iraq from Fort Bragg. Having graduated from Harvard University and Georgetown Law, Heath was an astute young man who joined the JAG Corps in 2001. He spoke slowly and deliberately.

Graner's hearing moved more quickly than Davis' had. Womack and Heath had filed essentially the same motions as the Davis team and sat through the earlier hearing. The debate quickly turned once again to the policy memoranda that came out of the Justice and Defense departments that discussed how the Geneva Conventions applied to the war on terror. Womack added his own twist to the defense's need for the documents.

Womack wanted the memoranda in order to advance a novel legal idea. He argued that these memos would show that the country's senior leadership had determined that the Geneva Conventions did not protect certain detainees in Iraq, specifically the prisoners in Tier 1A at Abu Ghraib. If that were the case, Womack argued that his client could not be held legally responsible for a crime since a soldier could not maltreat a person who was not protected by the Geneva Conventions.

Pohl was dubious. "You're saying that if there's a legal opinion to the effect that an individual in American custody is not protected by the Geneva Conventions, therefore it's okay to torture them? You can do anything to them?"

"Basically, that's what the law says, Your Honor. That is what the law says. If they're not protected . . ."

"What law is that?"

"Well, you can do anything that's not prohibited by law. If the Geneva Conventions do not protect someone, then they're not protected."

"Then you can just shoot them dead?" Pohl asked incredulously.

Without missing a beat, Womack emphatically stated, "Well, certainly, of course."

Pohl's eyes grew wide, and he shook his head in disbelief. "You seem to be saying it as a matter of law, that they're not protected by the Geneva Convention; therefore, you're free to do anything with those people in your custody. That's what you just told me, and what I'm telling you is, that would strike to me as not the law. There's no right to physically assault an individual who is not protected by the Geneva Convention. It happens all the time, true?"

Womack remained confident in his argument. "I intend to file that motion. These are not arbitrary individuals. These are the principal legal advisers to the commander in chief of all U.S. forces, to the chairman of the Joint Chiefs of Staff of all U.S. forces, the secretary of defense, the commander, or commanding general of the Multi-National Forces–Iraq, very important individuals directly in the chain of command of the MPs at Abu Ghraib. They have obtained, what I believe to be, competent legal counsel and correct legal counsel that certain individuals are not protected by the Geneva Conventions . . . that certain acts short of shooting someone do not constitute torture. These memos, Your Honor, I think, will help us flesh out the argument that under the facts of this case, involving these specific detainees from Abu Ghraib, it may be that there was no violation of U.S. law with regard to the way they were treated by these young MPs."

After a few minutes of legal argument, Pohl positioned the issue in a different light. "The accused is charged with violating a statute, true? The Uniform Code of Military Justice. And the fact that subcategories of the government, for example, the executive branch, interprets it in a certain way doesn't change the statute, true?"

"It actually does, Your Honor, because keep in mind that the U.S. Army is under the executive branch of the U.S. government," Womack answered. "The commander in chief, the president, is the commander in chief of everyone sitting in this room."

Pohl had the last say. "What I'm saying is . . . it's a matter of statutory interpretation. Does not a statute control over departmental legal opinions? And if in conflict, the statute controls over the legal opinion.

"I understand your position and I understand the liberal grant of discovery, but based on what I have before me, I don't believe you've shown sufficient relevance to warrant . . . looking at what lawyers at the Department of Justice or the Department of Defense did at the time. Subject to tying that into this case, your motion for that is denied."

Pohl had now made it clear in two hearings: if the defense counsel wanted to use national policy or legal opinions from Washington as a defense, they were going to have to show that their clients had read or known about these policies or opinions. They were going have to build their "abuse as policy" defense from the bottom up, starting from their clients' knowledge and working up the chain of command. There would be no wild speculation thrown around the courtroom.

✦

The final hearing of the day was for SSG Ivan L. Frederick, the highest ranking of the accused soldiers. Although Graner and Davis were both physically larger men, Frederick was clearly the most imposing figure of the group.

Standing an even six feet and weighing approximately 195 pounds, thirty-seven-year-old Frederick sported a buzz haircut, no facial hair, and the scowl one might call to mind if asked to think of an aggressive prison guard. Frederick had been the NCOIC of the entire hard-site prison facility during the night hours at Abu Ghraib. His past was quite different from Graner's: A small-town guy who grew up in the hills of Maryland and West Virginia, he was continuously in the Army National Guard or Reserve since high school and was known as a very professional correctional officer with a superb track record at Buckingham Correctional Facility in Virginia. He was quiet, almost stoic. Graveline had not seen Frederick speak to anyone, including his attorney or fellow soldiers.

Frederick faced a number of charges: two conspiracies to maltreat detainees, five counts of maltreatment, two counts of assault and battery, one count of aggravated assault, and one count of indecent acts. He had decided to be represented by both civilian and military defense attorneys. On this day, however, only the military attorney, CPT Robert Shuck, stood before the court. Shuck, with a ruddy complexion and reddish-blond hair cut close to the scalp, looked fidgety. Actually, Shuck was always fidgety, but on this particular day, he looked as if he was going to need Valium to calm his nerves.

Shuck's civilian partner, attorney Gary Myers, had been trying to move the court-martial out of Iraq for the last month. He began by sending a letter to Metz complaining that the court remained in Iraq for purely political purposes. When Metz responded that the trial would remain in Iraq, Myers tried again by filing an e-mail motion with Pohl requesting to represent his client by telephone for this particular June hearing. He based this new request on the grounds that his travel halfway around the world for a hearing that would take less than two hours would be too costly for his client and that he was not about to show up "in an inherently dangerous war zone" given his beliefs about why the court-martial remained in Iraq.

Pohl responded with an e-mail message that simply read, "Request denied."

Despite his absence, Myers had already had the biggest impact on any of the cases. Graveline was convinced that Myers had brought the abuse pictures to the media, having granted an interview to Dan Rather for the *60 Minutes II* piece and another to *New Yorker* contributing reporter Seymour Hersh. Graveline believed it was Myers' trial strategy to place his client and the abuse photos squarely in the media spotlight.

Myers had been a military defense counsel for more than three decades, first serving on active duty and then building a civilian practice around defending service men and women in courts-martial. Myers had spent time in Vietnam and defended one of the soldiers charged in the infamous My Lai massacre. It seemed he planned to employ one of the defenses used repeatedly during the My Lai trials: the chain of command, through either direct orders or unclear guidance, was more responsible than the individual soldiers were. However, before he could start his defense strategy in earnest, Myers wanted the court-martial moved out of Iraq. He was getting too old for this combat zone stuff.

None of the defense counsel wanted the courts-martial in Iraq. Bergrin and Womack had also filed motions to change the location to anywhere else—Kuwait, Germany, or the States. Witness availability, difficult travel conditions, the immense public pressure for a conviction in Iraq, and the supposed trouble in finding an impartial jury there were all legal reasons cited by the defense. In the end, however, the real reason was transparent: none of them wanted to try these cases in a combat zone where improvised explosive device (IED), mortar, and rocket attacks were common.

Graveline and Neill believed that it made the most sense to keep the cases in Iraq at this point for several reasons. Most of the potential witnesses were still in theater with the accused soldiers' unit, the 372d MP Company. The victims were primarily Iraqis. Still, they were not unsympathetic to the defense's position. If these trials were delayed for any length of time, most U.S. soldier witnesses would redeploy to the States. It would be difficult to justify bringing dozens of witnesses back into a combat zone, especially since most of them were reservists and would have returned to their civilian jobs by then. In addition, Iraq was already a dangerous enough place without the additional tensions of the abuse trials. There was no front line in Iraq—one could be in danger of attack riding in a convoy, walking in the Green Zone, or eating in the chow hall regardless of being a soldier or a civilian.

Just the week prior, several mortar rounds had shaken the courthouse and attorney trailer area on Victory Base. Graveline, who was working at a computer in the courthouse entryway, could not tell how close the rounds were hitting. The outside door of the building flew open, and Sergeant Brann and Captain Shuck sprinted in. Both men had been working out in the trailers and saw the mortars landing. The first hit in the small pond twenty yards behind the courthouse. The second one hit, shaking the ground, in the traffic loop about fifteen yards in front of the courthouse. To everyone's relief, that round did not explode; but after this second round, Brann and Shuck decided to make a run for cover in the stone building. They were completely out of breath. Fortunately, the attack ended at that point and no one was injured.

That attack seemed to clinch it for Shuck. He wanted out of Iraq. The Frederick defense team decided to take a stand in an attempt to move the trials out of Iraq as soon as possible. Now Shuck stood by himself in front of Pohl. The judge was not amused.

"Captain Shuck, where's Mr. Myers?"

"Sir, we have a motion to have Mr. Myers appear by telephone."

"I've already told Mr. Myers I've denied the motion." Pohl paused and began to read Myers' motion line by line: "'The United States has arbitrarily chosen to keep these proceedings in Iraq for what have become purely political reasons.'" The judge looked up from the paper he held in his hands. "Do you have any evidence of that?"

"No, Your Honor," Shuck mumbled.

Pohl continued reading. "'The United States has done so in the face of ever-increasing violence to include the recent mortar attack on Camp Victory. The accused has a right to civilian counsel.' I don't have any issue with that, do you?"

"No, Your Honor."

"'The accused should not be penalized by the government's venue selection. The cost of travel is prohibitive. Telephonic appearances in non-CONUS [continental United States] cases are a regular and ordinary event for Article 39(a) [pretrial motion] proceedings. It is not reasonable to expect that a military accused can afford to bring civilian counsel to every 39(a) in a non-CONUS setting.'

"Now, Captain Shuck, I can take judicial notice that I just did two hearings in this case with civilian lawyers, true? And both of those civilian lawyers came here for this hearing, true?"

"Yes, Your Honor."

After several additional pointed questions from Pohl, Shuck found his voice. "Your Honor, to appear today would concede to the fact that it's possible to try this case in a fair setting, and just like any other court-martial case in the United States or overseas, when in fact, the defense's position, it is not, that it is indeed a unique situation that places people in peril for their lives. And if we were to try this case like any other case, court-martial, then we do not want to give up those rights, will place civilian cocounsel into positions of peril."

"Mr. Myers' choice to come was a free and voluntary decision on his part, true? He didn't have to take this case, did he?" Pohl responded, unimpressed. "In his motion, he also states, 'The accused cannot afford to bring civilian counsel from the United States to Iraq for this brief proceeding.' Is that a legal basis not to show up?

"Now obviously, if you choose to hire a civilian from the States to appear here, there's going to be expenses incurred in traveling. So, why should I . . . is there some exception that if you go over X amount of dollars, then he doesn't have to show up?"

"Sir, I stand by my previous arguments," Shuck conceded.

"That's a wise course there, Captain Shuck."

Pohl turned to Frederick. "Mr. Myers is not present, and he's known for a week that he would not be allowed to appear telephonically, because quite frankly, I think that's an oxymoron. By that, I mean is, you either appear in person or you're not here. Do you understand that?"

"Yes, sir," Frederick responded quickly.

"And I told him that a week ago, and he's chosen not to come. But now, you're the accused in this case, and it's your right to counsel. Do you consent to proceeding today without Mr. Myers present?"

Frederick declined. He did not want to waive Myers' presence.

Leaning back in his chair, Pohl thought for a moment. "All right, we're going to continue this case until 23 July. On 23 July, Mr. Myers is either here or not here. And quite frankly, Captain Shuck, I know I'm looking at you and talking to you, but I decide who shows up and who doesn't show up. You tell Mr. Myers that's the date. I don't care how many bombs are going off, 23 July . . . well, rephrase that, I do care how many bombs are going off, but absent extraordinary circumstances, on 23 July, we're going to continue this hearing."

✦

Outside the courtroom, Bergrin and Womack began an impromptu press conference. Both emphasized their "wins" that day and their defense theories. Bergrin trumpeted the judge's ruling about preserving the prison as a crime scene.

"The president of the United States went before the American people, and he said, 'I'm going to tear down the Abu Ghraib prison. I'm going to destroy it and level it.' This judge had the integrity . . . to tell the president of the United States, 'You're not touching that prison.'"

Womack's comments focused more on the message he wanted the public to hear. "No one can suggest with a straight face that these MPs were acting alone." He went on to state that he was going to seek interviews of Secretary of Defense Rumsfeld and possibly President Bush.

Graveline and Neill walked away, unnoticed by the throng of reporters pressing against the defense counsel. The defense was desperate to try this case in the media.

"Anything to grab headlines and keep the focus off their clients and those pictures," Neill observed, shaking his head.

✦

After the court hearings, all the participants headed back to Victory Base in an armored convoy. Graveline sat in the back of a Humvee lost in thought.

Well, some good and some bad. We kept these cases moving forward. We don't have to go back and redo the pretrial investigations. But how are we going to get ten defense counsel in to see all these generals? It's not easy getting fifteen minutes on the CENTCOM commander's schedule, let alone time for five sets of defense counsel to interview him individually. And, to make matters worse, all of the military defense attorneys are here in Iraq working other cases, their civilian partners will all be back in the States shortly, and the generals are spread out all over the world.

How in the world are we ever going to pull these trials off?

4

UNEXPECTED REPENTANCE

Graveline's thoughts jarred to a halt as the convoy pulled to a stop back on the base. Robinson grabbed Neill and Graveline. "We better go tell Colonel Tate about the judge's order to the president and the interviews of the generals. He'll have some phone calls to make about those," Robinson declared.

As they walked into the large JAG office, they were greeted by a new figure.

It was Mike Holley. Smiling with his hand outstretched, the blond-haired man with small, rectangular glasses walked toward the trio.

Holley had arrived an hour before after flying up from Kuwait with Specialist Harman's civilian defense counsel, Frank Spinner. Harman's Article 32 investigation was scheduled to begin in three days.

This meeting had been a long time coming for all the men. Holley and Graveline had been in regular e-mail contact as Holley had prepared for the deployment. Holley had read all of the motions and Graveline's responses prior to the hearings and was dying to know what had happened.

"Let's go see the boss, so we don't rehash everything twice," Robinson interjected.

Tate was sitting back in his office. He had arrived in Iraq during the first week of June and had the benefit of a few weeks of overlap with his predecessor. Goetzke had flown out the previous weekend; it was now Tate's show to run.

Tate was a spark plug of a man, both physically and personality-wise. He was a short, sturdily built man with an endless store of energy. Raised in the 82nd Airborne Division, he bore the telltale signs of an Airborne soldier. Tough, persistent, and direct when the situation warranted, he was equally diplomatic, flexible, and smooth when a new approach was necessary.

For the first time, the government's team of attorneys was assembled. Robinson, Neill, Holley, and Graveline sat in a semicircle around Tate's desk.

Tate was extremely interested in the court hearings. He was much attuned to the political realities and interest that swirled around these cases. In his last assignment, Tate had been a legal adviser in the Pentagon's Office of Legislative Liaison. In that capacity, he had fielded the initial wave of questions over Abu Ghraib coming from Capitol Hill to the Army. He knew that the higher-ups at the Pentagon and in Washington would already be spinning out of control with news of the judge's rulings. He would have to be on the phone shortly with as many facts as possible.

Because of this immediacy, Tate kept the meeting short. But first he had a message to deliver to his team.

"Now that we're all here, I want to give you some guidance about these cases. First, put your heads together and come up with a list of whatever you're going to need. I'll take it personally to the chief of staff. Don't be bashful or hold anything back. There is no bridge too far. We can't do these cases halfway. They've got to be properly resourced and done right.

"And, most importantly, we are going to be entirely above board with these cases. We go where the evidence leads us. At the end of the day, there's going to be a lot of people second-guessing us. Regardless, we are going to conduct ourselves in such a way that we will be able to hold our heads high." He paused, looking around at each man with bold determination in his eyes.

"We are going to do the right thing, no matter where the evidence leads or who doesn't like the result. You guys get to the bottom of this thing, and I'll back you up."

As they walked out of Tate's office that evening, Holley was greatly heartened over the senior JAG's words. His own four-day-long trip from the States to Iraq had shown him that pulling off these cases halfway around the world and in this combat zone was going to be no small feat. Many times during his lengthy journey, especially in the two long days sitting idly in Kuwait, Holley had thought to himself that without the Army giving significant resources to these cases, failure was certain.

If it's this difficult to get just one person into Iraq, how are we going to get between fifty to a hundred witnesses, family members, and media to Baghdad on a specific date for a trial and ensure that the defendants get a fair trial and that everyone remains safe? Holley wondered.

But now with Tate's assurances, Holley was confident that at least his boss realized how difficult these cases were going to be and would be dedicated in securing the assets they needed in order to pull these trials off. But there was precious little time to relax.

While Graveline had the luxury of a few weeks to read the extensive investigations and gain his bearings when he arrived in Iraq, Holley had been dropped into the middle of frenzied activity. The defense counsel, with the exception of Gary Myers, for the five remaining accused were in Iraq for the next several days and wanted to travel to Abu Ghraib and interview detainees and other military witnesses. Specialist Harman's Article 32 investigation was set to happen in two days. There was the task of coordinating the defense counsel's schedules with the generals' for the interviews that Judge Pohl had ordered. Holley also needed to sort out who, apart from Graveline and Neill, would be helping out on these cases. They were going to need a support team.

Still, the top priority on Holley's list was to talk with Graveline. He wanted to assess his partner firsthand and try to divide up the work. It had been Holley's experience that an early division of labor was the best way to ensure that nothing fell through the cracks. Holley grabbed Graveline as the group walked out of the palace, the setting red sun reflecting off the placid lake.

"I'm going to get settled in a bit tonight, but let's meet tomorrow morning for breakfast," suggested Holley.

Graveline agreed, and early the next morning he sat waiting for Holley in the chow hall. The aluminum-sided, I-shaped building had a serving line set up on the far northeast wall and a salad bar, beverage coolers, and dessert table running through its center. The rest of the building was filled with a variety of circular and long rectangular card tables draped in checked red vinyl tablecloths and ringed with plastic chairs. Television sets were mounted high on the walls and were often tuned to ESPN, CNN, Fox News, or one of the British news channels. Graveline sat engrossed in the baseball highlights from the previous day.

Holley approached him as the younger JAG was polishing off some Frosted

Flakes out of a small plastic container. Holley had grabbed a plate full of french toast, eggs, sausage, and bacon.

Graveline could not pass up the opportunity to poke fun at Holley with his enormous plate of food. "You keep eating like that, and you're not going to be able fit into your Class A's for court," Graveline quipped, referring to the Army's dark green dress uniforms worn by soldiers on formal occasions and by JAG attorneys when they appeared in court.

"I know, I know, but I'm starving," Holley explained somewhat sheepishly. "Hey, we didn't get a chance to go too in-depth last night. Tell me about the hearings."

The two men talked for a while about the hearings, the defense counsel, and the judge's rulings. Holley had yet to meet Judge Pohl and was interested to learn what he was like in court. The conversation then turned to their preparation. By this time, Holley had finished his breakfast, and they were walking the quarter mile back to the palace.

"What are your thoughts about dividing up the work on these cases?" Holley asked Graveline.

"Well, what's worked for me and some of my partners in the past has been for the lead counsel to focus on proving our case and for the second chair to take care of all the motions and other distractions the defense tries to throw at us. So I was thinking that you could concentrate on getting our case ready, and I'll worry about taking as much off of your plate as possible—making sure the defense gets all the documents that they are entitled to in discovery, the time-consuming motions, expert witnesses, and figuring out how the defense is going to try to play their hand."

Holley liked the idea. "But that seems like a lot of work for you to bite off," he warned Graveline.

Graveline was quick to demur. "We can still split up the work as it comes in, but this plan can give us a rough framework and allows you to focus on the big picture. Essentially, you handle the MP side of the case, and I'll take the MI side."

"I think that'll work well, and we can adapt as the cases progress. I should be able to help map out where I think the defense might be going with some of their strategies based on some of my experiences as a defense attorney," Holley added.

By this time, the two had reached the palace. Holley had heard good things about Graveline from other JAGs who had worked with him before, but he was still very impressed with his young partner's grasp of the cases. The cases had so many difficult facets, and Holley knew he was going to have to rely on his cocounsel. He was confident that Graveline was up to the task—he would have to be.

Given Tate's meeting the night before, they wanted to send off a list of everything they thought they might need to Tate as soon as possible. Back in the office, the two sat at their neighboring cubicles and brainstormed out loud as Holley typed up the e-mail to Tate. The pair requested file cabinets, computers, and satellite cell phones.

The concave arc in the ceiling made it so the duo heard every conversation, however hushed, being held in the large JAG office space. This detail was very distracting, but more problematic in their minds was the fact that everyone else in the room could hear their discussions about these cases. They needed a place of their own—that request would go at the top of the list to Tate.

Holley and Graveline agreed that the two nonnegotiable items on their wish list were an area that afforded privacy with reliable telephone/computer access and SGT Jared Kary. The first was necessary because of their current office space and because the trailers frequently lost power. In fact, just the week prior, the trailers were without power for three days. With the pace of these cases and the need for communication with the defense counsel, they could not afford another three days of blackout. The second, and most critical in both men's minds, was the talented paralegal of the 16th MP Brigade, the unit that the accused soldiers had been assigned to after the investigation began. Kary had been with these cases from the very beginning, having arrived in Iraq the same week CID started its investigation into the abuse photos.

Sharp, quiet, and athletic, Kary had come to the Army via a slightly different route than most. After graduating college on a lacrosse scholarship, he had begun managing a golf course and supper club in North Carolina. Following the 9/11 attacks on Washington and New York City, the New Jersey native strongly felt that he needed to do more for his country. He enlisted in the Army.

Not one to back down from a challenge, Kary joined the XVIII Airborne Corps, graduated from Airborne school, and began work in one of the busiest

MP brigades in the Army. In his spare time, Kary was in night school studying for an MBA. He was the most motivated and competent young paralegal Holley and Graveline had ever seen. They were going to need his knowledge of the facts and his initiative to put together these cases. But it was going to take quite a bit of finesse to convince the MPs to give up this talented soldier.

Holley forwarded the list to Tate. He and Graveline knew it was ambitious. They were in a war zone where the priority of resources rightly went to the war fighters and electrical power was inconsistent. The entire JAG office of thirty attorneys, for example, had only two phone lines to use, let alone the satellite cell phones they had just requested from Tate. But maybe if they could receive a few of the items, it would go a long way toward moving the cases forward.

Tate sent a two-line e-mail in response: "Apparently, you intended this e-mail to go to the Home Shopping Network. OK, got it, and we'll work all this hard."

Two days later, workers began cleaning up a small room on the opposite side of the stone veranda from the main JAG office. Nine computer lines were dropped, worldwide phone lines installed, and furniture moved in. Sitting in the middle of all the commotion was Sergeant Kary, working on transferring digital evidence over to portable hard drives.

Thanks to the support from BG Bill Troy, III Corps' chief of staff, Tate was keeping his word.

✦

The remainder of the week was a whirlwind. After hatching their initial plan, Holley turned his attention to coordinating with the 16th MP Brigade to escort the defense counsel to the Abu Ghraib prison. Getting five soldiers and their eight attorneys out in a convoy to the prison twenty miles away was going to take some work. He called down to the MPs and spoke with Sergeant Kary and CPT Joshua Toman.

Toman had arrived in Iraq from Fort Bragg the previous week, assuming the prosecutor's duties for the MP brigade that John McCabe was vacating. An ambitious West Point graduate who, like Holley, had taken advantage of the Army's funded legal opportunity, he attacked every project given to him with tremendous energy, enjoyed the challenge of the combat environment, and took great pride in his organizational skills. He reassured Holley that he would organize everything and bring everyone back safe and sound from Abu Ghraib.

With the defense counsel taken care of, Holley focused on Harman's hearing. While he and Graveline had read a number of witness statements, neither one of them had interviewed any of the soldiers from the 372d.

At the time the photos came forward, the 372d's time in Iraq was coming to an end. The company had been scheduled to return stateside within days. However, with a major criminal investigation unfolding, they were going nowhere until more details about the abuse were known. The unit was relieved of its duties at Abu Ghraib and split up to perform other missions. The majority of the unit was conducting escort duty at the far side of Baghdad International Airport, more than a thirty-minute drive from the center of Victory Base. These escort duties, the difficulty of even the most minimal travel around Iraq, and the lack of good phone lines between Victory Base and the small base where the 372d was living meant Holley and Graveline were not going to talk to, or even meet, these witnesses until the morning of the hearing.

Never a good time to first meet a witness, thought Holley. *Nobody said trying cases in a combat zone was going to be easy.*

There is nothing attorneys hate more than to have a witness on the stand, under oath, and to have no idea what is about to come out of his or her mouth. Consequently, with the witnesses rolling in moments before the hearing was to begin, the two prosecutors decided to play it safe. They would put in Harman's confessions that admitted her presence on the night of the naked human pyramid and that she placed wires on the hands of the hooded man standing on the box, the confessions of her coconspirators placing her at the scene, and the pictures. That would be enough to get through this hearing.

Fortunately for Holley and Graveline, Harman's attorney, Frank Spinner, a retired Air Force JAG and experienced courtroom advocate, took the same minimalistic view of the hearing. This week was the first time he was meeting his client face-to-face, let alone any of the witnesses. He called a few witnesses but was very circumspect about the type of questions he asked. At that point, none of the lawyers knew enough about the facts of the cases, and they did not want to make a big mistake that could cost them dearly later at trial. The hearing, although taking up the greater part of two days, was uneventful.

✦

When not sitting in Harman's hearing, Graveline was busy trying to get his arms around the vast amount of documents associated with the investigations. Since arriving in Iraq, Graveline had focused almost exclusively on reading witness statement after witness statement in order to get up to speed on the important facts. His reading gave him a head start on the next critical, yet tedious, step of the process: figuring out what documents and evidence the government had and what had already been given to the defense. His preparation brought back to mind old lessons he had learned from his days in New Hampshire and at the 101st Airborne.

There are a thousand mind-numbing details to the legal process. You win cases by executing all of these little unglamorous details with precision. They are just as important, and oftentimes more so, than what happens in court.

Trial starts at the beginning of the investigation, not when the jury members are sitting in their box. If you think it starts with opening statements to the jury, you've already lost. Have your trial mapped out from the beginning. Thinking through the end goal will help in making the many strategic decisions along the way.

Contrary to trials portrayed on popular television shows, real-world criminal trials are not surprise events. Both sides are entitled to see all of the information the other side will present, and the government is required to provide all evidence collected, especially if it is exculpatory or helpful to the accused, whether it intends to use it or not. In a normal trial, this task entails simply obtaining the police file that usually contains crime scene sketches, witness statements, documents, and maybe a few expert reports; compiling those with a few other files that may have useful information about witnesses; and copying them for the defense. If a prosecutor fails to turn over all of the information, he risks having charges thrown out or the case being overturned on appeal. These prosecutions, however, were not the normal run-of-the-mill cases. Documents continuously seemed to be coming out of every conceivable corner, with unknown implications to all parties.

As if to underscore his thoughts, after the defense counsel's trip to the Abu Ghraib prison, Toman and Kary returned to the main JAG office and plopped down a long, rectangular cardboard box at Graveline's feet. The box was overflowing with folders, loose documents, and what appeared to be homemade weapons.

"What's this?" Graveline asked with an inquisitive look on his face.

"The guards took their attorneys down to Tier 1A, and they started collecting transfer logs, prisoner information, and other assorted items from down there. This is the complete collection," Toman replied. "I figured that we should turn all of this stuff over to CID since they have a way to secure evidence." Toman lifted up a four-inch-long bone with one side sharpened to a point and the other end wrapped in dirty scraps of fabric. "These are improvised shanks that the detainees made out of whatever they could get their hands on."

"Unbelievable," exclaimed Graveline. "I thought CID seized all the documents from down there at the beginning of the investigation." He turned to Kary. "Let's make sure CID gets this stuff, and then I want you to make sure we get all of it scanned and turned over to the defense."

There's got to be an end to the surprises in these cases, right? Graveline was amazed. He had never seen cases like these before. Every day it seemed a different soldier or person who had been at Abu Ghraib during the fall of 2003 was being interviewed in the press with new revelations that the team had never heard. *Surely, this is going to calm down . . . there can't be that many more twists and turns to these cases,* Graveline assured himself.

The next afternoon, Neill burst into the office and made a beeline for Graveline. Holley was not around. "You're not going to believe what's in the *Houston Chronicle*," Neill said excitedly. "I forwarded it to you on e-mail."

Graveline spun around in his chair and quickly pulled up Neill's e-mail. The first sentences of the report caught his eye.

The White House has decided to release a thick file of papers documenting its internal deliberations on rules for interrogating prisoners in facilities from Abu Ghraib in Iraq to Guantanamo Bay, Cuba. The two-inch stack of papers was to be released late today. It is intended to counter what White House aides fear is a growing perception that the administration authorized torture as an interrogation technique.

"The White House?!?" Graveline slumped back in his chair, his eyes searching the vaulted ceiling. "You've got to be kidding me!" The next line of the news account particularly sent Graveline into a foul mood.

"We believe it's important for the American people to have an accurate picture of the policies that we put in place and an accurate picture of the techniques that were approved by the Pentagon. It's important to set the record straight," said White House spokesman Scott McClellan.

"Do they think that maybe it's 'important' to let the prosecutors of these cases know about these documents? Maybe it's 'important' for the prosecutors to have 'an accurate picture' of the approved interrogation techniques? I know we're halfway around the world, but was anybody going to tell us about this?" Graveline vented to Neill. He was beside himself with anger.

Neill was equally frustrated. "It seems like we're learning more about these cases right now off the Internet than through our investigators. I don't even know if these documents have any bearing on the charges, but obviously someone in the administration thought they were important enough to hold a press conference over."

Graveline started calming down. "All right, we've got to figure out a way to get a handle on all of these documents floating around."

He grabbed his notepad and began scrawling down a list as he and Neill started to name every investigation or document they knew of.

First, there was the CID criminal investigation. They had most of the witness statements that had been collected to date, but they also knew that CID was still tracking down a number of leads and interviewing people around the world. There was also still the matter of all the forensic analyses the lab was doing on the soldiers' seized computers. They were going to have stay on top of the CID case agents to constantly give the prosecutors any evidence that became available.

They knew that MG George Fay was investigating the 205th MI Brigade's role in the abuses at Abu Ghraib. He and his team were located back in the States, although they had traveled to Iraq at the end of June. Fay had started his investigation in April and set a deadline of July 1. Both the defense and the prosecutors were eagerly awaiting the end of Fay's review as they hoped it would answer how deep MI's involvement truly was in the photographed abuses. Graveline had been pressing the legal adviser to convince Fay to release the witness statements but was rebuffed each time and told they would be released only when Fay's investigation and report were totally complete.

Neill and Graveline had read about Secretary of Defense Rumsfeld appointing an independent panel of investigators, led by former secretaries of defense James Schlesinger and Harold Brown, to evaluate the DoD's guidance and policy in detainee handling and interrogation. This panel had been appointed in May, and the prosecution team had not heard if it had reached any conclusions as of yet. Graveline made a note to see if he could find a contact on the panel who would be willing to talk.

Graveline was not sure if the Senate or House was conducting independent investigations. This is where Tate's previous assignment as a legal adviser to the Office of Legislative Liaison was going to come in handy. Graveline would ask his boss to reach out to some of his friends on Capitol Hill and in the Pentagon to find out if there were more investigations they were going to have to get their hands on.

The only completed investigation the prosecutors had in their possession was the one conducted by BG Antonio Taguba, and that entire investigation, to include the witness statements collected, was classified as secret. This elevated classification presented a problem since it meant the attorneys could only read the witness statements on computers reserved for classified information. While the civilian defense counsel had high enough security clearances to view the material, they did not have safes to house or secure locations to view the material back in the States. They could read only the information in or attached to Taguba's report on dedicated computers they did not have. Consequently, currently they could read the full report only by viewing the prosecutors' copy in Baghdad. Graveline jotted down another note—figure out how to get this information declassified so that we can handle it more easily, use it in interviews, and give the defense counsel physical possession of it.

✦

Brigadier General Taguba had come to his investigator role through command channels. While CID usually conducts investigations into criminal misconduct, under Army regulation, a commander can appoint an officer to conduct a fact-finding inquiry so the command can better assess how to deal with a particular situation apart from the criminal investigation.

After SPC Joseph Darby anonymously slipped the compact disk of photos under CID's door at Abu Ghraib, the CID agents on the ground ultimately identified the soldiers in the pictures as members of the 372d MP Company and immediately reported the discovery to the chain of command. The MP battalion commander, LTC Jerry Phillabaum, and the 372d commander, CPT Donald Reese, were both notified within hours of the discovery as CID started rounding up the suspects for interviews. Before long, news of these photos had reached the highest levels of command in Iraq, including the three-star commander, LTG Ricardo Sanchez.

These new allegations of detainee abuse were the last in a list of lapses and charges against the 800th MP Brigade, the higher headquarters of the 372d MP Company. Commanded by BG Janis Karpinski, the 800th was a theater-wide asset that had responsibilities stretching from the northern-most parts of Iraq all the way down to Kuwait. Given that its wide scope included more than the Iraqi area of operations, the brigade officially fell under the Coalition Forces Land Component Command (CFLCC—or known in military circles as C-Flick), whose mission was to coordinate and provide for the logistical needs of the coalition's efforts in Iraq and Kuwait. However, the subordinate units of the 800th in Iraq were tactically controlled by Sanchez.

The 800th had not been a particularly strong unit for several months with numerous escaped prisoners reported and accountability failures. With the discovery of these pictures, Sanchez decided that it was time for a systematic review of the overall fitness of the 800th, and on January 19, 2004, he requested that his higher headquarters, CENTCOM, conduct such an investigation. CENTCOM, in turn, directed Sanchez's request to the CFLCC commander, three-star general David McKiernan. McKiernan tapped one of his deputy commanding generals, two-star general Antonio Taguba, to investigate.

A short man with pepper black hair and a wide, generous face, Taguba had been born in the Philippines. His father was a career Army soldier who had survived the Bataan death march during World War II. Not surprisingly, Taguba sought a military career and had become the second Filipino American officer to reach the rank of brigadier general.

McKiernan's directions to Taguba were broad but clear: investigate the 800th MP Brigade's detention operations, specifically the facts and circumstances of the alleged detainee abuse at the Abu Ghraib prison; any detainee escapes; and the training, standards, and command policy and climate of the brigade. In order to complete the investigation, McKiernan gave Taguba a complete investigative team that included MP investigators, Army subject matter experts in detention operations, an Air Force psychiatrist, legal advisers, and support staff. But along with these assets came a short suspense—Taguba had thirty days to file his report.

Over the course of the next month, Taguba and his team interviewed fifty witnesses and compiled 106 separate exhibits. In the end, he produced a fifty-page report, buttressed with over three thousand pages of witness statements and documentary evidence that detailed a disastrous command climate in the 800th MP Brigade, a general laxness in military standards, and discreet acts of misconduct in the unit. Taguba made numerous findings as part of his report. The findings concerning detainee abuse depicted in the photos could be broken down into two basic critiques: (1) there was clearly criminal misconduct on the part of individual soldiers, and (2) the officers and senior leaders of the 800th and the 205th MI Brigade at Abu Ghraib—through a poor command climate, unclear command structure, and insufficient training—created an environment that was conducive to the commission of abuse.

In regard to the 800th, Taguba painted a picture of a dysfunctional military unit from top to bottom. He found a unit that lacked quality leadership, was not proficient in its mission, and was not getting the training for the mission it was actually handling. A U.S. Army Reserve unit based out of Uniondale, New York, the brigade's primary mission was to process and safeguard EPWs during the initial invasion and ground combat operations. With eight subordinate battalions spread throughout Iraq, the 800th had set up a primary internment facility named Camp Bucca in the southern part of the country. By the time President Bush landed on the deck of the aircraft carrier USS *Abraham Lincoln* to declare the end of major combat operations on May 1, 2003, Camp Bucca's population had risen to approximately seven thousand to eight thousand EPWs. The soldiers of the 800th believed that, with the end of combat, they would be allowed to go home once the detainees were released from Bucca. In the weeks following President Bush's announcement, these hopes were raised with the release of thousands of Iraqi prisoners. But as the Army's mission developed from being an offensive force to more of a static one during the summer of 2003, the 800th's mission transformed as well. Its new focus became running the Iraqi prison system and detention centers for individuals who had been caught taking actions against coalition forces. With the realization that they were not going home any time soon, the 800th's morale sunk.

The unit's morale problem was further exacerbated by the putrid conditions in which both the soldiers and detainees lived. Most of the prison areas were nothing more than tent camps surrounded with concertina wire. Supplies, food, and clothing for detainees were difficult to get and oftentimes never delivered. Taguba pointed to this discontent among the 800th soldiers as a significant factor in the unit's problems; however, he took the chain of command more to task for failing to mitigate this growing discontent.

Although unwritten, Graveline thought it apparent that Taguba could not have thought less of the officers running the MP brigade. The 800th had been brought into theater under the leadership of BG Paul Hill, who, in turn, handed command over to BG Janis Karpinski on July 1, 2003. In Taguba's opinion, Hill had left the brigade in poor condition, and Karpinski did nothing to improve the situation. Taguba found Karpinski to be a commander who failed in several key areas: training, instilling discipline, demanding accountability, and regularly visiting her troops. To make matters worse, many of the other officers, particularly those located at Abu Ghraib, were ineffective.

The detention facility at Abu Ghraib was the responsibility of the 320th MP Battalion. Leading that battalion was Lieutenant Colonel Phillabaum whom Taguba characterized as an "extremely ineffective commander and leader." According to a number of the soldiers in the 320th, Phillabaum tended to drift into the background and allowed his subordinates to run the day-to-day operations. Many of his soldiers stated that they rarely, if ever, saw the commander. Taguba found that the 320th, while experienced in EPW handling, had little or no previous training in running a prison facility and that Phillabaum offered nothing to remedy this deficiency.

After a particularly disastrous briefing over the security situation at Abu Ghraib to Lieutenant General Sanchez in late October 2003, Karpinski allowed Phillabaum to leave the prison for Kuwait for a few weeks to regain his composure. This absence particularly incensed Taguba and served as a clear example in his mind of the true level of dysfunction occurring in the 800th. Karpinski had Phillabaum, a battalion commander, leave the country and transfer his responsibilities to another commander, who was still responsible for his own battalion, without notifying Sanchez or his staff. Taguba reported that this move, spreading the leadership of two battalions incredibly thin without notifying higher command, was "without precedent in my military career." To make matters worse, the absence of this withdrawn leader from Abu Ghraib corresponded with a number of the most infamous abuses photographed by the soldiers of the 372d.

Compounding the incompetent chain of command in the 800th and the 320th, new challenges were rising, ones that would test the coalition forces: rocket and IED attacks. The command was attempting to stem the tide of these but was receiving precious little intelligence that could aid in this mission.

At that point, the military intelligence community was also struggling to transition from supporting offensive war fighting to gaining intelligence that could help the coalition rebuild Iraq. Intelligence operations were being conducted at several discreet locations with little or no coordination, leading to confusion and duplication of effort.

In late summer, two decisions were made in an attempt to help the MI units garner better intelligence. First, the majority of interrogation operations was consolidated to a central location, the BCCF, Abu Ghraib. Although the location was being used as a detention facility with minimal intelligence presence, the area was big enough to accommodate a larger operation, and the interrogators could take advantage of the standing prison area with cells to segregate detainees with potential intelligence value from the general population. Second, CJTF-7 requested that Washington send subject matter experts who could suggest ways to gain actionable intelligence.

Abu Ghraib is a city approximately eighteen miles west of Baghdad. Positioned between two major highways connecting Baghdad and Fallujah, the prison facility at Abu Ghraib was a massive complex taking up close to one square kilometer in a slanted rectangular formation. During Saddam Hussein's reign, it had been an internationally notorious prison used by the dictator to house, torture, and kill his political rivals. There had been numerous reports of mass executions and unspeakable cruelty, such as beatings and electric shock. The gallows still remained within its walls. In the prison's heyday under Hussein, as many as fifteen thousand prisoners were believed to have been housed there. However, shortly before the U.S. invasion in the spring of 2003, he had granted amnesty to the majority of prisoners and emptied the prison.

Given the prison's infamous reputation, especially among the Iraqi people, the Coalition Provisional Authority (CPA) was at first hesitant to utilize the complex as a detention facility when discussion first arose in June 2003. No one wanted the Americans associated with this prison's past or to operate a detention facility within a contested area. Yet, they needed a place to house Iraqi-on-Iraqi criminals, and Abu Ghraib was one of the few areas that had a standing prison with cells and an outer prison wall that was still mainly intact. With its central location, it was ideal for units throughout Iraq to access. Based on these considerations, the decision to use the prison was granted with the caveat that it would only be an interim facility until they could get a different prison ready.

The 800th was then tasked with preparing the prison for operation. It had been heavily looted after the invasion, many of its buildings had been damaged, and rubble was everywhere. The 800th put the 320th in charge of cleaning up the complex in order to hold both Iraqi civilian detainees as well as insurgents attacking the coalition forces. It was not until later that summer that CJTF-7 designated the prison at Abu Ghraib as its central intelligence debriefing center.

The 320th built three separate holding areas for different types of prisoners. The largest, Camp Ganci, was an encampment set up on the sandy dirt with dozens of Army-issued tents lined in rows and surrounded by strings of barbed, steel-gray concertina wire stacked on top of each other. The tents were ringed with tan sandbags and had plywood flooring. There were several covered, wooden guard towers encircling the wired-off area. This camp was primarily reserved for prisoners accused of Iraqi-on-Iraqi crimes. They were the car thieves, looters, rapists, and common criminals. Since, at this point, the Iraqis were not equipped to take control of these individuals, the job of holding these criminals fell to the 800th. The second detention area was another tent encampment, Camp Vigilant. A mirror image of the larger Camp Ganci, this section held former Fedayeen Saddam members and security holds who had attacked coalition forces.

The actual prison building, known by the American forces as the hard-site, was a two-story stone building. Its construction was similar to the laces on a football, with tiers shooting off to the left and right from a central corridor. Some tiers on the northern side of the building had been damaged and were unusable, leaving four tiers in the southern part of the building to hold prisoners. Tiers 2 through 4 had group cells capable of holding up to sixteen prisoners. Tier 1 had smaller individual cells and one isolation cell with a solid metal door and a sliding window as opposed to the traditional barred doors on the other cells.

All of the tiers had two levels with upper walkways running the length of the hallways. The walls were painted tan with the cell doors painted a slightly darker hue of brown. As the heat of the day warmed the prison, a foul smell arose from the floors and walls as evidence of years of unsanitary conditions. The MPs used Tiers 2 through 4 to house Iraqi-on-Iraqi criminals. Tier 1B was reserved for any juvenile or female prisoners as well as any disciplinary problem detainees from the camp areas. The MI units used Tier 1A to segregate certain detainees from the others. Of the entire sweeping Abu Ghraib prison complex with its thousands of detainees, it was this fifty-foot-long corridor, known as 1A, that was destined to become the epicenter of the abuse scandal that would shake the U.S. mission in the Middle East.

As the intelligence community was reorganizing its operations and consolidating interrogation elements at Abu Ghraib, an assessment team from Joint Task Force–Guantanamo Bay (JTF-GTMO) arrived on August 31 to review CJTF-7's ability to rapidly gain actionable intelligence. Consisting of approximately a dozen military subject matter experts in detention, interrogations, and computer systems, the assessment team was led by MG Geoffrey Miller, the commanding general of Guantanamo. Miller, a straightforward and abrupt man born and raised in Texas, was an artilleryman by trade but had spent the previous year running the U.S. detention and interrogation camp in Cuba.

After a ten-day visit, Miller and his team submitted a report and orally briefed Sanchez, recommending a number of ways they believed CJTF-7 could improve its strategic intelligence gathering. Most of the recommendations were aimed at changes in behavior for the intelligence community: think strategically instead of tactically (i.e., broad goals for the overall Iraq mission instead of how to only stop the local IED bombings) through a better flow of information between commands; have faster turnaround times by putting analysts in the booth with the interrogators; and get everyone on the same page by publishing a uniform interrogation policy that listed acceptable interrogation techniques. Miller's team also wanted to see more cooperation between MI and the MPs securing the detainees. Specifically, they suggested that certain MPs be trained in how to "set the conditions for the successful interrogation and exploitation of internees/detainees." The team tempered all of its recommendations with the acknowledgment that the Geneva Conventions clearly applied to the detainees being held in Iraq.

Taguba was particularly troubled by the team's suggestion that the MPs be utilized in setting conditions for intelligence gathering. He found this practice, which was in direct contradiction to the Army regulation governing MPs, led directly to detainee abuse.

Graveline scribbled a note to himself to look into Miller's visit more closely. The defense counsel had already claimed that the photos showed their clients setting the conditions for interrogations. Miller's visit seemed to be the first mention of MPs assisting with intelligence gathering. Finding out what happened during that visit would be the key to understanding what "setting the conditions" meant.

On the whole, however, Graveline found Taguba's report to be of limited use. It provided some general background information about the prison and the units that served there, and it identified the main players. Other than supplying witness statements, neither a prosecution nor a defense could be based on its findings. The general's report itself was problematic on a number of levels, not the least of which was the fact that the U.S. Congress had essentially taken it as the gospel truth of what had happened at Abu Ghraib.

People are going to expect certain actions be taken against particular individuals based on this report, and you just can't, thought Graveline. The problem with this report is that it's not specific enough; it's just too broad brush. The general throws around quite a few allegations and doesn't pin down enough specific evidence to justify them.

Graveline's mind raced. The report posed more questions than answers.

The report doesn't answer some basic questions. Were all of the photos showing MPs "setting the conditions"? When Taguba stated that certain acts done by the guards were "intentional abuse" or "sadistic," was he saying that any, or all, of this behavior was done at the direction of military intelligence? If they were done at the request of MI, how could the guards be held criminally responsible for following orders? Or did Taguba think the soldiers' actions were "criminal" simply because they were acting under orders that they should have known better than to follow?

The general also singled out four specific people linked with intelligence gathering at Abu Ghraib, including COL Thomas Pappas, the commander of the 205th MI brigade, and LTC Steven Jordan, the director of the Joint Interrogation Debriefing Center (JIDC), as being "directly or indirectly responsible" for the abuses at Abu Ghraib. *What specific abuses was he referring to? All of the abuses depicted in the photos? Other ones not photographed? Taguba could very well be right, but he didn't back these allegations up with specifics.*

Reading the report and the attachments, it seemed to Graveline that Taguba had not approached the investigation dispassionately. From time to time, Taguba lost his composure. Clearly, certain witnesses' responses did not sit well with him. This tendency was particularly evident in his interviews of Brigadier General Karpinski and Lieutenant Colonel Jordan.

Graveline put down the report in frustration. *General Taguba has left many loose ends for us to tie up.*

✦

The sun was shining directly into the JAG office at the back of the palace late Friday afternoon. As on most days between four and eight in the evening, the sun slanted through the large windows overlooking the main veranda and lit up the sizable room.

Wow, what a long week, thought Graveline. *Finally, the end's in sight. Well, as much of an end as you can have in Iraq when you're working all seven days. I hope Colonel Tate won't be too much longer. I'm starving.*

Holley and Graveline were sitting at their makeshift cubicles waiting for Tate to get off the phone with his contacts in Washington. It had become a nightly ritual for the trial team to walk with Tate to dinner at the chow hall, where they would rehash the day's events and get his take on their next steps. Tate had taken a liking to his young team, and these dinner conversations were one of the few times during the day he could relax.

As soon as the boss was ready, they would call Neill, who still worked in the trailers around the courthouse, so he could start his walk down for chow.

One of the young JAG enlisted soldiers approached Holley and Graveline. "There's somebody out in the hallway for you gentlemen."

Wonder who that could be, thought Holley.

As they opened the two large wooden doors leading to the hallway, the two attorneys squinted as their eyes adjusted to the dimly lit hallway. A tall figure dressed in desert camouflage stood partially shadowed a few feet down the hall-way to their right.

They were standing face-to-face with Staff Sergeant Frederick.

The guard's normally flinty, tan face flushed red. It was evident that he had been crying.

"I just want this all to be done. I want this to end," mumbled the sturdy prison guard.

Graveline and Holley were at a loss for words. They could not have been more surprised if Saddam Hussein himself had been standing there.

Holley broke the silence. "Listen, I would like to talk with you, but I can't without one of your attorneys here. If you want to talk with us, go get your at-torney, Captain Shuck, and bring him back up here." *Hopefully, Shuck is still down at his trailer,* Holley thought.

As Frederick walked away, Holley and Graveline hustled back into their office. They knew they had to think fast.

"Try to get Shuck on the phone," Holley instructed Graveline. "I'll get Colonel Tate."

Graveline could not reach Shuck. *Where are you, Rob? What else can you be doing on Friday night in Iraq?* He was becoming exasperated.

Graveline called down to Neill. He quickly explained the situation. "We need you to find Shuck and see if you can get him and Frederick together. We'd like to get them back up here tonight." Neill was on it; he would do what he could to find the off-duty defense counsel.

For their part, Tate, Holley, and Graveline were cautious and considered their next step. It was not every day that an accused soldier walks up to the pros-ecutors in tears, seemingly wanting to plead guilty.

What was certain was that Frederick's unexpected visit could be the big break they had been looking for. While Sivits was convicted and cooperating, he was still a young generator mechanic who had only witnessed two incidents of abuse in his time at Abu Ghraib. He was neither an MP nor a key player, but Frederick was an insider, the hard-site's NCOIC at night, and the most senior MP guard charged.

Robinson and Neill soon joined the three men in Tate's office. Neill had found Shuck and put him in touch with Frederick. Shuck told Neill that the two men would be up to the palace shortly. The five men talked animatedly over each other for several minutes.

Had Frederick talked to his lawyers prior to showing up in the hallway? If not, would Shuck even bring him back that night? What would Frederick's civilian lawyer's input be? If Frederick actually had spoken to his attorneys, what deal were they going to want? If Frederick wanted to plead guilty, how helpful would he be in testifying against the others? For their part, what deal would be acceptable to recommend to the general?

Tate focused them on the most pressing issue. "If I'm going to recommend a deal to my CG [commanding general], we'll need to know how helpful he's going to be with the other cases. I'm not too interested in cutting some deal with a guy who refuses to testify. We need a proffer from Shuck of what his client's going to say."

"That course of action could pose another problem," Holley interjected. "If he or Graveline talked with Frederick before a deal was worked out, there was the possibility under military law that they would have to disqualify themselves from the case based on what they elicited from Frederick if a deal fell through at a later date. Myers and Shuck could argue that the prosecutors learned certain facts from their client's interview and could now act on facts that they normally would not be privy to." Graveline thought Holley's concern was too conservative, but he also did not want to miss a chance to see these cases to the end.

Without a clear consensus on how to proceed, Tate decided the best course of action was for Neill to sit down and talk with Frederick and Shuck. Neill knew the case as well as anyone. He could ask the right questions and obtain the information necessary to decide whether to cut a deal with Frederick. Tate also tapped another captain, Joe Kobs, an administrative law attorney with no connection to the trial team, to sit in on the interview as a witness.

Another hour passed, still no Frederick or Shuck. *He's not coming back*, thought Graveline as he sat idly, surfing from one website to another on his computer.

Finally, Shuck appeared at the door. He nervously motioned Holley and Graveline over. Standing behind him in the dark hallway was Frederick, wearing the same sullen face that he had several hours before.

"We'd like to talk," he told the prosecutors.

Holley quickly ushered them down the long hallway and around the corner to a large conference room. As they walked, Shuck apologized for the delay, but it had taken quite a while for them to reach Gary Myers on the phone and talk over the options. They were prepared to give the government a proffer to all of the events Frederick could testify about. After the prosecutors had a chance to think through the proffer, Myers would contact Holley that weekend to go over the details of a guilty plea for his client. Holley agreed that the defense's proposal seemed a reasonable way to go and explained that Neill would take down the proffer to protect their client until the deal was complete. Shuck thanked Holley for his sensitivity to the situation. Holley closed the door behind him.

The next several hours dragged on for the four other prosecutors waiting in the main JAG office. As the clock crept past 2:00 a.m., they were all lost in their own thoughts. Tate sat in his office, responding to e-mails from the States. Holley sat with his legs kicked up on his desk, thinking about Sergeant Frederick. He could empathize with the man.

You don't have to condone his misconduct to feel for him, Holley thought. He could tell Frederick was hurting—from what at that point he did not know. *Anyway, isn't this how a justice system is supposed to work—have someone come to grips with where he went astray and come back looking to make amends?*

At the other end of the room, Graveline lay sprawled across a corner desk, pondering how Frederick's testimony could break open many of the questions surrounding the prison at Abu Ghraib. Robinson, who routinely woke up earlier than the others, sat half asleep, his head bobbing down.

From time to time, Neill would stroll back in to fill his coffee mug. The others would practically tackle him, peppering him with questions.

"How's it going?"

"No details . . . but are we getting anything good?"

Neill, a practical joker and always quick with a quip, smiled mischievously; quietly muttered, "It's all right"; and was back out the door and down the hall.

"You know I'm going to kill Chuck after tonight," Graveline moaned in exasperation.

The rest agreed.

5

HELL ON EARTH

Neill was taking his time, trying to draw from Frederick as much information as possible. He shared the rest of the team's hope that the staff sergeant was
about to break the entire Abu Ghraib scandal wide open, one way or another.
His interest was further piqued by a conversation he had had with Shuck a few
weeks earlier. If the government could come up with a reasonable sentence cap,
Shuck suggested that his client would be more than willing to come clean about
what happened. "You only know the tip of the iceberg," Shuck told Neill.

Hours earlier, as the interview began, Neill encouraged Frederick to speak
freely. He used a variety of interview techniques: asking very general, open-ended questions; giving nonverbal cues to suggest that he had not heard any of the
information before; and furiously taking notes on everything Frederick was relating. However, as the hours began to melt away, Neill started to seriously doubt
Shuck's "tip of the iceberg" comment. For the nights he was present, Frederick
could clearly explain to Neill and Kobs his actions and those of Graner, England,
and the others, but when it came to any senior officers' knowledge of the abuses,
he seemed to be simply speculating. After listening to Frederick for a while, Neill
decided to focus the soldier.

"What interactions did you have with senior leaders out there, for instance,
Lieutenant Colonel Jordan?"

Frederick hesitated and thought for a moment. "He would come down to
the hard-site all the time . . . ," he began.

Neill broke in. "Did he ever comment on what you were doing down there?"

"Well, one time, he came down and shook my hand. He said, 'You're doing a good job.'"

Neill was not impressed. *Officers go around all the time, shake soldiers' hands, tell them they are doing a good job, and have no idea what that particular soldier is actually doing,* Neill thought. He decided to press Frederick further. "Did Lieutenant Colonel Jordan know about any specific abuses, like the human pyramid?"

"No, sir."

After a few more questions, Neill wrapped up the interview around 3:00 a.m. Frederick and Shuck left the room, and Neill reflected on the character of the lengthy interview—it had been disjointed with Frederick leaping from one topic to another. *It was very difficult to keep him focused; he was definitely a stream-of-consciousness individual,* Neill assessed.

As Neill walked back into the main JAG office, Tate had only one question for him: "Does Frederick give us enough to justify pursuing a deal with him?"

Neill's first impression was that Frederick would not make a strong witness (he was simply too erratic), but they should strike a deal with Frederick, if possible, since he would definitely firm up the cases against the soldiers already charged. Without launching into specifics, Tate wanted to know whether Frederick had given them any new information about officer involvement.

"Definitely not," Neill replied.

Tate turned to Holley and gave the okay to broker a deal with Frederick and Myers. "But we can take that up in the morning . . . let's get some sleep," Tate suggested.

With the decision made to work with Frederick, the trial team began to wrestle with the dilemma of what sentence cap to offer the soldier. He was currently facing the possibility of sixteen and a half years. Myers would definitely want a lower number. In the military justice system, an accused soldier who strikes a plea deal with the government gets two bites at the apple to determine his sentence. First, the soldier and the convening authority, usually the unit's commanding general, agree on a sentence cap by placing a ceiling on the amount of jail time. With this agreement in hand, the soldier then goes to court-martial in front of either a military judge or a jury who will decide his sentence based on the maximum punishment allowed. This sentencing authority is not made aware of the previous agreement or cap. After the authority decides on an appropriate sentence, the accused soldier receives the lesser of the two, either the one adjudged at his hearing or the one previously agreed on with the general.

Prior to Frederick's surprise visit to their office, the team members had mulled over the desired end state for each of the prosecutions.

"I think we should view these cases as a ladder of escalating punishments with Ambuhl, probably the least culpable, at the bottom of the scale; Harman, Davis, and England in that order somewhere in the middle; and Frederick and Graner at the top," Graveline suggested. That paradigm seemed to fit the evidence that they had concerning the soldiers' involvement at the time.

Holley agreed but proposed a slightly different focus. "I think that's a good framework, but the way I see the evidence, Graner is the real bad guy in this group. He is involved in the most abuse and appears to be leading it. His is the really important trial . . . all of our strategic choices should be done with his court-martial in mind. The others won't matter much if we don't get his right."

Tate liked both Holley's focus on Graner and the general ladder strategy as far as punishments, but he reminded his young prosecutors of the desired result, just convictions in the cases that warranted them. While sentences definitely were important, that aspect of the trials was the least in their control.

Tate was reiterating something they all understood. There are no sentencing guidelines in military justice. The judge or jury can sentence a convicted soldier to no punishment all the way up to the maximum. During sentencing, the rules of evidence are virtually nonexistent, and all types of hearsay and speculation are brought in for consideration. Additionally, the soldier can also take the stand and make an unsworn statement regarding any topic he thinks important for the court to know. Sentencing proceedings in the military are oftentimes a crapshoot.

Despite understanding the realities of the system, the team realized that the sentences in these cases were going to be very important. Although unspoken, they all realized the tangible, numerical end results of these trials were going to affect the overall mission in Iraq. If the sentences were too lenient for these infamous crimes, it could send the wrong message to the victims, the Army, and both countries and potentially drive a greater wedge between the Americans and the Iraqis. While the sentences imposed by a judge or a jury were out of the prosecutors' control, the plea deals were not. They were only interested in recommending to Lieutenant General Metz plea deals that would reflect how seriously the command took the abuse.

With Frederick coming forward, the trial team needed to set the upper range of the sentences while, at the same time, making the deal attractive enough to convince Frederick to accept. However, Frederick's situation presented a difficult balancing act. On the one hand, based on their information from Sivits', Harman's, and England's sworn statements to CID, Frederick was one of the leaders. He had been the top enlisted soldier in the hard-site at night and had posed next to detainees who were either naked or in abusive positions. Frederick had been present for the infamous picture of the hooded man standing on the box with wires hanging from his hands and the night of the naked human pyramid; and on top of everything, he had physically assaulted detainees. On the other hand, having his cooperation would be a huge asset for the government. Frederick would give them a better view of the scope of the abuse and the complicity of MI and could fill in the details that Sivits was simply unable to provide.

Additionally, despite the benefits of a deal with Frederick, there were pitfalls to be avoided. If they agreed to a low number of years in prison, it would be very difficult to convincingly argue that Graner should serve substantially more time than Frederick or that the lesser players deserved roughly the same as one of the leaders. A sentence cap too low would possibly give the impression that Frederick could not be believed since the prosecution had "bought" the coconspirator's testimony for a "sweetheart of a deal." Any plea deal with Frederick was going to set the bar and determine how the rest of these cases would play out.

After hashing out these considerations, Tate told the group he was inclined to recommend no less than an eight-year cap to Metz. That would be half of what Frederick was currently facing and tough enough to address the seriousness of Frederick's role in the acts.

It was now up Holley to close the deal.

Creativity is going to be the key to these negotiations, Holley sensed. In order to entice Myers to agree to a high sentence cap, he knew that they had to be willing to concede to other demands they might not normally concede to.

Holley contacted Myers by e-mail the day after Frederick's late-night appearance. Myers suggested a Sunday morning telephone call to discuss a deal and how to reach him since he was on a short vacation in Rota, Spain.

So, in the early morning hours of June 27, Holley met Shuck in the main JAG office. Illuminated by only the faintest of morning sunshine in one corner, the room sat completely silent; most of the soldiers were either attending church services or taking in a few hours of extra sleep on their "weekend." Shuck brought along one of the new international cell phones Tate had obtained for the defense counsel's use. Clearly pleased with the new gadget, Shuck demonstrated the hands-free device to Holley. Holley could not have been more disinterested in the phone. He did not mind the early hour of the call (it was one of the few times one could talk privately on the phone), but it was too early for chatter about a cell phone.

As Shuck dialed the lengthy international number, Holley ran through his mental checklist of topics he thought might help convince Frederick and Myers that a deal would be beneficial: dismiss or let him plead to lesser offenses on certain charges, no argument over the number of witnesses to testify on Frederick's behalf, video-teleconference (VTC) for witnesses who did not want to travel to Iraq to testify, and agree to waive any pay forfeitures that may be part of the sentence and direct that money to Frederick's family.

Holley started off with some pleasantries and small talk about the difficulty of securing a good telephone connection out of Baghdad. He wanted to establish a congenial tone before springing the eight-year cap on Myers, an attorney he genuinely respected. He emphasized that the government was willing to accommodate Myers' presentation of mitigation and extenuation evidence during the sentencing hearing.

Finally, it came time to broach the sticky subject of jail time. Holley walked out of the office and onto the stone veranda overlooking the lake. He wanted to talk plainly to Myers about the sentence cap without anyone possibly overhearing.

Much to Holley's surprise, Myers seemed unphased by the eight-year offer. The discussion over the cap number was over in a matter of seconds. Myers seemed much more focused on the witnesses he was going to call and how to present them in Iraq without having them travel into the combat zone. He stated that he was not finished with his attempts to move the court-martial out of Iraq and was planning to appeal the judge's insistence on trying the court-martial in Iraq to the highest military courts in Washington, D.C. Holley replied that he understood the defense's position but that he still believed that the best place to conduct a sentencing hearing for Frederick was in Iraq, especially since the government was still deciding on whether to call some of the abused Iraqis to testify during the sentencing hearing. With Holley's reassurance that the team would do everything in its power to have Frederick's witnesses in front of the judge by video-teleconference, the phone call ended with a temporary agreement in place.

Holley hung up the phone with mixed emotions. He was thrilled that they had obtained exactly what they wanted. A deal was clearly possible since the two sides were apparently concerned about different objectives. Yet, there was still a long way to go before the deal was set in stone. In his experience, he had seen tentative deals in even the simplest cases fall through. He did not want to think they had a deal only to watch it evaporate weeks from now. Still, he could not wait to break the news to Tate and Graveline.

Graveline strolled into the office later that morning. Since he had slipped out of the office early the night before, he had no idea that Holley had scheduled a time to talk with Myers that morning. Holley spun around in his chair and excitedly told his partner about his conversation. Graveline was ecstatic.

"If we can get Frederick to roll, we might actually have a chance to wrap up these cases by the end of September after all." Anything that would move these cases along faster was a welcome relief.

The Frederick development was the first bright spot for Holley and Graveline. Both men had resigned themselves to the fact that there was no possible way these cases were going to be resolved in the "ninety to one hundred twenty days" they had originally been told. Normally, in the military, once a soldier is arraigned, he will stand trial within sixty to ninety days. However, it was quickly becoming evident to both of them that September would be the earliest the first case might go to trial and only if they pushed hard and caught some luck. There were just too many witnesses to be interviewed, too many leads to be tracked down, and too many cases to be resolved in a three-month time frame.

Worsening the situation in their minds, the two prosecutors sensed they had no control over how these cases were going to unfold or on whose time line. Six days earlier, Graveline had stood in court and informed Judge Pohl and the defense that they would have Major General Fay's investigation into the 205th

MI Brigade's conduct at Abu Ghraib by no later than July 1. But the day before Holley's conversation with Myers, they had learned from an Associated Press article on the Internet that Fay was not going to meet his July 1 deadline. LTG Anthony Jones, a three-star general, was replacing Fay as the lead investigator, since Fay had determined Sanchez should be interviewed as part of the investigation. According to Army regulation, an independent investigator must outrank the person being interviewed so that rank does not deter the investigator from asking difficult questions.

Even though pushing back the deadline was the correct decision, neither Holley nor Graveline was very happy with it. Fay had e-mailed Goetzke early in June, informing him that he believed his team had compiled a significant amount of information that was going to be of interest to both the prosecution and the defense. In Fay's assessment, no trials could proceed until both sides were given a chance to absorb all of the collected data. Graveline had already heard rumors that Fay's team had amassed more than seven thousand pages of documentary evidence. Additionally, Pohl had stated that these cases were not moving forward without the defense being given at least the witness statements from that investigation. It would now take a good deal of time for Jones to become familiar enough with the facts to ask Sanchez informed questions about CJTF-7's intelligence gathering. Until the prosecutors got their hands on this investigation, the cases would be delayed indefinitely.

This latest news was the proverbial last straw for Holley and Graveline. They knew they had to be more assertive if these cases were ever going to see the inside of a courtroom. The two of them hatched a plan to send Graveline back to the States for a few weeks to subpoena relevant documents from the various governmental and military agencies holding them. Although Graveline had already made contact with several of them, it was clear from the slow or lack of responses that the agencies were either content hiding behind red tape or hoping the prosecutors would not follow up. Plus being in the States would allow Graveline to set up the defense interviews with the chain of command there, such as Karpinski and some of her staff. It was time to take the idea to Tate.

At first, Tate seemed reluctant. The senior JAG was much more attuned to the inner workings of the Pentagon and the relations between governmental agencies. It would not be warmly received if a young Army prosecutor just appeared in the halls of the Pentagon or the Central Intelligence Agency (CIA), handing out subpoenas.

Graveline persisted. "It's too easy to blow someone off when they are halfway around the world talking to you on a fuzzy phone line. It's much harder to ignore that person standing in your office with a subpoena."

Holley was adamant as well. "If we have any hope of meeting the July 31 discovery deadline Judge Pohl gave us, we've got to go out and either persuade or force these agencies to start playing ball with us."

"All right, all right. If you guys think it's necessary, Chris can go," Tate relented. "But no subpoenas . . . at least not unless and until I give the word. I want you to get with Lieutenant Colonel Fair, figure out who has what, and write all of them a letter requesting the information. Tell them that you'll be in D.C. in a couple of weeks and will be stopping by to pick up the material. Let's see where that gets us." Tate paused and looked squarely across his desk at Graveline. "Let's make sure we're clear . . . no subpoenas until I give the okay."

LTC Karen Fair, a petite, sandy-haired West Point graduate, had arrived earlier that week to assume duties as Tate's deputy staff judge advocate. Coming from the Army's Office of the General Counsel (OCG) in the Pentagon, Tate figured she would have the most up-to-date information regarding which agencies were involved with the Abu Ghraib investigations. Fair assured Graveline that she would call her contacts in the OCG to see what she could find out.

The next day, Fair called Graveline over to her desk just outside of Tate's office and handed him a piece of paper. On the single page was a table listing the DoD's investigations into detention-related allegations. Consisting of several columns, it detailed who initiated each investigation, the name of the investigating officer or agency, the date it commenced, its purpose or scope, the status, and to whom the results of the investigation had been briefed. Graveline thanked Fair for the trove of information; it was as if she had handed him the key to a locked box containing vast wealth. Eleven investigations. The list was longer than Graveline expected, and it did not include other agencies, such as the CIA and Federal Bureau of Investigation (FBI) that he thought might have relevant information. Neither of these realities dampened his mood, however. For the first time, he knew what he had to get his hands on and where to find it.

List in hand, he walked down the marble hallway to the team's new office. Their new space, actually two small adjoining storage rooms, had been a work in progress for the last ten days, but the last touch—Internet connectivity—was now complete. While Graveline had been talking with Fair, Holley and Kary moved all of their material into their new workplace. They set up their work areas back-to-back and laid out folding tables in each corner of the entry room, next to the electrical plugs. The interior room contained a safe for classified documents and file cabinets in the left corner, a computer work area complete with a scanner set up on a long table for Sergeant Kary, and two other long tables stretched along the far wall for binders and boxes of candy and goodies from home.

Graveline sat down at his computer to put the final touches on the letters notifying these agencies that he would be coming to gather their investigations. The main message was in his second paragraph:

The Government's prosecution team has become aware that your agency is currently conducting an investigation that could have relevant information to these courts-martial. As the Government representative, I am requesting that your agency provide a copy of any relevant investigations for inspection and possible dissemination to the defense counsel. The Government believes that the release of the investigation, especially witness statements obtained during the course of the investigation, is an essential step in expeditiously resolving these cases. It is the Government's goal that the extensive pretrial discovery issues can be resolved informally without resort to the Court's subpoena power.

The language was a watered-down version of Graveline's original letter (he and Fair had gone around and around on the nuances late one night much to Holley's delight, as he laughed at his young partner's exasperation). *It's definitely more politically deft than my first draft, with just enough of a threat for a subpoena,* Graveline eventually conceded. The letters went out attached to e-mails on July 1 and 2, 2004.

Graveline scrambled to get ready to leave Iraq. Staff Sergeant Brann worked his back channels to have the requisite paperwork approved unusually fast and received the necessary permissions for Graveline to fly. But even with Brann's connections, the true challenge would be traveling from Baghdad to Kuwait.

It was not uncommon for a soldier to sit for days at the airport, waiting for the next Air Force flight to take off. For force protection purposes, the air controllers would not give exact flight times over the phone, only "show times," which could vary from an hour to several hours before the flight's actual departure. Additionally, the Air Force would not know how many passengers it could take, or who would take priority, until immediately before departure based on what cargo had to go on the C-130 airplane. Combine all of these variables with numerous soldiers itching for the chance to leave Iraq for even a few days of R&R, and the passenger "terminal" (or three large canvas tents set up with crooked rows of cots and folding chairs) was a miserable place to be.

This uncertainty compounded the difficulty of booking flights out of Kuwait. Graveline was reluctant to purchase a commercial airline ticket without knowing for sure when he would leave Iraq. Sergeant Kary and Staff Sergeant Brann had been trying all week to pin the Air Force down on an available flight out of Baghdad. After yet another futile attempt, Kary spun around in his chair.

"What if we try the British or Australian transports? They leave out of the airport and fly down to the same airfields in Kuwait. You can then book your follow-on tickets to the States with the travel agent on Camp Doha in Kuwait." Kary paused, then added jokingly, "And I hear they serve better food on the British flights, sir."

Kary's idea proved to be a great success. On July 5, Graveline approached the British Air Force counter in the passenger terminal. A young twenty-year-old British soldier informed Graveline that he would be leaving within the hour. Soon, Graveline was strapped into one of the British transport's red canvas seats, peering out the small, round window at Baghdad below.

Two days later, Graveline stepped off another plane, this one a jumbo jet at Washington Dulles International Airport. Fortunately for Graveline, an important ally in the Army JAG community was taking care of the Washington side of his trip. LTC Mike Mulligan was widely recognized within the DoD as *the* case prosecutor for the Army. Known for his aggressive manner, he had prosecuted a two-star general, high-profile murderers, and a gang leader in the course of his stellar military career. Mulligan, a block of a man whose graying crew cut accentuated his square facial features, was now the head of the Trial Counsel Assistance Program (a centralized agency the JAGs had set up in Arlington, Virginia, to help young prosecutors around the world). Beyond the usual rigors of his job, he was also leading a team that was prosecuting a capital murder case out of Fort Bragg against a soldier who had wounded and killed his brigade's leadership prior to the Iraq invasion.

Most importantly, Mulligan was a close personal friend of Tate's and wanted to help the team in whatever way he could. Given his already intense workload, the JAG leadership had decided not to assign Mulligan to these Abu Ghraib cases. However, they had sought his advice on whom the prosecutors should be, and Mulligan had been one of the senior JAGs to recommend both Holley and Graveline for the prosecution team. Graveline and Mulligan had crossed paths a few years earlier when Graveline had been the appellate attorney working on Mulligan's gang prosecution. As the captain's assignment officer, it had been Mulligan who had arranged Graveline's move to Heidelberg in 2003. Now he was working out the details and finding Graveline office space and a hotel room, and setting up meetings for him.

Graveline's first stop in the States was Mulligan's office. The energetic lieutenant colonel sprang to his feet to shake the younger man's hand, his enormous hand easily enveloping Graveline's.

He had only one question: "What can I do to help?"

With Graveline off to the States with his list of tasks, Holley turned his attention toward his side of the case, the 372d MPs. While he had read their witness statements taken by CID and had spoken briefly to a few of them at Harman's Article 32 investigation, he sensed that there was much more information to be gleaned from these men and women. They had been there, presumably seen the same things as the accused soldiers, been given the same training prior to deploying, and were their leaders and friends. However, when CID had interviewed them, to very open-ended questions they had given mostly nondescript answers, such as "I never saw any abuse" or "It was crazy there."

If I can pin them down with some details, it'll go a long way to figuring out who these soldiers are and how much the chain of command knew, Holley pondered. *These soldiers are going to hold the key to discovering the full picture of what happened at that prison. They are the case.* Holley had heard rumblings that these soldiers knew more than they were saying, but no one had "asked the right questions" yet. This news did not surprise him since very few of these soldiers had been interviewed, or only in a very cursory manner, by CID or other Army investigators. He had to meet these soldiers face-to-face.

On Wednesday, July 7, Holley coordinated with Captain Toman and SFC Michael Bostic, the rail-thin, quiet chief paralegal for the 16th MP Brigade, to travel to the 372d location, Log Base Seitz. While Seitz was technically a part of the Victory Base/Airport compound, it was a thirty- to forty-minute drive from Victory Base's center. The black Ford Explorer bounced along the pothole-filled dirt roads with Bostic driving, Toman riding shotgun, and Holley sitting in the back. Dust kicked up heavy and thick behind them. All three men were loaded down in their flak vests and Kevlar helmets as they rode along the base's perimeter.

It was mid-afternoon when they arrived at the remote location. A solitary soldier stood manning the gate under a tiny makeshift canopy just wide enough to protect him from the direct rays of the blazing sun. Bostic slowed to a halt, and the soldier raised the single-bar gate. As they drove onto the base, Holley could not believe what he saw.

Seitz looked like some kind of dock, or a junkyard, with odd stacks of equipment, pieces of vehicles, barrels, pipes, tires, generators, and scrap metal strewn throughout. Every building, without exception, was heavily sandbagged and razor-wired off. Throughout camp, there were a number of high blast walls constructed of sand-filled canvas blocks wired together and numerous mortar bunkers that formed mazes approaching and separating buildings. The bright sun cast bizarre shadows off the piles of debris and gray-colored walls, giving the camp an otherworldly feel.

This place is like a scene out of Mad Max, Holley thought, calling to mind the postapocalyptic world depicted in the famous Mel Gibson movies. In his decade in the Army, Holley had never seen such chaos in an Army-run operation.

The vehicle pulled up to the 372d company area. As the men walked into the company headquarters building, it took a few minutes for their eyes to adjust to the change in lighting. The single room was lit exclusively with fluorescent lighting, the windows having all been blocked to the top with sandbags. There was a folding table and a few metal chairs in the center of the room, and a map of the local area pinned to the far wall. Waiting for them in this makeshift headquarters were the company commander, CPT Donald Reese; company 1SG Brian Lipinski; and SFC Shannon Snider.

Reese, in his late-thirties and a window-blind salesman in his civilian life, was a rugged-looking man with a pronounced jaw and salt-and-pepper black hair. He walked over to Holley and shook his hand. Holley looked him squarely in the eye.

He looks flat worn out, Holley thought. He knew that the company leadership, particularly these three, had been through a lot since the pictures surfaced. Within weeks of discovering the abuse photos, they had been suspended indefinitely, removed from Abu Ghraib, and sent to live on Victory Base. No one had let them know their status, how long the investigation would take, or if they would be rejoining their unit or sent back to the States. They had spent their days fishing for carp in the lake around the Al Faw Palace and waiting, never sure if the next day was going to be their last at Victory or in Iraq. This uncertainty for both them and their unit had clearly taken a toll on Reese and Lipinski. Holley sensed they were overwhelmed by the fervor over the photos and were close to their respective breaking points.

The group moved from the center of the room and began to talk. Holley focused the conversation on which soldiers had specific duties in the hard-site at Abu Ghraib. He wanted Reese and Lipinski to re-create how the company was organized at the prison in October and November 2003 in order to identify the key soldiers he needed to interview.

Reese and Lipinski laid out how the platoons were set up and who was in them. They explained how they had been short on manpower when they arrived at the prison and had taken soldiers from the headquarters platoon to fill the other four platoons. The company had then spread out to work different missions. First platoon had received the mission to run Camp Vigilant, one of the two tent encampments at the larger Abu Ghraib facility. Second platoon had moved into the Green Zone in Baghdad to run protective service missions for the CPA. Third and fourth platoons had been cross-leveled, with some of third platoon running escort missions into Baghdad and the rest of these two platoons in charge of the hard-site prison. Reese had moved Graner and Frederick from the headquarters platoon to fourth to utilize their experience as prison guards.

As the commander and first sergeant continued to talk, Holley started piecing together the chain of command and hard-site operations. After a few minutes, he had decided who he needed to talk to that day: SFC John Boyd, Graner's platoon sergeant, as well as SSG Christopher Ward and SGT Hydrue Joyner, Frederick and Graner's counterparts from the day shift in the hard-site.

First, though, Holley wanted a few minutes alone with Snider. His name had come up numerous times in Holley's reading and conversations with other 372d soldiers. He had been the night shift's top enlisted soldier, and Holley had pointed questions for him. In particular, Holley had to know what Snider witnessed on November 7, the night the seven detainees had been brought into the hard-site from one of the outside camps, stacked in the human pyramid, and forced to masturbate. This night was the basis for a number of the charges against the accused soldiers.

Holley walked the slim guard outside. "I need to know exactly what you did and saw the night of November 7."

Snider did not hesitate. "I was on the top tier and saw Davis bring his leg up pretty high and come down in a stomp. I couldn't really tell if he stomped on a detainee or not, but I told him to knock it off."

"Back up to the beginning. When you brought the detainee you were escorting into the tier, did you throw him down?"

"No, I put him on his knees. Look at me . . . I can't be throwing people around," Snider immediately responded. Holley sized up the small man. *It's true. He can't be any more than five-foot-six, 160 pounds.*

Snider continued. "I then went up to the top tier . . . into the office. I looked down and saw Davis bringing his leg up."

"Did you see Davis jump on top of the pile of detainees?" interrupted Holley, referring to claims by other witnesses that Davis had "body slammed" the hooded men.

"No, sir. I only saw Davis stomping and told him to stop. I then walked downstairs and saw Davis out in the main hallway. When he saw me, he said, 'That was no worse than what happened to me in college.' And that was the end of it. I didn't see anything after that."

Holley was generally satisfied for the moment with Snider's answers. He still did not know what entirely to make of Snider's involvement regarding the Abu

Ghraib abuses, but he did not sense the MP was holding anything back regarding that particular night. He asked where he could find Joyner. Snider pointed him toward the sleep area.

Holley had already heard quite a bit about Sergeant Hydrue Joyner from other soldiers and was looking forward to finally talking with him. Given that Joyner ran Tier 1A during the day and Graner at night, he seemed to be the key to understanding what really went on there. If anyone would know about MI involvement on that tier, it would be Joyner.

Holley, Toman, and Bostic walked into the rectangular trailer that served as the company sleep area. The room was lined with rows of bunk beds. At the far end of the room, remnants of a shattered dry erase board littered the floor. Holley found Joyner sitting on a bunk facing the door. He walked over, shook his hand, and introduced himself. Since Holley expected Joyner to be guarded about talking with the prosecutor, he tried to break the ice by asking Joyner about his background.

Joyner, a large, physically strong man with a wide face and an engaging personality, opened up immediately. He had been born in North Carolina but raised in Washington, D.C., in a tight-knit, religious family. A security guard in his normal civilian job, he was married and had had five years of experience in the Army Reserve. He had enjoyed his time in the 372d but had found his job at the hard-site to be very stressful. Having never been a prison guard, he had been out of his element in the hard-site, unsure of what to do on a day-to-day basis. So he improvised and did the best he could, Joyner told Holley.

Holley found him good-natured and liked him right away. *He seems very open and honest,* Holley thought. *If he turns out to be deeply involved in abuse, I'm going to be very surprised and disappointed.*

Joyner had arrived at Abu Ghraib on October 12, 2003, two days before Tier 1A was turned over to him. Anywhere between twenty to sixty people were usually housed in the tier at any one time. His biggest concern was keeping the cell block clean, using whatever soap, toothpaste, or disinfectant he could scrounge up out of care packages sent to the soldiers from home. He had found the detainees to be, by and large, cooperative and friendly. He would walk through the tier and make conversation with them in his broken Arabic and their broken English. Not being familiar with many of their actual names, Joyner began giving the detainees friendly nicknames, such as "Spider Man," "Big Bird," or "Groucho." In fact, Joyner related to Holley, some of the detainees felt hurt if he did not give them a nickname, and they would eagerly ask for one.

Joyner stated that he had seen detainees naked in their cells, usually when he came to relieve the night shift. Graner would tell him the naked men had had their clothes taken away as punishment for having a weapon or food that they were not supposed to have. He could not remember a time when MI had asked him to strip anyone, but MI had asked him to help keep detainees awake when they were running their sleep programs. Initially, these requests had been verbal, but over his time in Tier 1A, they were written in a formal memo. MI had asked him once to play loud music for a particular detainee, and that request had been in writing.

Holley turned Joyner's attention to some of the specific detainees. Joyner had been on the quick reaction force (QRF) the night of November 7 and had heard about the riot in the outside tent camp. He knew that seven men had been brought into the hard-site to go to Tier 1B, but he had not been present when they came in.

"What did you know about the detainee on the end of the 'leash' held by Lynndie England?" Holley inquired. Joyner identified that naked detainee as "Gus," a distinctive man whom Joyner would not soon forget. Gus "refused all things": clothes, medicine, food, water—everything. He would turn down food and water until the point of dehydration, all with the signature line, "I refuse!" Although he also would threaten Joyner and every other guard, Gus was too small, and generally too weak, to hurt anyone. He would sometimes swing at Joyner, but the swings were along the lines of a cartoon character: wild, comical, not dangerous.

Joyner eventually attempted a diplomatic approach to Gus. He put a table in the middle of the tier with two chairs and a little food. Joyner invited Gus to have a seat. Gus initially refused but then started to devour the food on the table. Joyner warned Gus to slow down, but Gus naturally "refused" and ended up vomiting. When he regained his composure, Gus told Joyner that Joyner was "okay," but he would still shoot Joyner with a rocket when given the chance.

Joyner told Holley that he was flattered Gus would use an entire rocket just on him.

Holley laughed. The extroverted guard filled in many of the gaps. However, Holley was still sure there was more to learn from him. But the JAG's time was running short, and he needed to catch up with other soldiers before leaving.

The JAG trio wove around the labyrinth of bunkers to the base's chow hall. Inside, Reese and Lipinski found a few more soldiers: SFC John Boyd, Graner's original platoon sergeant; SSG Christopher Ward, Frederick's day shift equivalent; and SGT Robert Jones. As Holley sat down with these soldiers, he found them to be very willing to talk on any number of topics: the accused soldiers, their chain of command, their deployment to Iraq, and their current assignment.

However, he also found that this company was in disrepair, and the soldiers were struggling to keep their sanity. Their collective spirit was broken, and any semblance of "unit" came from their own personal commitment to each other—and even that was flagging. Holley could not help but sense whatever pride these soldiers had when they began their trek to Iraq had greatly diminished. The soldiers he interviewed kept repeating how ashamed they were to be members of the 372d.

We forget how much we play up unit pride in the Army, Holley reflected. *That's great and effective—until it's gone.*

As his interviews continued, Holley began to understand the sources of the frustration, anger, and disgrace these soldiers felt. The 372d, at that point, had been in Iraq for a long time, beginning its tour in May 2003. The soldiers had initially deployed to a tiny town south of Baghdad, called Al-Hillah, with the mission of conducting "normal law-and-order" patrols around the city, establishing a police academy, and running the local jail.

Arriving in Al-Hillah shortly after the American offensive operation, they discovered living conditions were primitive at best. The company set up its living area in an abandoned date factory, pitching long lines of cots with mere inches separating each one. The stagnant desert air hung motionless as the summer heat slowly turned the building into a giant sauna. The factory had no running water or electricity. Birds and bats built nests in the rafters, regularly dropping excrement on the soldiers' personal belongings and beds below. A "lucky" few, including Graner and Frederick, lived in a tent planted a short distance from the main building. Despite these hardships, the 372d soldiers remembered Al-Hillah with pride. They had seen much progress, the townspeople loved them, and the unit had received a good deal of praise from the 800th's chain of command.

As their time in Al-Hillah drew to an end, many of the soldiers believed that they would be heading home. Then came the news that they were heading to Abu Ghraib to help run the prison facility there. While the overall mood sank, morale was still high coming off their positive Al-Hillah experience. The company broke in two, with half heading directly to Abu Ghraib in the first days of October and the other half traveling to Kuwait to replenish supplies. In the first wave was the company leadership, including Reese and Lipinski. The second group, which included Joyner, Graner, and Frederick, arrived at Abu Ghraib between October 12 and 15, 2003.

Getting resources had been a real problem at Abu Ghraib. The 372d had continuously asked for better food and clothing for the detainees. All the soldiers related to Holley that they had seen some naked detainees, but their nudity had generally stemmed from a lack of supplies. They simply did not have enough jumpsuits, or even underwear, for every detainee. Each request for more supplies had taken weeks to arrive, or was received with the wrong items, or had simply never been filled. In fact, the reason many male detainees were issued female underwear was not to humiliate them, but because when the unit had requested men's underwear, boxes and boxes of women's underwear had been sent instead. That was all they had to give the prisoners.

Holley also broached their interactions with MI. Some soldiers who had worked the hard-site stated that MI had asked them to help keep detainees awake by yelling at them. Others had no similar dealings with MI.

Holley perceived that the general consensus among these soldiers was that Abu Ghraib was a difficult and confusing experience on many different levels but that Graner and his posse had completely screwed up and ruined things for the unit. He also began to get his first real feel for the character and personality of the accused soldiers.

Graner: a smart, charismatic, funny rogue who did his own thing
Frederick: an average noncommissioned officer (NCO) with no striking traits, a
    follower who was never on time
Davis: an aggressive, "high-speed" soldier or thug, depending on whom you
    asked, although everyone agreed that he saw most things from a "racial"
    perspective

Harman: a brand-new, somewhat hapless, and shy soldier who was friendly with
children and had an odd obsession with dead things
England: reputed to be mentally slow and would follow Graner anywhere
Ambuhl: quiet, somewhat a void of a soldier
Sivits: a good worker who was extremely well-liked

The group of accused soldiers was especially tight knit as well. Harman and
Ambuhl had spent much time together during the pre-deployment at Fort Lee,
Virginia. Graner and England had also begun dating at Fort Lee and were always
together. In Al-Hillah, Graner, Frederick, Ambuhl, and England had always
hung around in Graner and Frederick's sleep tent. They had grown even closer
working the night shift at Abu Ghraib.

The 372d had been a few short days away from heading home from Abu
Ghraib when the investigation kicked off. Almost immediately, the redeploy-
ment was on hold, and Reese, Lipinski, and Snider had been suspended and
moved to Victory Base. With their leadership gone and fellow soldiers under
intense scrutiny, the remainder of the 372d was in the dark about its future.
Rumors abounded. At the beginning of February, the decision had come: the
majority of the company would head for convoy security duty at Log Base Seitz
and a small detachment would perform escort duties in Tikrit. Morale could not
have been lower as the 372d arrived at Seitz; the soldiers were under the worst
stigma imaginable with dissension in their ranks caused by several soldiers still
under investigation. Although Reese and the rest of the company leadership had
rejoined the unit at Seitz, everyone was listless and shared the sense of resignation that Holley detected earlier that day in Reese and Lipinski.

Seemingly shunned by the Army and their leadership, the soldiers vented
their frustrations to Holley. As he talked to soldier after soldier, Holley began to
sympathize with what had been their lonely fate for nearly six months. *Most of
these soldiers have done nothing wrong, but they are now being treated as outcasts—
leaderless, forgotten, without hope. And now they're stuck in this place.*

The current assignment had only sunk the 372d further into despair. Log
Base Seitz was a prime mortar target, and the buildings all reflected this fact.
One story in particular really struck Holley as a reflection of the 372d's life and
spirit at Seitz.

Sergeant First Class Boyd, one of the 372d's older, grizzled veterans who had been with the company for over twenty years, related to Holley that on one occasion, as another of the numerous mortar attacks started, one of the MPs began to run for a bunker. When he came to the first one, he found it filled with soldiers; he could not get in. So he ran for a second bunker some distance away. It was clearly a hard run as he lumbered in the heat, his Kevlar helmet bouncing and heavy flak vest weighing him down. As he reached the second bunker, he found this one full as well, every last inch stuffed with soldiers. With mortars raining down, the soldier started to sprint toward yet another bunker. But, after several paces, he just stopped and sat down. He had given up— resigned to his death.

Fortunately, the soldier was not hurt.

Boyd went on to tell Holley that mortars fell very, very heavily there, throughout each day and every night. The attacks occurred with such frequency and regularity that the 372d had actually started planning the day's work around them: wait for the morning mortars, do some work, wait for the afternoon mortars, complete the rest of the work. The soldiers were convinced there were two mortar crews. One that fired wildly, everywhere, sometimes not even landing them in the compound. The second crew was much better and could "walk" the mortars down the long, rectangular junkyard. Boyd recounted another story. One night, the soldiers heard mortars hitting the ground, immediately followed by the sound of tanks. Apparently, the QRF pursued and made contact with the insurgents. The MPs heard the main tank gun and persistent machine-gun fire. They cheered as though it were the Super Bowl.

No wonder they cheered so loudly, Holley thought to himself. After only a few hours at the base, it was clear that the mortar situation at Seitz was really, really bad. Holley noticed that even with all the force protection measures, they had yet to protect every building and were still working to get the existing protection even higher. The absence of any sandbag protection could be seen on the sides of the metal buildings in which the 372d slept. The long open-bay barracks had been cut through with shrapnel holes. Some holes were very small, the size of a quarter, while others were much larger, the size of a softball. Holley noticed the holes were everywhere, allowing sunlight into the buildings and giving them the look of being large, white sieves.

As much as the frequent mortar attacks dampened morale, what really dispirited the 372d was its day-to-day job. Most of its soldiers were assigned convoy security duty for the tractor trailers that came in and out of the base. They rode along in the cabs to deter ambushes. However, these trucks were operated by Kellogg, Brown & Root, a subsidiary of Halliburton, and were driven by third-country nationals, usually Pakistani or Egyptian, who could not speak English. The soldiers felt helpless in their task, trying to protect their cargo against attacks, such as IEDs, small-arms fire, and rocket-propelled grenades (RPGs), without being able to communicate effectively with their drivers. One of the soldiers told Holley how the vehicle he had been riding in was hit with an RPG. He had not been injured, but it definitely added to the sense of futility he had about his situation.

Daylight was fading, and Bostic was eager to get the two attorneys back to Victory Base. Like all good noncommissioned officers, Bostic saw it as his responsibility to get his officers where they needed to go safely. Bostic took this duty very seriously, and he suggested to Holley that they hit the road.

Shortly after dusk, Holley, Bostic, and Toman pulled away from Seitz, the faintest edge of the setting sun hovering on the horizon. Holley sat in the backseat, gazing blankly out the window. *Lost in all this mess is the fact that there are some really great guys in this company. And some who had been overlooked so far in the investigation of these abuses. Ward and Joyner were two soldiers who were closest to what happened in the hard-site but had been seemingly missed by investigators. It's clear from their actions that Tier 1A was run far differently from the day shift to the night shift. Both give details that weren't written anywhere else and genuine insight into how things really worked in the company.*

More than any thoughts about the cases, however, Holley's thoughts continually returned to the 372d's situation. With his experience as an MP officer, he readily identified with the men and sympathized for their current fate. *Fair or not, those guys had been used and abused. I hope sooner or later the rest of the 372d gets some credit for sticking with it.*

Am I glad to leave that place. I just wish these MPs could leave with me.

6

A LITTLE HELP FROM OUR FRIENDS

On the other side of the world, the morning sun was cresting over the broken horizon of gray high-rise office buildings and smaller brick homes in Arlington, Virginia. As Graveline jogged along a tree-shaded trail, he could not believe how relaxing this early morning run was, even though the trail paralleled one of the D.C. area's busiest highways, Route 66. *It's just nice not to worry about where to find cover if mortars start falling,* he mused as he passed another mile marker post. While it was definitely safe to jog around Victory Base (several members of the coalition forces had recently finished a ten-kilometer race in conjunction with Atlanta's Peachtree Run on the July Fourth holiday), a soldier had to keep his guard up since most runs' routes at one point or another came close to the post's outer walls. The occasional mortar attacks seemed to most frequently occur during the morning jog time.

Despite the beautiful day and the peaceful surroundings, Graveline could not help but feel a strong sense of guilt. Ever since he had left Iraq, the simplest luxury (a well-prepared meal, a soft bed, a run along a shady lane) had caused intensely conflicting sentiments to well up in him. Leaving Iraq had heightened his senses and made him appreciate the little things in life that are so easily taken for granted—how great it was to talk with Colleen on the phone without a two-second delay or echo in the background, to walk down a city street without fearing where the next explosion might come from, or just how good a cold, draft beer tasted on a hot summer day.

Graveline remembered a similar experience after a six-month deployment to Kosovo with the 101st Airborne Division in 2001. But, unlike his return from Kosovo, this time he had left other members of his team in a combat zone. *Holley, Tate, Kary, Neill . . . none of them can enjoy this,* he lamented. *They're still in Iraq, away from family and friends and living in austere and dangerous conditions.* He found himself wanting to deny himself any indulgence, to live in the most spartan conditions he could muster on this trip, finish his work in the States as quickly as possible, and return to the team in Iraq. As it was, Graveline faced a tight schedule as he tried to gather the necessary information, arrange the defense interviews of the generals, and be on a plane to Iraq by August 2. Mulligan had laid the initial groundwork by helping Graveline schedule meetings with several people he needed to collect documents from: Tuesday—Naval Criminal Investigative Service (NCIS); Wednesday—Army inspector general (IG), Navy inspector general, and the panel being headed by Secretary Schlesinger. He had also lined up several defense counsel to meet with COL Marc Warren, Lieutenant General Sanchez's legal adviser, on July 26, and he hoped to have at least three more witnesses ready to be interviewed that same day.

The only bump in the road so far had come from LTC Steven Jordan. Graveline wanted to talk to Jordan for a number of reasons: he had been the senior MI officer at Abu Ghraib for most of the fall of 2003, the director of the Joint Interrogation Debriefing Center, and a person identified by Brigadier General Taguba as being responsible for the Abu Ghraib abuse. However, the lieutenant colonel informed Graveline through an e-mail from his lawyer that he had invoked his right to remain silent. *Don't know what to think about that,* pondered Graveline. Jordan's name came up regularly in sworn statements taken by Taguba and CID. It was widely suspected that the reserve lieutenant colonel was neck deep in the mess. The question in Graveline's mind was whether Jordan had actual knowledge of the abuses, despite Frederick's statements that the senior officer lacked such awareness.

Yet, the invocation of Jordan's right to remain silent caught Graveline by surprise. *He's already given a long statement to Taguba, and I think he talked with Major General Fay, so if he's worried about exposing himself to some criminal liability, he's probably already done it. And it's never good when a senior officer invokes, especially in this situation where the enlisted soldiers are claiming that they were or-*

dered to take the actions they did. Still, he's one of the guys Taguba specifically pointed out as a source of the problems there. We'll have to figure out what role, if any, he played as this thing unfolds.

For the moment, however, Graveline realized he had more pressing tasks with the discovery deadline fast approaching at the end of July. He put Jordan aside, determined to investigate him further at a later date.

✦

Holley hunched over his laptop, stewing. His worst fears about the investigations were coming true. While these cases were getting into full swing in the courtroom, the CID agents in Iraq were anything but actively engaged. Since arriving in country, Holley had found the lead CID investigator possessed a troubling mind-set. Little, if any, meaningful work had been accomplished on the case during the month of June. The prosecutors sensed that the case agent was more interested in writing the final report than in following any new investigative leads. Now, as the afternoon of July 13 was winding down, Holley found himself exchanging testy e-mails with this investigator.

A few weeks earlier, during Harman's Article 32 investigation, Graveline stopped the agent outside the courthouse. "Can you take some handwriting samples from Ambuhl and send them to the lab? I'd like to know whether it was her or Graner writing the entries in the logbook the MPs kept down in Tier 1A for the night shift."

The agent, who was slightly taller than Graveline with his head shaved bald and sporting a thin mustache, looked annoyed. "Sir, is that necessary? I think these cases are getting blown way out of proportion, and any more time spent on these abuse cases takes away from my other mission at the prison," the agent replied from behind his tinted sunglasses. "We've done our job, and these cases are pretty clean, kind of open and shut."

"I understand that you've already put in a lot of time on these," Graveline responded, "but we're going to need some of the information in the logbook to get beyond a reasonable doubt and we need to know who wrote which entries."

The agent shook his head and unenthusiastically answered that he would get on the job of collecting the handwriting samples. Now, three weeks later, neither Holley nor Graveline had seen any movement on this request or the case in general. Holley had had very little contact with CID since his arrival in

Iraq, finding the agent nonresponsive to e-mails and phone calls. Holley chalked many of the unreturned messages up to the poor communications network in Iraq since the agent was out at Abu Ghraib, where even more frequent power outages occurred than at Victory Base. Still, in order to pull off these cases, the team needed to be fully connected to the investigators. With this thought in mind, Holley arranged a convoy to the prison on July 11.

Toman, who regularly visited Abu Ghraib as part of his legal adviser duties for the 16th MP Brigade, was able to get Holley on convoy headed to the facility. As they approached the confinement facility, Holley was struck by its castle-like appearance, mostly owing to its extremely high, brownish-hued walls and towering guard mounts encircling the camp. *This place is enormous,* observed Holley as the vehicles rumbled through the gates, revealing in the distance rows and rows of tents surrounded with barbed wire and interspersed with smaller stone buildings. Abu Ghraib reminded Holley a bit of Log Base Seitz.

The convoy came to a halt within a walled compound inside the main walls. Holley was taken aback by how stark and dreary the place was, as it appeared decrepit and abandoned. He jumped out of the back door of his Humvee, sweating profusely from being buttoned up inside the vehicle. He headed toward the CID office on the far side of the compound. In the afternoon heat and weighed down in his flak vest and Kevlar helmet, sweat continued pouring down Holley's face and back as he traversed the ankle-twisting rock and gravel path. As Holley entered the CID office, a simple one-story building made of white cinder block, he found their case agent and two other agents working in a single large room crammed with several folding tables serving as desks for the agents' computers and other electronic equipment.

Holley pulled up a chair alongside the investigator and began talking at length about remaining targets of investigation and what steps Holley thought were still necessary in the investigation. The agent rocked back in his chair, unenthusiastically listening to the JAG's pitch. Finally, the agent chimed into the one-sided conversation and expressed the same reluctance he had conveyed to Graveline weeks before.

"Sir, we have the pictures showing these guys there and the sworn statements of England, Harman, and Sivits confessing to the crime. That evidence should be more than enough," he argued.

"Actually, England's and Harman's cases will probably be some of the last to be finished, so they won't be testifying in the other courts-martial. If they're not available to take the stand, we can't use any of their statements against the others," explained Holley.

"Then, why do we waste our time taking sworn statements?!?" exploded the agent. "Are you telling me that all of these sworn statements we've taken are worthless now?"

Holley sensed he needed to calm the agent down. He knew that the case agent had been in Iraq for quite a while, and he perceived the agent was tired, a bit frazzled, and ready to go home. "Not at all. Those statements will be very important in England's and Harman's courts-martial. However, in the other trials, the accused soldier has a constitutional right to confront the witnesses against him. In fact, the Supreme Court has just come out with a case saying the government can't just put a witness statement taken by the police into evidence instead of actually calling that witness to testify at trial. Since it's unlikely England and Harman will be testifying as witnesses in Graner's trial, we can't use their statements because Graner's lawyer won't be able to cross-examine them. We'll need to build our case against Graner and the rest using other witnesses and circumstantial evidence. Plus, if there are any legitimate defenses to these charges, we have a duty to seek them out. That's why we need CID to help us fill in the gaps."

The conversation ended with the agent silently accepting the attorney's explanation, but Holley could tell he was not pleased. So, the next day, he crafted an e-mail to the agent praising his and CID's work to date and detailing why the prosecutors could not simply put in the sworn witness statements. After hearing nothing from the investigator after another day, Holley sent another e-mail to confirm the previous one had been received.

The agent's response was immediate and terse: "Got it. Thanks."

Holley responded by asking about the status of the handwriting exemplars. The agent answered with another quick e-mail: "MAJ HOLLEY, that is on the list of things to do. Will get it as soon as possible."

Holley could not contain his frustration with the agent's nonchalant attitude and dashed a demand: "OK. I need to know what's on your list, what Abu leads you're following up on, and when the exemplars are going to be sent off. If you run into resource problems, let me know. Thanks, MAJ Holley."

Instantly after sending that message, Holley caught himself.

We can't afford to get into a battle of wills with the only CID agent in country working on these cases. There is still an enormous amount of work to be done. The defense teams will all have their own investigators soon, and literally dozens of reporters are going to start digging up evidence and other witnesses—they already have.

He struggled to find just the right words that would both motivate and strike a conciliatory tone at the same time. However, those right words were slow in coming as he strove to suppress his irritation with the situation.

While a mediocre effort from a case agent can be compensated for by the prosecutor in your average run-of-the-mill case, Holley pondered, *we're going to need more than a mediocre effort to help us, or we'll never get beyond a reasonable doubt.* As he stared at his computer screen, he contemplated how much more complex these cases were going to become over the next several months. As both he and Graveline became more familiar with the facts of the case, they had begun to identify a number of investigative leads that still needed to be tracked down, including thorough backgrounds of the accused soldiers, which had not been started yet.

Holley started typing.

"That last e-mail from me came across wrong . . . these cases are the most important cases either of us is ever likely to be part of . . . there's a lot of things that you'll have to take care of to make sure it's done right . . . if you need anything to do your job—phone, vehicle, more people to include more agents, anything—you've just got to tell me . . . bottom line is if we need something, we're coming to you first and last."

Hopefully that will get the point across and make him feel like he's part of the team, Holley mused as he hit the send button. However, Holley was already mulling over how to have an investigator assigned personally to the prosecution team similar to the ones the convening authority had given the defense attorneys—be it another CID agent or some other alternative. *I know he's tired and frustrated, but if he doesn't want to throw himself into this, then we'll find someone who will.*

✦

By the end of his second week in the States, Graveline's initial optimism started to wane. The main prize Graveline sought was Major General Fay's witness statements. He knew that if they had any hope of starting these trials in

September, he had to get his hands on these statements as soon as possible. Prior to leaving, Tate and Fair suggested that Graveline work through the four-star general who appointed Fay, Army Materiel commanding general Paul Kern. The two JAG colonels believed Kern's legal adviser, COL David Howlett, would understand the urgency for the prosecutors to obtain these statements more so than if they approached Fay directly.

Graveline's first meeting with Howlett was not promising. As they sat in his Fort Belvoir, Virginia, office, Howlett seemed sympathetic to the Iraq team's need for the information but stated that none of the witness interviews would be released until all were finished and the report complete. When pressed on a release date, Howlett responded that he was not sure, that the generals conducting the investigation would set the exact dates.

Graveline continued to push. "We really don't care about Fay's conclusions in the report. We're after the substance . . . the statements he's collected and the documentary evidence he's gathered."

Howlett did not see any way that the evidence would be released prior to the report's completion, especially given the defense counsel's apparent willingness to leak information to the media.

Graveline suggested that the government could ask Judge Pohl for a protective order from the court to guard against a release of the information. Howlett agreed that the order would be a must, but he added that he was skeptical that the command would release the information until the final report was complete, which under his best guess would be the end of July. With that, he ushered Graveline out, thanked him for stopping by, and suggested he check back in a few days.

Graveline's failure to extract any information out of the Fay team seemed to set the tone for his remaining appointments, which all followed the same predictable, bureaucratic form:

- a warm welcome from the agencies' attorneys, who would tell him how much they wanted to help;
- Graveline identifying the documents he needed from that agency;
- the lawyers responding with a "Let me take it to my boss, and I'll get back to you";

- Graveline leaving empty-handed with a promise of a phone call "sometime soon."

Ten days after arriving from Iraq, Graveline had only obtained a few CID reports. To make matters worse, he was struggling to marry up the schedules of senior, war-fighting generals and twelve defense counsel who were scattered throughout the world. *I'm treading water,* sighed Graveline. *At this pace, these cases might get tried sometime next year.*

He had his first taste of success July 20, when an attorney from the DoD's Office of General Counsel got word to him that his documents were awaiting him at the Pentagon. These were the ones Graveline and Neill had read about on the Internet in June, released by the White House and DoD, and sought by Bergrin and Womack during the hearings in Baghdad. The two-inch-thick stack traced the U.S. interrogation policy as the highest levels of government debated its boundaries during 2002 and 2003. Graveline did not like turning over documents to the defense that he had not read previously, but a speedy turnaround was the only way to keep these cases moving. He scanned the documents onto CDs and sent them out. He then grabbed the stack and headed to his hotel.

Graveline had been looking forward to this moment since he was assigned to the cases. After reviewing the evidence collected by CID, he was convinced that most of the abuses at Abu Ghraib seemed to be sick jokes for the MPs' amusement; however, he could not at this point eliminate the possibility that MI had played a larger role than initially indicated. Despite seeing numerous examples throughout his career of how perverse the human heart can be, Graveline was still finding it difficult to comprehend the all-important "why."

Why stack naked men in a human pyramid? Why make them masturbate? Why put a leash around a man's neck? Why have snarling dogs leaping at a naked man? Could these acts really have only been for laughs? Graveline was still unclear how many photos, if any, were depictions of "softening" detainees for interrogations. With all the controversy swirling around the administration in the national and international press, he decided it was time to figure out for himself what role, if any, U.S. policy formed at the Pentagon had in the abuses at Abu Ghraib.

Graveline settled into the couch in his room at the local Holiday Inn with a notepad, sticky tabs, and Diet Coke. He slowly began piecing together America's interrogation policy development from September 11, 2001, through Afghanistan and Guantanamo Bay and on to CJTF-7's mission in Iraq. Soon, the couch and floor were strewn with documents.

According to the documents, the first major step in the policy was a February 7, 2002, presidential memorandum concerning the treatment of al Qaeda and Taliban detainees. The memo was addressed to President Bush's key staff and the principals of the federal agencies involved in Afghanistan: the vice president, secretary of state, secretary of defense, attorney general, his chief of staff, director of the CIA, the national security adviser, and the chairman of the Joint Chiefs of Staff. The two-page document laid out the president's thinking on the treatment of prisoners and the applicability of the Geneva Conventions in Afghanistan.

The logic was straightforward in its treatment of al Qaeda. The Geneva Conventions apply only to conflicts between "High Contracting Parties" with "'regular' armed forces fighting on behalf of states." Al Qaeda was clearly not a "High Contracting Power"; therefore, the formal protections of the Geneva Conventions would not be afforded any al Qaeda captured in Afghanistan. The Taliban forces were a closer call, with the president coming down on the side that "provisions of Geneva will apply to our present conflict with the Taliban" while at the same time determining the Taliban were "unlawful combatants" engaged in an "international" conflict and would not be eligible for Articles III and IV protections. Despite these legal determinations, the president also set a clear bottom line: "our values as a Nation . . . call for us to treat detainees humanely, including those who are not legally entitled to such treatment . . . as a matter of policy, the United States Armed Forces shall continue to treat detainees humanely and, to the extent appropriate and consistent with military necessity, in a manner consistent with the principles of Geneva."

With the discovery of the Abu Ghraib abuse pictures, controversy had erupted over this particular decision by the president to not apply the strict protections of the Geneva Conventions to al Qaeda and Taliban forces. Many commentators had viewed this act as the first step toward Abu Ghraib. At first blush, however, Graveline did not think this particular order was all that controversial.

The Geneva Conventions are fairly narrow legal constructs whose protections are phrased in language that presuppose a conflict between nations or an easily recogniz-

able adversary. It would be difficult, actually close to impossible, to comply fully with the conventions in a war where it was difficult to distinguish where al Qaeda ended and the Taliban began, contemplated Graveline. *It seems to me that the real question will be how this policy was implemented practically—what would treatment "consistent with the principles of Geneva" look like in reality? The devil's always in the details.*

He continued to scour the stack of paper looking for those details. A memo dated November 27, 2002, for Rumsfeld from the DoD general counsel, William Haynes, had addressed counter-resistance techniques to be used at Guantanamo Bay. The memo was a cover sheet from the two-star commander, JTF-GTMO, through the four-star commander of Southern Command (SOUTHCOM), requesting a wider array of interrogation techniques that could be used on the detainees housed there. The additional eighteen techniques were broken up into three categories in a separate memo dated October 11, 2002:

Category I—if the detainee is determined by the interrogator to be uncooperative, the interrogator may use the following techniques:

(1) Yelling at the detainee (not directly in his ear or to the level that it would cause physical pain or hearing problems)
(2) Techniques of deception:
   (a) multiple interrogator techniques
   (b) interrogator identity. The interviewer may identify himself as a citizen of a foreign nation or as an interrogator from a country with a reputation for harsh treatment of detainees

Category II—used with the permission of Officer in Charge, Interrogation Section

(1) The use of stress positions (like standing), for a maximum of four hours
(2) The use of falsified documents or reports
(3) Use of isolation facility for up to 30 days [this technique would require approval by the director, Joint Interrogation Group]
(4) Interrogating the detainee in an environment other than the standard interrogation booth

(5) Deprivation of light and auditory stimuli

(6) The detainee may also have a hood placed over his head during transportation and questioning. The hood should not restrict breathing in any way and the detainee should be under direct observation when hooded.

(7) The use of 20-hour interrogation

(8) Removal of all comfort items (including religious items)

(9) Switching the detainee from hot rations to MREs [Meals Ready to Eat]

(10) Removal of clothing

(11) Forced grooming (shaving of facial hair, etc.)

(12) Using detainees individual phobias (such as fear of dogs) to induce stress

Category III—techniques in this category may be used only by submitting a request through the GTMO chain of command, with appropriate legal review and information, to Commander, SOUTHCOM. [The memo went on to say that these techniques are only required for a very small percentage of the most uncooperative detainees and that they may be utilized in a "carefully coordinated manner to help interrogate exceptionally resistant detainees."]

(1) The use of scenarios designed to convince the detainee that death or severely painful consequences are imminent for him and/or his family

(2) Exposure to cold weather or water (with appropriate medical monitoring)

(3) Use of a wet towel and dripping water to induce the misperception of suffocation

(4) Use of mild, non-injurious physical contact such as grabbing, poking in the chest with the finger, and light pushing

Haynes had recommended Rumsfeld to authorize the SOUTHCOM commander "to employ at his discretion, only Categories I and II and the fourth technique listed in Category III." Rumsfeld accepted his counsel's advice and approved the techniques' use at GTMO on December 2, 2002. Below his signature, Rumsfeld had scrawled a message:

However, I stand for 8–10 hours a day. Why is standing limited to 4 hours?
D.R.

Graveline quickly turned to the legal analysis that was attached to the request. *Where did some of these new techniques come from? What could have been the possible legal justification for some of the techniques listed in Categories II and III? Threatening a person's family with death? Exposing a person to cold weather or water? Using "phobias" to induce stress?* Many of the approaches in those two categories seemed, on their face, patently abusive to the young JAG. Even the ones that were not over the top, such as the forced standing pointed out by Rumsfeld, seemed to lack any specific guidance.

This lack of clear limitations on interrogation approaches had been gnawing at Graveline for a while. He had read the Army interrogation field manual and had found it to be of no assistance in figuring out what was clearly off-limits during interrogations.

There seems to be very little guidance about what is meant by a particular interrogation technique. How does an interrogator force a detainee to stand for four hours? What if the person gets tired? What if he refuses? Could the interrogators physically grab him and hold him up? Is handcuffing that person to a door acceptable to keep him standing?

What about use of phobias? What does that mean? Holding a person off the side of a building and threatening to let him go? Snakes? Rats? Unmuzzled dogs right next to him? It seems as if the policy was drafted with little thought about what would happen at 2:00 a.m. in the dark recesses of some little camp halfway around the world.

Are the pictures from Abu Ghraib simply examples of interrogations gone wrong? Is the naked human pyramid or forced masturbation just an example of an interrogation approach? How about the detainee on the end of the strap held by England? Another approach? What about the pictures of the unmuzzled dogs pinning the naked man against the wall? Was that exploiting his phobia for interrogation purposes?

The legal analysis had been drawn up by LTC Diane Beaver, an Army JAG for the GTMO joint task force and one of Miller's team members on his trip to Abu Ghraib in September 2003. Graveline had interviewed Beaver by telephone the week prior. During that conversation, Beaver had given the impression that the detention conditions were so poor and the intelligence collection so rudimentary that Miller's visit became more focused on the basics of both aspects: maintain clean detention areas, keep prisoner counts, establish a database to maintain all the information collected during interrogations. She related that the team left with a particularly unfavorable opinion of the 800th MP Brigade's professionalism and of its officers, especially Brigadier General Karpinski. However, their conversation had never touched on particular interrogation techniques utilized at GTMO.

Graveline now pored over her memo, devouring its reasoning. Beaver had recognized that some of the Category II and III techniques were problematic in the sense that they potentially sanctioned assault, communication of a threat, maiming, or cruelty and maltreatment—all violations of the Uniform Code of Military Justice. Her solution, however, had been truly unique.

Beaver had recommended that "it would be advisable to have permission or immunity in advance from the convening authority of military members utilizing these methods [grab, poke in the chest, push lightly, placement of wet towel or hood over detainee's head, threatening with death]." She had gone on to emphasize that the techniques in the second category were "legally permissible" as long as there was an "important government objective and it is not done for the purpose of causing harm or with the intent to cause prolonged mental suffering." As for the third category, Beaver had acknowledged that threatening a person with death was specifically mentioned in the United States' anti-torture statute as an example of infliction of mental pain and suffering, but she still concluded this technique was legal, mentioning the statute only as a "caution" to be considered. She had also suggested "caution" when using the "misperception of suffocation" technique since foreign courts had opined about the mental harm that technique might cause. In her final paragraph, Beaver attempted to soften her analysis by advising that the Category II and III techniques be subjected to a legal, medical, behavioral science, and intelligence review before they were utilized.

Graveline was beside himself as he read the legal piece. *Prospective immunity from prosecution? What kind of recklessness is that? We're going to grant a soldier immunity before we know what he is going to do? You would effectively give him carte blanche to commit all kinds of misconduct. What if a detainee dies or is seriously injured when the soldier crosses the line? What will you do then since he already has immunity?*

Yet, more than what he considered shoddy lawyering, Graveline was concerned with the fact that, while these particular techniques had been requested by SOUTHCOM for GTMO detainees, he recognized a number of the Category II techniques as ones on the CJTF-7's interrogation rules of engagement (IROE) for use in Iraq. He made a mental note to recheck which ones had made their way from GTMO to Iraq.*

The harsher GTMO techniques approved by Rumsfeld did not stay on the table for long. The very next record Graveline turned to was a document signed by Rumsfeld on January 15, 2003, titled "Memorandom for Commander USSOUTHCOM." The three-paragraph memo rescinded Rumsfeld's December authorization; emphasized the continued "humane treatment of detainees, regardless of the type of interrogation technique employed"; and promised further guidance. Next to that memo was another from Rumsfeld, also dated January 15, establishing a DoD working group to study the "legal, policy, and operational issues relating to the interrogation of detainees held by the U.S. Armed Forces in the war on terrorism."

Graveline was baffled. *I wonder what happened in those forty-four days between his first authorization and the establishment of this working group? You usually do not see policy issued from the SECDEF's office turned around so quickly.*

It was getting late, and Graveline liked to be in the office by 6:00 a.m. to call the team in Baghdad during the duty day.** With one last fling of papers to the floor, Graveline crawled into bed, eager to talk with his partners the next day about this new information.

Holley was not in the office when Graveline called the next morning. After a few verbal jabs from Sergeant Kary about Graveline's "tough" duty, he passed the phone to Neill.

"You're not going to believe some of the legal arguments in these DoD documents," Graveline exclaimed as he related the arguments for prospective immunity and the aggressive interrogation techniques.

---

* At that point, the CJTF-7 IROE was classified as secret and was being kept in a locked safe near Graveline's office. This document was eventually declassified. All of the documents being discussed in this chapter have been declassified.
** Eastern standard time (U.S.) is eight hours behind Baghdad, Iraq.

"That's just cra-z-y . . . ," Neill trailed off, his voice rising an octave to emphasize the last word. From the beginning, Neill had been concerned about the MI aspect of the cases, especially since there was so much they did not know about the MI soldiers and civilians at Abu Ghraib. Most intelligence operators there at the time of the photos had long since redeployed, were spread out around world, and never interviewed. In fact, when he had learned that III Corps was bringing in Holley and Graveline, Neill had feared they would be prosecution "true believers," so convinced of the accuseds' guilt that they would be unwilling to entertain or fully investigate the notion that MI or the chain of command could be complicit in the abuse. Much to his relief, he found the two men had taken the defense's claims seriously and aggressively pursued the leads that had come up thus far.

Graveline cautioned against jumping to conclusions too quickly. "There's still no evidence tying these documents to what we've seen coming out of Abu or that any of the accused were briefed on these arguments," Graveline warned. Nonetheless, these documents were the first time the prosecutors had seen for themselves that certain members of the DoD and federal government seriously argued for, considered, and authorized harsher interrogation techniques above and beyond the approved Army manual. Neither attorney knew how these documents would fit into the grand scheme of the prosecutions. However, one thing was clear—there was still much investigating to do before they would know the truth.

✦

Being "off work" is a foreign concept for deployed soldiers given their amount of work and lack of compelling outside interests when thousands of miles from family, home, or a car. The trial team's deployment was no exception. Seven days a week, Holley and Kary arrived at their small office before 8:00 a.m. and worked usually through midnight. Neill, Robinson, and Tate worked in different areas but kept similar hours. While their work was fast paced, days of the week became indistinguishable from one another, a prime example of what deployed soldiers call "Groundhog Day"—a reference to the Bill Murray movie in which he relives the same day over and over again. As a result of this reality of deployment, Holley spent very little time in his sleep tent, normally grabbing what rest he needed in the morning and not returning until late at night.

Late one night, however, as he was sitting on his metal cot getting ready for some much-needed sleep, Holley noticed the soldier next to him was wearing an MP armband on his uniform. Given his hours, Holley had had little opportunity to meet any of his tentmates, so he introduced himself, referenced his prior MP service, and asked the man where he worked.

"Staff Sergeant Richard Russell," the soldier replied. "I'm working for Colonel Bradley in the Provost Marshal's Office here on Victory." A compact man with spiky brown hair and mustache, Russell was never at a loss for words or a big dip of tobacco tucked into his lower lip. He went on to relate his frustration with his current job. "I volunteered for Iraq with the hope of leading my own squad. Now, I'm just sitting behind a desk instead of being out where the action is."

After September 11, 2001, Russell was mobilized for a year, performing MP duties at Fort McCoy in Wisconsin. Russell then served a second year-long tour in Iraq during the initial phase of the war. He had volunteered for a third deployment because he felt a strong sense of patriotism and that "one tour just wasn't enough." He was the consummate volunteer who looked at the Army Reserve not as a part-time job but as a full-time commitment to serve his country. But this commitment came with a heavy price; Russell had a wife and two sons at home. Holley was struck by Russell's passion.

As their discussion progressed, Russell mentioned that he was a qualified military police investigator (MPI). Holley perked up. During May and June, Davis' and Graner's defense teams had asked the government to assign them a CID agent or MPI soldier to track down leads and interview witnesses. While the defense is not normally assigned their own investigator in the military process, Graveline had persuaded Goetzke and Tate that this highly unusual request was not unreasonable given the scope of the cases. Tate agreed and went to COL Charles Bradley, the corps' provost marshal, to ask if he had enough investigators to cover such a tasking. Bradley had seemed lukewarm to the idea but assured Tate he would try to find the manpower for this assignment. With that understanding, Graveline had explained to Judge Pohl during the June motion hearing that the government intended to assign these investigators by no later than June 30.

Several weeks had elapsed since Tate's request, and Bradley had still not identified any specific investigators. Holley knew they had to break this logjam immediately or face the wrath of Judge Pohl and further delay these cases, which already seemed stuck in molasses. Plus, he was still on the lookout for an investigator whom they could assign solely to the prosecution team as well. He saw an opportunity with Russell—would he be interested? Did he know any other MPI soldiers who might be?

"You bet I would," Russell said, jumping at the chance, "and I know another investigator up north around Mosul who could use a change of scenery. He just lost two of his friends in a bombing, and on top of that, he is really butting heads with his unit commander. He's a reservist too, a former U.S. Marshal, and a federal agent back in the States, when he's not busy manning police academies and running MP operations in Iraq. I'm sure he would love to work on these cases."

Russell dug through some papers and produced a scrap of paper with a phone number. "His name is Master Sergeant Mike Clemens. Just tell him that I said to call him."

Holley thanked Russell for the information, exchanged phone numbers, and assured him that he would be in contact soon if he could get him pulled for the Abu Ghraib assignment. As Holley lay in bed trying to fall asleep, he wondered if the team had finally caught a break.

In the cot next to him, Russell, too, was lost in thought. *What are the chances of this ever happening? Here I am, in a tent, somewhere in the middle of Iraq, looking for a chance to be a real MP, and this major assigned to the biggest Army prosecution ever is sleeping in the cot next to me. Talk about a strange twist of fate.*

Russell had known Master Sergeant Clemens for about eighteen years, the two having served together in many MP assignments throughout their military careers in Wisconsin. Most recently, Russell had served as an investigator under Clemens at Fort McCoy. They had become particularly close after he had attended some investigation courses taught by Clemens. Clemens had become a mentor to Russell, always looking out for the junior MP. *Now, it's time for me to return the favor.*

✦

Graveline continued to track the DoD's interrogation policy over the next several days, both in the office and in his hotel room. The members of the working group had taken longer than the fifteen days Rumsfeld had originally granted them. Instead of January 30, they had delivered their analysis to Rumsfeld on April 4, 2003. Headed by the Air Force general counsel Mary Walker, the group had rendered a lengthy seventy-one-page legal opinion that contained discussions of applicable federal and international law, possible defenses to criminal charges for individual interrogators or their supervisors, and analyses of the requested interrogation techniques.

As Graveline read through the document, he was struck by its tone and emphasis. *It reads like a treatise on how to step beyond preexisting interrogation limits without ending up in jail,* he thought. First, the group had tried to limit the federal law against torture by defining torture as narrowly as possible. As written in the statute, torture is an "act committed by a person acting under the color of law specifically intended to inflict severe physical or mental pain or suffering . . . upon another person within his custody or physical control." Given that definition, the group had focused on the words "specifically intended" to argue that "even if the defendant [interrogator] knows that severe pain will result from his actions, if causing such harm is not his objective, he lacks the requisite specific intent" to commit torture. The group had also narrowed the law's prohibition against mental pain and suffering by emphasizing that such pain must be "*prolonged, intentional, calculated* to disrupt profoundly the senses or personality, or in the case of threatening death to the detainee or one of his family members, that the threat must be *imminent*" (emphasis in report).

Graveline let out a low whistle. As a prosecutor, he was having a difficult time wrapping his mind around this argument. *Aren't they essentially telling interrogators that as long as your "objective" is to get information, then inflict whatever pain you want, and it won't be considered torture? So some interrogator can poke a detainee in the eye with a red-hot poker or cut off a detainee's finger, but since his "intent" is to get intelligence, rather than just inflict pain for pain's sake, he's not committing torture?*

Moving from the anti-torture law, the working group had shifted its focus to possible defenses for interrogators or, as its members had phrased it, "legal doctrines under the Federal Criminal Law that could render specific conduct, otherwise criminal, *not* unlawful." This portion had started with the argument that any effort by Congress to regulate interrogations of unlawful combatants would violate the president's authority as commander in chief, and therefore the torture statute "must be construed as inapplicable to interrogations undertaken pursuant to his commander-in-chief authority." Even if the torture statute applied, the group had proposed that the legal defenses of necessity (i.e., committing a crime to prevent a greater crime) or self-defense (to include the defense of others) could apply for the individual interrogator.

This section left Graveline shaking his head. *Why are they pushing so hard to use these interrogation techniques? All these arguments push basic legal concepts too far. They claim the president's power as commander in chief is so complete that it would allow him to order the torture of an individual with no constitutional way for the Congress or courts to constrain or review that decision. It runs counter to one of the first cases they teach in law school when the Supreme Court cut back a similar argument made by President Truman during the Korean War. And the defenses of necessity and self-defense are both predicated on the doomsday scenario where a terrorist has the information that will stop an imminent attack on a large population center. Why bring them up when trying to set policy governing a wide range of detainees that such doomsday situations may never apply to? Those are the exceptions, not the rule. This is a dangerous road we're going down.* *

It appeared to Graveline that the group had attempted to end its work by limiting some of its earlier conclusions. It had pointed out that all interrogation techniques should be "implemented deliberately following a documented strategy designed to gain the willing cooperation of the detainee using the least intrusive interrogation techniques and methods" and keeping in mind the culture and tradition of the armed forces to treat prisoners humanely. It was during this final section that Graveline read for the first time that "for routine interrogations, standard U.S. Armed Forces doctrine will be utilized" and that "interrogations involving exceptional techniques . . . may be applied only in limited, designated settings approved by SECDEF or his designee."

Taking this analysis, Rumsfeld had published new guidance to SOUTH-COM two weeks later on April 16, 2003. In the cover sheet for this latest GTMO interrogation policy, Rumsfeld had authorized the use of twenty-four techniques (listed *A–X*) that were to be used with specific safeguards. He had

---

* It was only later that Graveline would discover all the Judge Advocate Generals of the four armed services and the office of the General Counsel of the Navy had voiced strong dissents to this working group's product.

also reiterated that "U.S. Armed Forces shall continue to treat detainees humanely and, to the extent appropriate and consistent with military necessity, in a manner consistent with the principles of the Geneva Conventions." Rumsfeld had ended the memo by specifically asking for prior notification before four methods were used—incentive/removal of incentive, pride and ego down, Mutt and Jeff (or good cop/bad cop), and isolation—and leaving open the possibility of other techniques being used if they could be justified.

Of the twenty-four techniques, many came straight from the Army field manual governing interrogations. Five other methods not found in the manual were added: dietary manipulation, environmental manipulation, sleep adjustment, false flag, and isolation.

Despite the secretary's statement that "use of these techniques is limited to interrogations of unlawful combatants held at Guantanamo Bay, Cuba," when Graveline put the April 16 and the previously approved November 2002 memos alongside the CJTF-7 IROE published on September 14, 2003, he found large portions of the Iraq policy matched the GTMO memo word for word, especially the approaches that went above and beyond the field manual:

Dietary Manipulation: Changing the diet of a detainee; no intended deprivation of food or water; no adverse medical or cultural effect and without intent to deprive subject of food or water (e.g., hot rations to MREs).

Environmental Manipulation: Altering the environment to create moderate discomfort (e.g., adjusting temperature or introducing an unpleasant smell). Conditions would not be such that they would injure the detainee. Detainee would be accompanied by interrogator at all times. (Caution: Based on court cases in other countries, some nations may view application of this technique in certain circumstances to be inhumane. Consideration of these views should be given prior to use of this technique.)

Sleep Adjustment: Adjusting the sleeping times of the detainee (e.g., reversing sleep cycles from night to day.) This technique is NOT sleep deprivation.

False Flag: Convincing the detainee that individuals from a country other than the United States are interrogating him.

Isolation: Isolating the detainee from other detainees while still complying with basic standards of treatment. (Caution: The use of isolation as an interrogation technique requires detailed implementation instructions, including specific guidelines regarding the length of isolation, medical and psychological review, and approval for extensions of the length of isolation by the 205th MI BDE Commander. Use of this technique for more than 30 days, whether continuous or not, must be briefed to 205th MI BDE Commander prior to implementation.)

In addition to these techniques, the September 14, 2003, CJTF-7 interrogation policy included five other techniques not found in the Army interrogation manual:

Presence of Military Working Dogs [MWDs]: Exploits Arab fear of dogs while maintaining security during interrogations. Dogs will be muzzled and under control of MWD handler at all times to prevent contact with detainee.

Sleep Management: Detainee provided a minimum 4 hours of sleep per 24 hour period, not to exceed 72 continuous hours.

Yelling, Loud Music, and Light Control: Used to create fear, disorient detainee, and prolong capture shock. Volume controlled to prevent injury.

Deception: Use of falsified representations including documents and reports.

Stress Positions: Use of physical posture (sitting, standing, kneeling, prone, etc.) for no more than 1 hour per use. Use of technique(s) will not exceed 4 hours and adequate rest between use of each position will be provided.

In the cover memo to the IROE, Sanchez reminded the intelligence community in Iraq that they were operating Mutt and Jeff in a theater of war where the Geneva Conventions applied and expressly stated that seven certain techniques—incentive/removal of incentive, pride and ego down, presence of military working dogs, yelling, loud music, light control, and stress positions—required his written permission prior to usage. Sanchez had published this IROE with the intent that they be implemented immediately.

Graveline knew the September IROE had only been in effect for less than a month in Iraq. By October 12, Sanchez had published new guidance to his interrogators. The October IROE limited the approved interrogation approaches to only those found in the Army field manual, thus removing the ten harsher techniques. Sanchez left open the possibility of other unidentified approaches but stated that all approaches not listed in the memo would have to be submitted for his approval. This policy remained unchanged throughout the fall of 2003.

With all the policy memos spread over his office desk and floor, Graveline jotted down several questions he wanted to ask COL Marc Warren, whom he was going to see that week. *Of all these documents, how many actually reached CJTF-7 prior to the formation of this policy? How did Warren view these "exceptional" techniques? How often and for what purpose had the MI community in Iraq asked permission to use harsher techniques?*

Warren was widely recognized within the Army JAG Corps as, if not the best, one of the foremost experts in the law of war and Geneva Conventions. He had taught the subject for years at the JAG school and had applied his knowledge in hot spots such as Grenada, Kuwait, Bosnia, Kosovo, Central America, and now Iraq. Having been the CJTF-7 staff judge advocate, Sanchez's primary legal counsel, and lead U.S. Army attorney in Iraq during the initial invasion and reconstruction effort, Warren was one of the officers the defense counsel had selected to interview. His session was the first one scheduled: July 27, 10:00 a.m. The young prosecutor knew Warren well after having worked for him at the 101st Airborne Division and V Corps, and the older JAG had become a mentor and friend to Graveline. Now he hoped Warren could sort out the command's intent with the IROE and explain exactly how the policy was developed and implemented.

The morning of the twenty-seventh, Graveline walked into Mulligan's office to find Warren seated across the desk, drinking coffee and chatting with Mulligan. He had arrived an hour early. Graveline saw an opportunity to have his questions answered.

"Let me back up and give you the big picture of what was going on in Iraq last summer. That will give you a better idea of the genesis for the policies," Warren started. Ever since Graveline had met him five years prior, Warren had always spoken very deliberately, carefully choosing the right word to convey his ideas. The law and the facts mattered to Warren, and he wanted both to be expressed as accurately as possible. "At that point, the command was facing two major issues. The detention mission in Iraq was largely broken and getting worse, and second, the insurgency was increasing, attacks were frequent, and we needed more intelligence to help curb the violence.

"There were many factors contributing to the detention mess. First, the population in the detention facilities was exploding. Our units were capturing large numbers of people, sometimes with very little discernment, and sending them to the confinement camps with scarce or no paperwork. In fact, I was at a camp one day and saw a group of prisoners being dropped off. One of the men being brought in had a card hung around his neck that said 'murderer' on it. That was it—not where the murder allegedly occurred, not who the capturing unit was, no names of witnesses, nothing.

"So CJTF-7 started prodding the units to fill out an apprehension form that would give the MPs some minimal information to help discern the level of threat a particular detainee posed and to determine how long to keep or release that person. The units in the field were understandably upset. We were asking already tired soldiers fresh off of a firefight to fill out witness statements and more paperwork. But we had to come up with some kind of process since we were receiving enormous pressure from what seemed like all sides. On the one hand, there was the ICRC [the International Committee of the Red Cross], and on some days the CPA and the media, saying you need to release these people as soon as possible or demanding to know the evidence against them. And on other days, our units in the field, the CPA, the media, and many times the Iraqis, were asking us to make sure we didn't release a dangerous person back into community. Given the realities of the situation, the detention board often came down on continuing to hold a detainee under the rationale 'better safe than sorry.'"

Warren took a slow sip of his coffee, looking deep in thought. He then began again.

"The personnel we had running the mission didn't help either. Early on, the CPA tried bringing in some prison experts from both the United States and Great Britain, but once those guys saw how underfunded the mission was and the difficulties of moving around Iraq, it became a revolving door of senior advisers coming in for sixty or ninety days, making their assessments, and leaving.

The problem continued to fall back into the military's lap, primarily on the MPs and JAGs. At first, we thought the 800th MP Brigade was going to be the answer to our problems. They were seen as the subject matter experts since they specialized in detention."

"General Karpinski to the rescue?" Graveline asked sarcastically. He had yet to talk to anyone who had had anything positive to say about her.

"I don't put the blame for the 800th's faults at the feet of any single person. General Karpinski had a very difficult mission that she was trying to perform with a less-than-adequate headquarters and a number of competing missions, Abu Ghraib not being the only detention facility that she was responsible for. We were all very short staffed and underresourced. There never seemed to be enough supplies or bodies to go around, and no more were coming. DoD designated us a joint task force complete with a 400-person staff requirement, but we essentially remained manned with our 175, plus or minus, Corps assets. In fact, I had asked CENTCOM on a number of occasions for more judge advocates to help with the detention and interrogation missions and was told that those weren't JAG missions and we weren't going to be getting any more.

"General Karpinski was attempting to accomplish one of the most difficult missions in the history of the MP Corps and lost her deputy commander, who was not replaced because the reserves don't do individual replacement and her command sergeant major had to be relieved." Warren paused. "Don't get me wrong, General Karpinski has her faults and lacked control of her units. But the MPs on the whole lacked senior leadership in their officer corps in Iraq and, consequently, couldn't make things happen at the operational level. Worse yet, many of the reserve MP officers throughout Karpinski's command complained all the time since they thought their job was done once the prisoners of war at Camp Bucca had been released. She got dealt a very difficult hand with a tough mission and a number of unprofessional people under her who were not up for the task at hand."

The colonel caught himself rambling a bit. "I'm sorry, Chris. I'm afraid I went far afield from your original question."

"That's fine, sir, I need to know as much of this background information as I can," Graveline replied. "I believe my original question had to do with the development of the interrogation policy."

"Right, right . . . with these difficulties in the detention operation and the lack of good intelligence, General Sanchez sent a request up the chain to ask for some assistance. This request prompted the visit from Major General Miller and his team of experts from Guantanamo. One of that team's findings was that any number of interrogation practices and techniques had begun to creep into use in Iraq from Afghanistan and various special forces units. They suggested that the command come up with a comprehensive interrogation policy to cover the universe of acceptable interrogation techniques. The idea was to constrain the number and kind of techniques used in theater in order to get everyone on the same page. I tasked a couple of my staff attorneys to work with the MI section to see what we could come up with. I believe Miller left the policy memo that they were working from at GTMO to act as a template."

"Was there ever any question about whether the Geneva Conventions applied to interrogations in Iraq given the interaction with the folks from GTMO?" Graveline asked.

"Never. If there was one thing that our legal staff was clear on, it was that the Iraqi theater of operations fell squarely under the Geneva Conventions. In fact, I distinctly remember General Miller's first in-brief with the task force staff. During that meeting, I reminded both his team and our people that we were in a different legal posture than GTMO since Geneva applied to us fully. No, we did our own analysis of the interrogation policy that we presented to General Sanchez in September."

"Do you remember seeing the DoD working group memo or Department of Justice memos talking about interrogation techniques or legal justifications for aggressive interrogations?"

Warren shook his head. "I've seen them now over the past couple of weeks, but not while I was in Iraq."

"I've also found several different drafts of this policy, sir, during the months of September and October. Why so many versions?" inquired Graveline. He showed Warren interrogation memos dated September 10, 14, and 28 and October 5 and 12.

"The first one dated the tenth was a draft that was forwarded to the pertinent staff sections and MI units for comment. It was not the final product. The September 14 memo was the one that Sanchez actually signed and published,"

Warren explained. "After he signed it, we sent it up to CENTCOM, saying that if we didn't hear any objections that the policy would be going into effect. After a few days, the JAG cell up at CENTCOM called with some reservations about a couple of the listed techniques. So over the course of the next few weeks, several drafts circulated among the staffs of CENTCOM, CJTF-7, and the MI units refining the policy until it was decided to narrow the policy to state that only the techniques out of the Army manual were permissible unless specifically authorized by General Sanchez. So the final October policy, dated October 12, simply restates the Army manual's interrogation techniques, leaving open the possibility of other techniques if requested up to Sanchez. Once again, the idea was to constrain what the interrogators could do, to give them good right and left limits. The only two actual policies were September 14 and October 12. All the others are only drafts."

"Did you ever see any requests for 'harsher' techniques sent to Sanchez by the interrogators?"

"The only ones that I ever saw were requests to keep a detainee in segregation past thirty days," Warren answered. "I'm confident that I would have seen any others if they existed since even the ones requesting extended segregation required a JAG review."

Graveline looked at the clock and realized they were about to be late for the colonel's interview with the defense counsel. "Sir, we better get going."

Warren rose from his chair but stopped at the door. "Chris, I would be shocked if those pictures have anything to do with the CJTF-7 interrogation policies. When General Sanchez first saw those photos he was horrified and ordered an immediate investigation. None of those scenes was consistent with his intent for interrogations. I can honestly say, as a person who saw 99 percent of the documents that went in for General Sanchez's signature, that there were never any requests that made it to the general for holding people at the end of leashes, putting women's underwear on their head, or placing wires on their hands. These were not actions sanctioned by the CJTF-7 command."

As Graveline followed Warren out the door, he contemplated the situation in which the command had found itself in Iraq. *Sanchez, and in his own way Colonel Warren, have been raked over the coals for these photos, and in the two months I've been on the case, I've yet to see one piece of evidence linking any actions they took to the photos.* He was beginning to sympathize with both Sanchez's and Warren's predicament. *When you stop and think about what these two men were faced with, it really was a "mission impossible." Sanchez had started the war as a two-star division commander, gets his third-star, assumes command of a "joint task force" of more than 130,000 troops but with a staff half the size it needs to be, and gets handed a failed state with no government, electricity, or running water and a raging insurgency smack dab in the center of the world's most violent area. He had to rely on his subordinate commanders, like Karpinski and Pappas, to enforce the standards since he couldn't be everywhere at once. Now, he gets second-guessed by any number of congressmen and women and media analysts who have never even sniffed a combat zone for not knowing what was happening on the night shift at one prison miles away from headquarters in a war zone. Great job to have.*

✦

The phone rang. Holley reached across the table and snatched the receiver off its base. An unfamiliar voice was on the other end.

"Hello, sir, my name is Master Sergeant Mike Clemens."

Russell had called Clemens the day after his conversation with Holley. Clemens, though, had waited a day or two before calling Holley so as not to appear overeager. "I hear you have a situation that you may need some help with," volunteered Clemens.

Holley paused, uncertain on how much to divulge to the MP he had never met and was not yet sure he could trust. "Yes . . . yes, I think I do." Still searching for the right words, Holley offered, "Why don't you tell me about some of your experience?"

Clemens described his early work history as a corrections officer, deputy sheriff, narcotics and vice detective, and deputy U.S. Marshal. He also served over twenty years as an MP soldier and investigator in the Army Reserve and had been asked on several occasions to head up sensitive "missions," the most recent of which was helping to create a new MP investigations and antiterrorism unit in Wisconsin.

As Clemens rattled off his impressive resume, Holley listened intently. Within minutes, he recognized that Clemens was a professional in every sense. *This guy is the answer to my prayers. He could really close the gap between us and defense in terms of knowing the behind-the-scenes story.*

Holley asked about the investigator's issues with his commander. No matter how talented Clemens was, he could not afford to have the team dragged down. Clemens explained that his commander had been out of the reserves for several years and had been working as a security guard before being called up for active duty. No matter how hard he tried, Clemens could not convince the inexperienced officer to listen to the advice of seasoned NCOs. The two had also clashed over the commander's insensitive response in dealing with the deaths of soldiers in their unit.

Clemens' explanation of his fallout with his unit commander eased Holley's concern. *This seems to boil down to a personality clash between him and his commander. That can happen in any unit. But his commander handled some of these issues very poorly. I think we can make this thing work.*

The JAG moved to a description of what he was looking for from an investigator. "Are you interested?" queried Holley.

Clemens, suddenly reinvigorated, could barely contain his excitement. "I'd love to work on these cases."

"I think your experience is exactly what we need. Give me a couple of days, and I'll let you know," Holley reassured the MP.

As he hung up the phone, Holley knew the sales job on this request was not going to be easy. Even though Clemens was eager to end the tension with his commander, getting investigators for the defense team had been like pulling teeth. Colonel Bradley was not going to be receptive to giving up yet another MP investigator, especially the operations NCO in Mosul. He had to come up with strong justifications to land Clemens for the prosecution.

Holley started an e-mail to Tate in order to arm his boss with the necessary arguments to persuade Bradley. "With regard to our investigation, and help in that arena, here's my no kidding assessment of where we are and what we need to do. Our investigation of the facts, the facts that really matter, is seriously deficient. The original CID investigation was very narrowly focused and limited to about half the people that need to be interviewed . . . There's a large number of witnesses, and as you know, they're spread to the four winds.

"Our CID agent is tired and worn out . . . I think this unique situation—the whole world watching, every little fact important, a lot riding on the outcome, us significantly behind the power curve, deployed environment, etc.—demands a unique solution. I think this guy Clemens is that solution. I know this isn't a typical approach to the problem, and, yes, the 'right' thing to do is try to make the system work with CID. But I'm convinced that the best course of action is to pull Clemens up here.

"As Colonel Bradley points out, CID is a cut above MPI. That's true. But this guy is a cut way above CID. I like CID, think there's a lot of good agents, and I've worked closely with CID agents for most of my eleven years. But I guarantee you there's no one in the Army's CID command with Clemens' skill set. Or likely ever to be. Sir, please take a look at this guy's résumé—just a review. If we get this guy, I'm confident we can truly be masters of that courtroom.

"Sir, that's my pitch. I guess I'll end this way—I know this is going to cause trouble, I know it's not typical, and I know it's a little bit of a gamble, but at the end of the day I think this is the guy we want if we want to do this trial 'world class.' If I had an ace, just one, this is when I'd play it."

While the JAGs awaited a response on Clemens, the CID case agent appeared at the JAG office with a new agent. Special Agent Art Simril, a CID warrant officer assigned to the CID operations section at Fort Belvoir, had been sent to Iraq for a "few weeks" to review the case file, identify leads, and help in any way he could. The new agent had clearly brought a can-do attitude with him, and Holley even sensed an infusion of energy and direction in the original case agent with his arrival. The sturdily built Simril was a welcome relief to Holley. In addition to Simril, Bradley agreed Clemens should also join the team. In a matter of days, the team had gone from minimal investigative assistance to having two highly dedicated and talented agents.

We might actually have a fighting chance at these cases after all, thought Holley for the first time in a long while.

7

THEY WEREN'T TERRORISTS

Right before lunch on August 12, Graveline was trying to finalize the interview schedule with the remaining generals for the upcoming trip to Germany when an e-mail popped up on his computer screen. It was from a CID agent whom Graveline was unfamiliar with, Special Agent Rusty Higgason.

"Sir: I have discovered a document on the Abu Ghraib SIPRNET server that I need to get to you ASAP . . . please contact me."*

I wonder who this guy is, Graveline thought as he noticed the agent's phone number had a Northern Virginia area code. Graveline picked up the phone and called Higgason. The agent introduced himself as one of the agents on the detainee task force working out of CID's headquarters at Fort Belvoir, Virginia. Graveline had visited CID HQ in July and had met many CID agents, but he had no specific memory of Higgason.

"Sir, I think you're going find this document really interesting," stated Higgason cryptically. He was obviously referring to classified text. Graveline replied that he would drive to Belvoir that afternoon.

Higgason met Graveline at the front desk of the headquarters. As they walked down a narrow, carpeted hallway to the detainee task force's office, the thin, young-looking man with close-cropped brown hair, sharp facial features, and a "Joe Friday" demeanor explained to Graveline that he had been given the job of going through the CJTF-7 classified server allocated to the units at Abu

---

* SIPRNET is the network used by the military to convey classified information.

Ghraib. Graveline was surprised to hear about this investigative effort; he could not remember anyone mentioning it to either him or Holley.

The pair walked into the office, which was the size of two conference rooms partitioned off with temporary walls and a number of file cabinets. Higgason led Graveline to his desk and handed him a three-page statement. It laid out yet another specific allegation of abuse—this time a detainee claiming five prison guards had beat him at the direction of his interrogator. While the report described the abuse in detail, the detainee gave a very generic description of the soldiers delivering the blows.

After reading the statement, Graveline asked Higgason if CID could conduct more background investigation to identify the suspected soldiers. While this particular allegation was still far from developed, it piqued Graveline's curiosity.

"Where did you say you got this from again?" he inquired.

"The Abu Ghraib SIPRNET server . . . earlier this summer, as part of their investigation, General Fay's team went looking for some of the SIPRNET e-mail correspondence between MI personnel at the prison," Higgason offered as he elaborated on the forensic computer examinations. "They found some items they thought we might be interested in.

"Around the same time, another member of Fay's team interviewed Chief Warrant Officer Jon Graham, one of the MI warrants working at Abu. Graham had kept all of his e-mail files on a compact disk, and he gave the Fay group a copy. We've found some pretty interesting stuff on there as well." Higgason rummaged through some papers and gave Graveline the printed copy of an e-mail.

Consisting of a three-message string sent August 14, 2003, the first note had been penned by an Army captain, William Ponce, working in the intelligence section of CJTF-7. Ponce had sought input from other members of the intelligence community in Iraq for interrogation techniques they would like to see approved. As Graveline scanned the document, several lines caught his eye:

The gloves are coming off gentlemen regarding these detainees, Col Boltz has made it clear that we want these individuals broken. Casualties are mounting and we need to start gathering info to help protect our fellow soldiers from any further attack.

Originally sent to two recipients, this e-mail had been forwarded around the MI community in Iraq apparently in order to solicit input from the MI soldiers participating in interrogations on the ground. The third e-mail in the chain was a response to the captain's search for suggested techniques and dripped with bravado:

> I spent several months in Afghanistan interrogating the Taliban and al Qaeda. Restrictions on interrogation techniques had a negative impact on our ability to gather intelligence. Our interrogation doctrine is based on former Cold War and WWII enemies. Todays [sic] enemy, particularly those in SWA [Southwest Asia], understand force, not psychological mind games or incentives. I would propose a baseline interrogation technique that at a minimum allows for physical contact resembling that used by [redacted]. This allows open handed facial slaps from a distance of no more than about two feet and back handed blows to the midsection from a distance of about 18 inches. Again, this is open handed. I will not comment on the effectiveness of these techniques as both a control measure and an ability to send a clear message. I also believe that this should be a minimum baseline.
>
> Other techniques would include close confinement quarters, sleep deprivation, white noise, and a litnany [sic] of harsher fear-up approaches . . . fear of dogs and snakes appear to work nicely. I firmly agree that the gloves need to come off.

This final e-mail, written by CWO Lewis Welshofer, struck Graveline with its tone and explicit endorsement of violence as an effective technique. Since starting on the cases, Graveline had spoken with a number of interrogators, all of whom had laughed off the need for physical violence to elicit the information they sought. Each had told him that the most effective technique was the simplest: talking to the person and appealing to what he or she held dear (home, family, status). They had all stated that physical coercion would only produce slanted and inherently unreliable intelligence. "A person will tell you whatever he thinks you want to hear if you're hurting him" had been the common refrain from the pros.

As Graveline neared the end of the e-mail, Higgason broke in: "That guy, Welshofer, is currently being investigated in the death of an Iraqi major general during an interrogation. That didn't happen at Abu Ghraib, though. Welshofer was at a different camp."*

Graveline asked if Higgason had found any other e-mails responding to or condemning the techniques Welshofer had suggested. He and his team had found nothing.

Higgason continued to lay out his efforts. "After we received Graham's e-mails and the information about the deleted accounts, we went out and imaged the hard drives for that portion of the server that Abu Ghraib used. I've been going through the digital documents for the last couple of months, piecing together any evidence we can find."

Graveline then inquired how many documents he had left to review, to which the buzz-cut agent answered, "Sir, we're talking hundreds of thousands of documents. I've reviewed several thousands of pages, but we've really only started to scratch the surface."

"How many guys do you have looking through this server?" Graveline questioned.

"Right now, me and one or two other agents . . . as we have time between tracking down other leads. But I'm the only one who spends the majority of time on it. You have to understand . . . this task force is looking at all detainee abuse cases, not just those out of Abu Ghraib. We're getting pulled in a hundred different directions as new claims of abuse surface out of both Afghanistan and Iraq."

Graveline was dismayed. *This database could bring the progress on our cases to a screeching halt. But we've got to get it done. This e-mail is a perfect example of the type of document we have a duty to turn over to the defense. It fits right into their argument—the U.S. command in Iraq had turned up the pressure on getting actionable intelligence and advocated more aggressive tactics to get it.* Graveline paused. *Solutions . . . think of solutions. It's not going to do any good to vent my frustration on Higgason.*

---

* Chief Welshofer was convicted at Fort Carson, Colorado, in January 2006 of negligent homicide and negligent dereliction of duty for his role in the death of the general. He received a sentence of sixty days of restriction, forfeiture of $6,000 pay, and a reprimand.

"All right, I need you to bottom line this for me. Realistically, how many documents are we talking about?"

Higgason did not have an exact answer. "Several hundred thousand . . . maybe a million," he said with a shrug. "It's hard to give an exact number since I can open some folders and find several word processor or data files."

"And at any one time, we have at most three agents reviewing them? Let me ask you this: if this was your full-time job, without any other distractions, when do you think you could have this server done?"

"December," came the reply.

Graveline pressed Higgason. "If I were able to get you more manpower, say three to four more agents, how soon do you think you can get this done?"

"If we get more people, I think we may be able to get it done by the end of October. But we're really shorthanded, so I don't know where you're going to get the help."

"Leave that to me," reassured the JAG as he stood to leave. *Actually, I have no idea where I'm going to find extra help*, Graveline thought exasperatedly. "Anything else I need to be aware of before I take off?"

Higgason walked Graveline around one of the partitions. "We've been going through the detainees' dossier files and face sheets trying to line up the dates of abuse with any subsequent interrogations," Higgason stated as he pointed to a spreadsheet that hung on the wall. "We haven't found any interrogations for the seven detainees photographed in the human pyramid and forced masturbation."

The words struck Graveline like a lightening bolt.

"Never interrogated?!?" Graveline could not believe his ears.

"Everybody interrogated at Abu Ghraib had a dossier file on the server with interrogation reports, interrogation notes, detainee photographs, and various other documents," Higgason explained. "I did queries using all of the variations of their names and magistrate numbers, and I have not found any records or dossiers pertaining to these detainees."

The agent continued. "During the initial CID investigation, the agents at the prison were able to identify these seven men based on the MP logs and detainee interviews." Higgason moved closer to the spreadsheet, motioning toward the numbers next to the men's names. "These seven guys only had magistrate numbers. The MPs at Abu Ghraib also had coalition force captures, enemy prisoners of war, civilian internees, or detained persons, all of whom had an actual internment serial number. Those detainees were generally the people military intelligence was interested in. These particular seven detainees only had magistrate numbers; they were all Iraqi-on-Iraqi criminals—car thieves, rapists, burglary, or in for assault. They were not of any military intelligence value. Actually, most of the abuse victims were never interrogated. The man on the end of the leash held by England or the detainee they referred to as 'Shitboy' was never interrogated. They were both mentally ill guys who were being held in Tier 1A/1B to give them their own cells."

Graveline studied the spreadsheet intently. *This changes everything,* he mulled, excitedly contemplating the implications of the evidence. *The fact that none of the detainees these guards are charged with abusing were ever interrogated puts a stake in the heart of their case.*

Graveline spun around quickly with a huge smile on his face, holding out his hand to Higgason.

"You've just made my year. I'll work on getting you some more help with the computer server."

Graveline's head was spinning as he walked out the front doors of the CID building. *Wow! How's that for a twist? I probably just received the best and worst news I've heard since I've been on these cases. Sure, there's a couple of hundred thousand pages of discovery to go through well after our deadline—Judge Pohl's going to love that—but this "we're just following orders from MI" defense is done. How can the defense possibly sell that with a straight face after we put on this evidence?* He could not wait to deliver the news to Holley and Neill.

✦

In late July, based on multiple requests from the defense counsel citing scheduling conflicts, Judge Pohl had agreed to move the next round of motion hearings to Germany. He emphasized to all parties that it was to be a one-time move, and they could expect the trials to remain in Iraq. Pohl set the hearings for August 23–24 at Taylor Barracks, one of the small U.S. Army installations scattered around the south-central German city of Mannheim.

Moving the hearings out of Iraq was both a blessing and a nuisance for the trial team. First, the defense counsel immediately relaxed, which allowed Graveline flexibility in scheduling the senior generals' interviews with the defense. The prospect of spending a week in Germany as they met with their clients, litigated legal issues, and conducted in-person and VTC interviews with the generals was much easier for Graveline to sell than a week in Iraq.

As a personal perk for Graveline, Mannheim is located only eleven miles from Heidelberg, so the change of venue put Graveline near his home post among friends who could help. He called MAJ Brad Huestis, who immediately assisted Toman and Kary with logistics: hotel and barracks rooms for the accused and their attorneys, rental cars, and courtroom access. LTC Rich Gross locked down the Sanchez interview and reserved the main V Corps' conference room for the VTC interviews of Generals Mark Kimmitt, Geoffrey Miller, Thomas Metz, Barbara Fast, and John Abizaid.

The trip to Germany also allowed Holley, Kary, and Toman a chance to see their wives for a couple of days. As soon as he had received Pohl's e-mail moving the hearings, Graveline started a lobbying campaign with his team members to bring their spouses or families to Germany for the week. Kary, who had not seen his wife since his deployment in January, immediately jumped at the suggestion. Toman, too, quickly lined up an airline ticket for his wife. While not dampening his subordinates' enthusiasm, Holley was less inclined to bring Renee to Germany given the amount of work to be done and his need to focus on the hearings. Nevertheless, Graveline pressed his colleague to bring Renee for a short visit, emphasizing that they had no idea how much longer these cases might last. Holley reluctantly agreed, and Renee happily researched ticket prices.

For as many good opportunities that would come out of this trip to Germany, there remained the difficulty of moving five accused soldiers, three noncommissioned officers from the MP brigade to serve as escorts, and the prosecution team out of Iraq. Understandably, the local German government was concerned about the impact of bringing the Abu Ghraib defendants to its area, especially given the substantial Muslim population in and around Mannheim. The Germans informed the command that they wanted to know every time the accused soldiers would be off post and in the local community. The burden of coordinating all these military and civil tasks fell squarely on the shoulders of Toman, Kary, and Brann.

The team assembled in Mannheim the third week of August. Graveline arrived first and went immediately to Heidelberg in order to finalize the arrangements for the VTC interviews. The Iraq contingent of Holley, Toman, Kary, all the defendants, and their military counsel flew the next day from Baghdad to Frankfurt.

Clemens, the newest member of the team, flew into Frankfurt on August 21. The weeks following his initial call with Holley had been a whirlwind for him. That call had come right before Clemens' scheduled two weeks of designated R&R leave. He had planned to visit his wife, Jennifer, and daughters after many months apart, and Holley insisted he do so before joining the team in Germany. Consequently, Clemens had flown from Mosul to Kuwait (where he checked his military gear with an MP unit), through Germany and Atlanta, and finally to his home in Wisconsin. However, when he was booking his return flight, his Army superiors in Iraq, in true Army bureaucratic manner, deemed it necessary for Clemens to sign back into the Iraqi theater to pick up his equipment before joining the rest of the team. So his return trip went from Wisconsin, through Atlanta and Frankfurt, and to Kuwait, only to turn back around for Germany.

Now 18,568 miles sure is the long way to get to Germany, Clemens thought as he added up the miles and landed in Frankfurt for the second time.

Despite this roundabout itinerary, Clemens was eager to start. As he drove his rental car through the tidy Army post in Mannheim, he was taken back to his old days as an MP in Germany. He had been a young man hoping to see and experience everything the country had to offer. Now several years older and wiser, he was about to embark on another adventure. Clemens jolted back to reality as he approached the courthouse. The parking lot was filled with media satellite trucks and reporters from every network imaginable. The world was watching this case unfold.

Inside, as he climbed the curved stone staircase, he heard more and more voices down the hall to his left. Clemens entered the office and was greeted with a flurry of activity.

Lots of officers in here, was his first thought.

Almost immediately, Sergeant Kary walked over and introduced himself, not missing the name and rank on Clemens' desert uniform.

"Master Sergeant Clemens, we've been waiting for you," Kary stated while ushering him toward an officer standing a few feet away. "Major Holley, you have a visitor."

Holley introduced himself with a firm handshake and a warm smile.

"I am so glad you're here," he started. "I hope your flight was all right. I'm really sorry about you having to go all the way back to Kuwait to get your gear. Why don't you get settled in and come back over when you have gotten some rest?" As usual, Holley was more concerned about taking care of soldiers than dictating immediate work. In Clemens' mind, these words were a welcome change and set the tone for the task ahead and a strong relationship.

Clemens was ready though. "Just tell me what you want me to do, sir."

Holley cocked his head with a grin. "There must be a few thousand pages of case file over there to get you started. We can work out all of the details of your assignments as we go along. I'm going to trust your judgment; if you see something, let us know what you think we should do. Sergeant Kary," Holley then turned to his young paralegal, "make sure Mike gets whatever he needs."

Clemens walked over to the imposing boxes of files. They were everywhere. The office was little better than organized chaos, with people moving in and out of the area with a sense of purpose. Clemens could not help but think that he had simply walked into one of the biggest criminal cases in military history.

Clemens began to digest the materials in front of him. The accused soldiers seemed "normal" on the surface, but Clemens just could not shake the notion that normal people do not do such abnormal deeds. After a few hours, Clemens reached the Graner file. Initially, nothing jumped off the pages. Graner was an average soldier in the military, had attended the usual military schools, deployed to Iraq during Desert Storm, been promoted, and had a civilian career as a correctional officer. Clemens flipped through the records and found Graner's test scores dating back to when he enlisted in the Marine Corps.

During his or her initial entry into the Army, every soldier is given an Armed Forces Vocational Aptitude Battery (ASVAB). The scores help determine a candidate's military occupational specialty. After the soldier is tested on a variety of subjects, the scores of each subtest are averaged together to produce a general technical (GT) score. The highest score anyone can achieve is a 130.

Clemens stared at Graner's test scores. *You have got to be kidding me.* He walked straight to Holley's office.

"Sir, you are not going to believe this, or maybe you will . . . ," Clemens began. "Do you know what Graner's GT score is?"

Holley looked up from his own stack of files with a smirk and a glint in his eye. "No, tell me."

"It's 129 out of a possible 130."

Holley leaned back in his chair, clasped his hands behind his head, and smiled broadly. "You know, Mike, you just might fit in around here."

✦

The defense teams began working together by coordinating strategies, sharing witness interviews, and joining together on issues they saw working for one another. This collaboration shaped the motion hearings in Germany with each of the various counsel emphasizing a different key issue that all the teams wanted: Womack focused on the release of the Fay report and other investigations, Bergrin homed in on forcing the government to grant officers immunity to testify, and Myers took up the cause of moving the trials out of Iraq.

Prior to the beginning of Graner's formal hearing, Pohl assembled Womack, Heath, Holley, and Graveline in his chambers to hash out any last-minute issues before going on the record. The attorneys filed into the white-walled, L-shaped room and stood before the judge's desk.

"How's that Fay report coming, Captain Graveline?" Pohl inquired with a slight smirk as he pulled on his robe. The judge had apparently closely followed Graveline's regular e-mail updates to the defense counsel and the court—messages that always seemed to promise progress any day now. The older JAG seemed to know full well the troubles the prosecutors were having moving the Washington bureaucracy and how slowly it could work if the bureaucrats did not believe complying was in their best interest.

Graveline shrugged sheepishly. "They've completed all of their interviews. It's just a matter of finishing the report and sending it through the proper channels for review. I've been told they're not going to release anything until the SECDEF has had a chance to review it first."

"So, what you're telling me is that the government has evidence in its possession that could have exculpatory evidence for the accused, but they're not going to hand it over until the SECDEF has his talking points worked out?" Pohl retorted, reading between the lines. "But obviously someone has no problem leaking favorable portions of it to the *New York Times*," he said, referring to an article that had appeared the week before. "Defense, what do you have to say about that?"

"Clearly, this is outrageous, Your Honor," Womack sprang to life. "How can we possibly prepare for a trial when the government won't give us the necessary information? The only answer is to dismiss all of the charges until such time that the government is prepared to give us all of the relevant information."

"Why shouldn't I give the defense what they want, Captain Graveline?" asked the judge.

"Sir, this information is going to be forthcoming in the near future. It's a matter of days, not months," Graveline offered.

"Haven't we all heard that before? First, this Fay report was going to be done by July 1, then it was the end of July, and now it's when SECDEF gets done reading it," Pohl stated.

"Sir, you have to understand. Every time I go asking these various people for information, whether it's the Fay team or the CIA, the first question they ask me is, 'What exactly did the judge say?'" explained Graveline. "They're not interested in giving me one document before they have to. I need you to yell at me on the record about the pace of discovery. I mean, really give it to me."

"Oh, that's too easy, Captain Graveline," Pohl chuckled.

Holley chimed in. "Sir, seriously, it would help us tremendously if you yelled at us and gave us very specific guidelines for what is discoverable and deadlines for the release of those documents."

"All right, let's go on the record and take care of that . . . ," Pohl said. He stood up from behind his desk and headed toward the door.

"Sir, one more thing." Graveline wanted to brace Pohl about CID's search through the SIPRNET server. He quickly outlined the new issue for the judge.

Pohl shook his head in disbelief as he ushered the attorneys out the door. "Let's go."

Womack had an additional issue of his own for this hearing. CID had seized the computer from Graner's room during the first night of the investigation, and Womack wanted the resulting evidence suppressed. Graner had consented to the search, but now Womack argued the consent was involuntary because Graner had been too tired to okay the search. Both Holley and Graveline thought the motion was a waste of time, since the government had multiple copies of the abuse photos from the other accuseds' computers. Even if Womack won this motion, it would not matter in the long run. Moreover, the prosecutors considered Womack's argument factually absurd as he tried to argue that an MP, whose job is to know the legal requirements for searching a person's belongings, would be so fatigued that he wouldn't be able to understand that he could refuse a search of his own property.

For Womack to get this evidence suppressed, he was going to have put Graner on the stand under oath. *How this cross-examination goes might shape what the trial's going to look like,* thought Holley. *If I can get to him here, Womack might think twice before putting him on the stand during trial.* From his own experience as a defense counsel, he knew that a client's testimony could be very useful in the right circumstances. *Even a well-prepared prosecutor could have a tough time cross-examining the defendant since it is the one witness the government cannot interview beforehand.*

Plus, Graner's smart. He has one of the highest GT scores I've ever seen. If he gets on the stand during the trial and starts throwing around allegations about one of the officers who has invoked his right to remain silent ordering him to do everything down there, we might have a real problem rebutting that testimony. No, this cross-examination is going to have to send a message that we're going to be ready for him at trial.

Every corner of the small, sparse courtroom was filled with spectators, other attorneys, and reporters as Graner's military attorney, Captain Heath, began the direct examination of his client. More reporters were stuffed into an adjacent room, watching the proceedings by closed-circuit television. First, Heath had his client paint a picture of the stressful work environment of a combat zone: seven-day-long work weeks, work days that stretched from before sunrise until well after dark, the perceived—if not ever-present—danger compounded by the unit's lack of armor. Then Graner focused on the day the investigation had started; he testified that he had worked a sixteen-hour day the day before the search and had only been sleeping a few hours prior to his company commander, Captain Reese, entering his room around 3:00 a.m. to inform him that CID wanted to speak with him. He related that he was brought to the CID building, where an agent read him his rights, and he invoked his right to remain silent. Graner stated that the agent asked him whether CID could search his room. He swore that he told the agent no but relented after the agent convinced him that the search was going to happen one way or another and that it would look better for him if he consented. As a result, Graner summarized that he had only given his consent because he was tired, was overly stressed by the combat environment, and had thought the search was a "done deal" based on the agent's authority as a law enforcement officer.

Holley was on his feet with a series of rapid-fire questions for Graner about his life experiences. Within the first minute, Holley established that Graner was thirty-five-years-old, a high school graduate with two years of college education, and had been married for over ten years with two children. Further, he had been trained as an MP in the Marine Corps in the late 1980s and knew the lawful authority of an MP, knew how to take a statement from a witness or suspect, and knew the basics of search and seizure and securing a crime scene. Holley shifted to Graner's experience as a prison guard in the Pennsylvania correctional system and as a combat veteran of Desert Storm. Soon, Graner admitted that he was used to working in stressful and dangerous environments. Graner also conceded that he knew how to "project authority" and not back down in the face of a stressful situation and that he had performed all of his duties well as a Marine in Desert Storm despite any fear he had.

The prosecutor handed Graner the CID form the defendant had signed authorizing CID special agent Manora Iem to search his belongings. "He didn't physically force you to consent to search?" Holley asked Graner.

"No, sir, he did not physically force me to consent."

"And he explained to you where he wanted to search, right?"

"He explained that he wanted to search my quarters and my person, yes, sir."

After a few questions about the information in the form, Holley pressed Graner further. "Now, whose signature, just to be clear, whose signature is that in block six, over signature of person granting consent?"

"That would be mine, sir."

"Where on the form did you indicate that your consent was not voluntary?"

"Where did I indicate on the form that my consent was not voluntary?" Graner retorted, somewhat confused.

"Correct."

"Nowhere, sir," admitted Graner reluctantly. Still, Graner insisted that the CID agent made it sound as if he had no choice but to give his approval. "Agent Iem portrayed to me that searching my quarters was a done deal."

Holley seized upon that point and asked Graner to recount specifically what Agent Iem had said about the CID obtaining authorization regardless of whether he consented. In response, Graner attempted to characterize what he took Iem to mean. Holley asked again for the specific words Iem had used. Graner responded with the conclusion, "He had the authority to search my room."

At this point, Pohl broke in, "Well, Specialist Graner, can you answer that question?"

Graner turned back toward Holley. "Ask me one more time. The third time's a charm."

Holley paused, gathering himself in this battle of wills. "Special Agent Iem informed you that if you refused to consent that he *could* go get authorization from a commander, yes?" Holley inquired, emphasizing the future action the agent would have to take.

"Yes, sir."

"Special Agent Iem did not tell you he already had authorization from a commander, correct?"

"I don't believe so, sir," Graner stated flippantly.

"Well, did he tell you that or not?" Holley questioned forcefully. He was not willing to allow Graner to hedge.

Graner's answer remained the same—"I do not believe so, sir"—but the response this time was much more subdued.

Graveline sat at the prosecutor's table becoming more and more impressed with the skillful questioning. He had come to enjoy working with Holley a great deal. Still, Graveline had been eager to see his partner in action in the courtroom—it was one thing to be a good conversationalist and another to be a good courtroom attorney.

This is a masterful cross-examination, marveled Graveline. *He appealed to Graner's ego by boosting him up on how well he completed his jobs under dangerous and stressful conditions. Then, without Graner even suspecting it, Holley got him to admit that he consented to the search and that the CID agent only said he "could" get a warrant—it hadn't been a done deal.*

Pohl seemed to agree with Graveline's assessment and denied the motion to exclude the computer images seized from Graner's computer. The judge then turned to the main issue of the day, asking, "What's the status of the Fay investigation?"

Graveline rose to his feet. "It is currently in Washington, D.C., Your Honor. It has not been provided to the prosecution team. From what I understand, the investigation is complete and is being provided to senior leadership within the Army and the Department of Defense and will be released sometime in the near future."

"Why can't you give a copy of the evidence to the defense now?" Pohl inquired.

"Because . . . ," Graveline tried to choose his words carefully, "to be honest, the prosecution doesn't have it, Your Honor."

"I didn't ask you that, Captain Graveline. I'm not asking whether you have a copy, that's not my concern. My concern is . . . you've talked about this two months ago. And two months ago, when this thing was supposed to be wrapped up by 1 July . . . what's your legal basis for not giving it to them?"

The young JAG knew that he had no good answer, and any attempt to tap dance around the question would be unsuccessful. "There is no legal basis, Your Honor."

"Then why don't you do that?"

Graveline tried to explain some of the delay in releasing the evidence Fay had collected, but Pohl interrupted: "What you're telling me is all the government is doing with this investigation is vetting it . . . and perhaps, leaking it. Mr. Womack, you're standing."

"Sir, we would propose that Your Honor use your good office and order them to release it or abate the proceedings," the defense counsel stated.

After a brief conversation between Pohl and the counsel, he ordered the government to produce all of the governmental reports (Fay, Schlesinger, and Church) since they were all due to be discussed in congressional hearings on September 9. "Given that once it goes to Congress, I know it will be in the *New York Times*. I'm going to slide your date to 10 September, and that's it."

Pohl turned his attention to CID's search of the classified computer server. "Now, what are we talking about here in terms of . . . you got one guy sitting at a computer screen pulling up one document at a time, looking at it to determine what it is, and then move on to the next document? How many documents are we talking about here?"

"Several hundred thousand."

"And [in] what millennium is this going to be done?" retorted the judge, which prompted laughter from the audience. "What you're telling me is CID apparently doesn't see this as a priority if they've only got one guy on it."

"What they have is a task force looking into all detainee abuse cases, to include any potential detainee abuse cases in the Afghanistan and Iraq areas of operation . . . ," Graveline attempted before simply conceding, "Yes, Your Honor."

Pohl wanted concrete solutions from the government. "If I gave you a suspense date of say, 20 October, are you going to meet it?"

Graveline found himself caught in a dilemma. While he intended to keep these cases moving as quickly as possible, he did not want to commit to a date only to come back with a request for more time as he had with the Fay information. "I highly doubt it, Your Honor. I would think that the more realistic suspense date would probably be 1 December. I will push them to get it done prior to that, and yes, I would prefer it's done by 20 October, but I don't want to sit here and make the representation . . . ," he stammered.

Apparently, Pohl decided to take Holley and Graveline up on their request to yell at them on the record and give very specific deadlines. "Here's what we're going to do. You can tell CID this: they can use their assets like they want to, but if this thing isn't done by 1 December, I'm going to seriously revisit Mr. Womack's request [to dismiss the charges]. The charges in this case were preferred on the twentieth [of] March. This case has been moving rather slowly for obviously a lot of reasons.

"I'm not holding you guys responsible, referring to trial counsel, but as I've told you before, I shoot messengers . . . and that's you. But the Fay report was supposed to be done on 1 July. Now we're talking maybe 10 September. The Church and Schlesinger thing we never talked about, but, of course, those are still ongoing. This new thing of looking at hundreds of thousands of things now not due until 1 December. It strikes me that the government has to figure out what they want to do."

"You think Judge Pohl put that strong enough?" Graveline asked Holley after the hearing. The younger attorney rolled his eyes and flopped down in a chair in their makeshift team headquarters in Mannheim.

"Let's hope so," Holley returned. "There's already a report up on the CNN and BBC websites, so I'm sure we'll be getting angry calls from D.C. any time now."

No sooner were the words out his mouth than Kary walked into the room. "Sir," he said, looking at Graveline, "you've got a lieutenant colonel from CID headquarters on the phone for you."

✦

The next morning, August 24, it was time for Bergrin and Captain Dunn to raise their arguments on behalf of Sergeant Davis. Like Womack and Heath, the Davis team attempted to have Judge Pohl suppress evidence against their client, this time a statement Davis had given CID on the first day of the investigation. Davis fared no better against Holley's withering questions. By the end of the cross-examination, Davis admitted he knew exactly what he was doing when he gave his statement to CID, which made Pohl's decision to keep it in evidence easy.

The real battle of this hearing was the defense's attempt to force the government to grant immunity to some of the officers from Abu Ghraib. Under the Uniform Code of Military Justice, the convening authority can grant a military witness the ability to testify and not have his words used against him in any future prosecution. While immunity does not necessarily mean that a witness cannot be prosecuted for the incident he is testifying about, it does make it difficult since the government still must show that it developed the case against that person without any reference or assistance from his testimony. Practically speaking, granting immunity to any of the officers would be akin to handing them a "get out of jail free" card.

Bergrin wanted the convening authority, Lieutenant General Metz, to grant testimonial immunity to Colonel Pappas, the MI brigade commander; Lieutenant Colonel Jordan, the officer in charge of Abu Ghraib's Joint Interrogation Debriefing Center; CPT Christopher Brinson, the MP officer in charge of the hard-site; and 1LT Lewis Raeder, an MP platoon leader who replaced Brinson in December 2003. The defense counsel had submitted the immunity request to Metz the week prior, which he denied. Bergrin now asked Pohl to order Metz to immunize these witnesses or dismiss the charges against his client.

To convince the judge to take that step, Bergrin needed to show that the witnesses were going to invoke their right to remain silent, the government had only granted immunity to certain witnesses to gain a tactical advantage, and the witnesses' testimonies were exculpatory for the accused soldier and could not be obtained from any other witness or piece of evidence.

In the weeks leading up to this hearing, Holley and Graveline had spent several hours on the phone discussing this very issue. They were of one mind: Metz was not yet in a position to make informed decisions concerning who had clean hands in this mess. At that point, they could not rule out prosecutions against anyone who had been at Abu Ghraib, including the officers. The last thing they wanted to do was grant a person such as Colonel Pappas or Lieutenant Colonel Jordan immunity only to find out later that he had given orders to the MP soldiers to commit acts of abuse. It was clear to them that the safe course was to recommend denial of the immunity request for now and revisit the requests as the evidence firmed up. Despite these arguments, both prosecutors were concerned about how the denial of immunity would appear.

From the beginning, Holley and Graveline had insisted the defense be given every resource possible in order to eliminate later claims that the government railroaded these soldiers. The defense counsel could now use these denials of immunity to argue that the government was hiding critical evidence that would clear their clients.

After discussing this subject yet again on a call with Holley, Graveline walked down to Mulligan's third-floor office to get his take on the immunity problem.

Mulligan suggested they look at the Abu Ghraib cases as they would a prosecution of a major drug smuggling and dealing ring. "These prosecutions are going to take patience. First, you'll need to convict this first level of soldiers, who are kind of like the street dealers and middlemen. Once you've got them, we can pump them for what they know about any higher-up involvement and see if they can't give us that next level. What the Army needs to do is to keep you and Holley together with Colonel Tate, consolidate all of the soldiers and officers who were out at Abu Ghraib under III Corps' jurisdiction, and work through these cases as you get the evidence."

Graveline nodded in agreement. "The problem is that the Army's just not set up to do a major criminal prosecution that spans several jurisdictions and commands. The JAG Corps, as an institution, doesn't have the experience with complex prosecutions like the Department of Justice or major DA offices," Graveline opined. "We've got over fifty potential defendants and witnesses spread out over a dozen different units both on active duty and in the Army Reserve. If we don't merge these cases, we'll have a number of convening authorities making different charging and immunity decisions that could negatively impact cases in other jurisdictions."

"I'm not getting the vibe in the leadership to consolidate these cases," responded Mulligan, "but I'll keep working my connections to try to coordinate, as much as possible, the prosecutions that will fall out of the Fay investigation. For now, though, I suggest that you don't foreclose any future action by granting immunity at this time . . . and your position that you're only granting people immunity after they've gone to trial is a good line in the sand. It's a commonsense approach and shows that your team is serious about getting convictions against whoever may be responsible for abuses."

Graveline was happy to hear reinforcement from the experienced prosecutor. He thanked Mulligan and immediately relayed the conversation to Holley.

"I think that's right," considered Holley. "I've already started talking to Colonel Tate about some level of coordination between JAG offices once Fay releases his report, but we haven't decided the best way to go about that yet. Anyway, I think our recommendation about the immunity is set."

Tate agreed and advised Metz of his legal opinion. Metz denied Bergrin's immunity request for the officers.

Holley now stood before Pohl justifying that decision.

"Colonel Pappas, Colonel Jordan, Captain Brinson, and Lieutenant Raeder are currently being investigated by the United States government to determine if they have committed any wrongdoing. We have reason to believe that they may have. We are waiting, and we suspect that upon release of the Fay report, some of those questions will be resolved. Independent of the Fay report, we still have reason to believe that there may be misconduct that needs to be resolved. The convening authority has not elected to immunize these individuals until he can resolve that question. It's not a discriminatory use of immunity. We immunized Specialist Sivits . . ."

Pohl was beginning to lose patience with the government's refrain of "wait for the Fay report" and stopped the prosecutor mid-sentence. "Major Holley, this appears to be a frequent occurrence in this case, is that you're telling me now . . . 'Well, we're not sure about these guys,' and now almost nine months later, we're saying, 'Well, we're almost done investigating this case, and until we get done investigating it, don't let these guys, don't grant them immunity, because if you gave them immunity, that would preclude their prosecution.' Is that what you're asking me?" The judge understood the law, and he was not letting Holley off easy on this point. "Why can't you give them immunity and then still prosecute them?"

"That vastly complicates our prosecution, as the court is aware."

"Complicate doesn't mean prevent, though."

"It does not prevent, sir, but it does complicate."

Holley and Graveline knew full well that this was the weak point in their argument. Nothing in the law prevented their convening authority from granting immunity to a witness and then another convening authority in a different jurisdiction from still prosecuting that person as long as the latter convening authority was not privy to the information received through the immunized testimony. However, both prosecutors strongly suspected that if they agreed to give immunity to one of the MI officers, they would be giving that officer's convening authority an obvious reason to drop any charges against that person. The JAG lawyers in another jurisdiction could point to how difficult separating that testimony from the rest of the CID case file would be and fail to pursue any further prosecutions. The thought that one of the officers would slip through the cracks because of some action the team members had taken had been a source of major concern for them.

Pohl was not finished grilling Holley. "Are you standing up there and telling me . . . that there's thought to criminally prosecute these individuals?"

"Yes, sir."

"And as such, they shouldn't be given immunity in this case?"

"That is correct, Your Honor."

"And when is that decision going to be made?"

Holley paused since he had no good answer. "I apologize for going back to old ground, but the Fay report was focused on the MI side of the house, which really involves most of these witnesses . . . we are going to take that information to make our charging decision from there. And, Your Honor, we are just as frustrated as the defense and, no doubt, the court with the delay . . ."

"Judge, we have to really plead with this court to send a message," Bergrin inserted, unable to contain himself any longer. "We need to prepare this case.

We're defending the rights and the liberty at this time of Sergeant Davis . . . these four individuals have materially relevant information that could lead to the vindication, hopefully, of Sergeant Davis." The New Jersey defense counsel was just getting warmed up. "We ask the court to order the convening authority to grant these individuals immunity, so that we can question them. We can have them come forth to tell the truth and the whole truth and nothing but the truth as to what happened at Abu Ghraib prison. And that's the only way we're going to get it, Your Honor."

Pohl moved to gain control of the discussion by bringing the hearing back to the central themes. First, he declared that, given the defense's contention that the chain of command condoned Davis' actions at the prison, Pappas', Jordan's, and Brinson's testimony would provide critical information given their unique leadership positions. Pohl found Raeder only able to give tangential information, since he took over Brinson's position after the dates of the alleged offenses. Consequently, he told Holley that he had until September 17 to demonstrate why he should not grant immunity to Jordan, Pappas, and Brinson.

Although this ruling did not sit well with the prosecutors, it was vintage Pohl. Under a strict reading of the law, the defense had not come close to meeting its requirements for having the court order immunity. Regardless, Judge Pohl liked to ensure an even playing field. Still, Holley and Graveline did not want to be pushed into a position where someone, particularly the officers, would not be prosecuted before they could discover the full story behind the abuses.

✦

Despite the courtroom happenings, Frederick and Myers grabbed international headlines. On the first day of hearings, August 23, Myers stood before a cluster of microphones and cameras that lined the courthouse steps and read a prepared statement from his client: "I have accepted responsibility for my actions at Abu Ghraib prison. I will be pleading guilty to certain charges because I have concluded that what I did was a violation of law." For his part, Myers commented that they were "making prudent choices."

Before Pohl the next day, Myers wanted two rulings in order to make the guilty plea more advantageous for the defense: move the trial out of Iraq, and get the court to appoint a world-renowned psychologist, Dr. Philip Zimbardo, to their team as an expert witness. When a soldier pleads guilty, that person is allowed to present witness testimony and other extenuating and mitigating evidence in a hearing before the sentencing authority (either the judge or a jury). These hearings often become very lengthy, mainly owing to the various methods that can be used to present sentencing evidence to the court: live witnesses, letters of support, videotaped statements, or video-teleconferences. Military law encourages these different forms of evidence so that the service branches may conduct sentencing hearings aboard ships at sea and in distant foreign countries without bringing U.S. civilians overseas.

Since Myers planned to call more than a dozen witnesses to testify on his client's behalf, he wanted Frederick's sentencing hearing out of Iraq. Since the hearing in Iraq where Pohl chastised Shuck for Myers' absence, the defense had filed a motion to change the location of the sentencing hearing. Given the geographical spread of the attorneys and the judge, both sides agreed that the judge could decide the issue without holding a hearing. Prior to everyone's arrival in Germany, Pohl had ruled the sentencing hearing would remain in Iraq, stating that "the defense has failed to show the accused would be prejudiced by the trial occurring in Iraq."

In court, Myers now wanted to persuade Pohl in person that the judge needed to reconsider his ruling. He started with his baseline contention—the civilian witnesses he wanted to testify would not fly to Iraq because of its danger level.

Pohl pointed out that he had recently conducted a trial in Tikrit, Iraq, where family members for both the accused soldier and the victim had flown into Iraq to participate. "There is the physical capability of transporting them to Iraq if they so chose to go."

"It is not a question of whether they [the civilian witnesses] are willing to come," Myers responded. "It is a recognition that no one need to go into a combat zone to discharge their responsibilities as a witness if there is an alternative that can meet the ends of justice."

"Mr. Myers, wouldn't that apply to every case in a forward and deployed environment? What you're telling me is that because these witnesses choose not to go to Iraq because they believe it's too unsafe, they've now chosen where the trial is going to be . . . the bottom line is, they can't be forced to go anywhere outside the continental United States, which tells me is the end result of this logic that you're giving me is that when defense sentencing witnesses don't want to come to a particular location, therefore, we move the trial to where they will come."

Myers had been waiting for this fight and had saved his best rhetoric. "No, Your Honor, it's far more complex than that, far more complex than that. Am I supposed to ask the warden of this prison to zip into Iraq so that his family can be exposed to that? Or the prison guard, do I tell him this meets the ends of justice, sir? 'I know that you could be dead. Tell your wife and kids that you'll be back in five days'? I mean, what do I say to these people, Your Honor, that they're making a bad choice? This isn't a choice. This is an opposite choice . . . you need to hear that this man is not some rogue," Myers said motioning to Frederick seated at the defense table. "You need to hear that for his entire life he's been a good and decent person, that he was corrupted in a corrupt circumstance and is willing to admit it, that this takes a form of courage. I'm not trying to elevate him to a higher status than he deserves, but he does deserve to have these people who have cared about him and loved him there to tell you these things in something other than a deposition.

"It can't be done, and it can't be done with this expert, either, who will explain to all of us what the whole world has asked, how could this have happened with a guy like Chip Frederick? And judges are good at cutting to the chase, but they're not divorced from emotion or from compassion or from understanding what witnesses say. I submit to you respectfully, Your Honor, that in this case, because it is sentencing, that the material question you must ask yourself and answer is, what does all this mean in terms of a sentence? And we submit to you that these are essential witnesses within the meaning of the rule and that their absence would be a fatal flaw in the proceedings, and therefore, we ask you to abate these proceedings in Iraq and cause the convening authority to move them elsewhere."

Myers continued unabated, "I'd just say this to you, Your Honor, this is a good system of justice. I've believed in it for thirty-seven years, and it works. And it would be a tragedy if we did anything to make it appear that it doesn't work. And I humbly suggest to you that the best way to do that is [to] balance the interests, the political interests against the interests of the individual, move it out of Iraq, create the transparency that you need, and have a fair sentencing proceeding. We have no disagreement with what we're doing here. My client has made a determination that he is, in fact, guilty of certain charges and specifications. We simply ask, Your Honor, that we go to a place that is consistent with

American justice. Many with M16s [are] in a courtroom in a convention center that has been jury-rigged to look like a court with perils of death coming in and out. Your Honor, I also have worn the uniform in this country a long time ago. I'm very proud, I might add. But we cannot ask our citizens who are civilians to go into a war zone and subject themselves to the pain and penalty of death merely to discharge their responsibilities, and I hope that you will take that into account as you rule on this motion. I rule this motion as critically important, not only for the near term, but also for the long term, and I want to thank you for allowing me to take the time to talk with you."

Despite Myers' passionate plea, Pohl saw the issue as one easily resolved by the different alternatives that military law allowed for sentencing evidence, especially given the prosecutors' willingness to set up video-teleconference equipment in Iraq to take the witnesses' testimony. He stated once again that trials do not simply move because certain witnesses are unwilling to attend in a particular location. "Be all that as it may, it started in Baghdad. The offenses occurred in Baghdad. The convening authority has directed Baghdad as a site, and so everybody's on notice that this is where it's going to be."

If he was angered by the judge's decision, Myers did not show it as he moved on to his second request. Myers had asked that the government pay Dr. Zimbardo $25,000 for five days of work. A well-credentialed psychologist and professor at Stanford University, Dr. Zimbardo would examine Myers' client and testify as an expert witness on his behalf during sentencing. Holley knew if the court found this type of evidence necessary, then the law required the government to produce Dr. Zimbardo or provide an adequate substitute. Consequently, he had already selected a psychologist and a psychiatrist to offer the defense. With these alternatives, neither he nor Graveline seriously thought Pohl would order the production of Dr. Zimbardo for such an exorbitant amount of money—the equivalent of a third of his annual salary for five days of work.

Dr. Zimbardo had earned notoriety in the 1970s for conducting an experiment known as the Stanford Prison Experiment in which college students were either guards or prisoners in a mock prison. By the end of the first week, Zimbardo and his colleagues observed that the guards had become verbally and physically abusive to the prisoners. Based on these observations, he extrapolated that psychologically normal people, put in positions of extreme power over others, i.e., prison guard/prisoner, can and will become abusive. Myers wanted him to explain to the court how Frederick, a man with no criminal record or serious prior disciplinary issues, could have committed such heinous acts. Myers flatly rejected the government's proposed experts.

"There is no one who possesses Dr. Zimbardo's depth of understanding. He's been teaching and working and studying for forty-six years in this area. He is the go-to guy. There isn't anybody else who equals him in this area," Myers insisted. "There's no adequate substitute in the United States Army for this guy. The Army goes to Phil Zimbardo for advice, Your Honor."

Despite Holley's arguments to the contrary, Pohl seemed inclined to give Myers Zimbardo's services, citing his very specific expertise. However, before granting the request, he tried to convince Myers to concede on the cost. "I'm just trying to figure out, what's the five days of preparation, other than just reading stuff he apparently has already read."

Sensing his victory, Myers scaled the request back to three days for $15,000. The defense had their high-paid expert.

✦

Interspersed with the hearings, the defense attorneys, prosecutors, and Clemens took advantage of being colocated for the first time in months to schedule a number of the general officer and senior leader interviews that had been ordered by Judge Pohl. Because of its video-teleconference capability and spaciousness, Graveline reserved the V Corps commander's conference room—complete with a large, round wooden conference table surrounded by black high-backed chairs—to facilitate the many attorneys, witnesses, and court reporters. Prior to arriving in Germany, defense counsel for the various defendants had interviewed COL Marc Warren (CJTF-7's head lawyer), COL Ralph Sabatino (a reserve JAG attorney with multiple past experiences with the 800th MP Brigade and who worked for the CPA in prison/detainee operations in Iraq during 2003), and BG Janis Karpinski (the 800th MP Brigade commander). Many of the highest-ranking officers on the defense's list remained to be questioned, however.

Even with the attorneys all in one place with their schedules free, Graveline and Kary still found it challenging to coordinate interview times with the generals' staff. Finally, they pieced together a schedule in the following order: BG Mark Kimmitt (CJTF-7's spokesperson) by VTC from Tampa, Florida; MG

Geoffrey Miller (the former Guantanamo Bay commander) and LTG Thomas Metz (the MNC-I commander and general responsible for the courts-martial) by VTC from Iraq; MG Barbara Fast (CJTF-7's top intelligence officer) by VTC from Arlington, Virginia; GEN John Abizaid (the CENTCOM commander) from VTC from Tampa, Florida; and, finally, LTG Ricardo Sanchez (CJTF-7 commander) in person in Heidelberg. Looking over the final schedule Kary had prepared, Graveline shook his head in disbelief. *These are definitely not your run-of-the-mill courts-martial . . . I don't think I'll ever see another case where the defense gets a chance to interview the four-star CENTCOM commander.*

The defense counsel eagerly engaged the generals in hours-long, wide-ranging interviews with each defense team having the opportunity to query the officers. The questioning meandered from one topic to another: the generals' knowledge of the interrogation techniques used by CJTF-7, the abuse photographs and when they became aware of them, chain-of-command relationships, what involvement any Pentagon officials had in interrogation tactics, and the decisions being made in reference to the pending courts-martial. For all of their enthusiasm over Judge Pohl's decision to mandate these interviews, the defense counsel found little from the senior officers that was helpful to their defenses. All were clear that the Geneva Conventions applied in Iraq and that the abuses displayed in the photographs were beyond the pale. Not one of these senior leaders stated that he or she recognized legitimate interrogation techniques depicted in the photographs or identified any link between the Pentagon and what happened at the Abu Ghraib prison.

✦

As the summer of 2004 began to fade, it became obvious to everyone that the five remaining cases would not be resolved until the end of the year—at the earliest. As the time line grew longer, it presented real problems for Graveline in particular. He had left several cases open at V Corps, and there was no plan on how to cover his position after the summer. On top of those professional concerns, Colleen was due to give birth in December, and the couple was uncertain where the delivery would happen.

Graveline had spoken with Mulligan, Huestis, and Holley to work out a plan. All agreed that Graveline should ask for a change of station from Heidelberg to Washington, D.C., to work for Mulligan. Since the move would free up his job in Germany, the Army could assign another JAG to Heidelberg, which would put Colleen back in the States and closer to family and friends in case her husband could not be present for the birth. Holley approached Tate with the suggestion. Tate, the former head of the JAG personnel division, thought the idea was feasible and offered to call and pave the way for the move.

Weeks of back-and-forth phone calls and e-mails ensued among personnel, Graveline, Mulligan, Tate, and the new V Corps staff judge advocate COL Michelle Miller, until it was agreed that the move would happen while Graveline was temporarily back in Germany for the motion hearings. Colleen left their young son with her parents and flew back to Germany as the hearings were finishing to help pack up their home. However, they could not schedule the movers or clear post until the Army actually gave Graveline written orders to move, and he had yet to see them. Time was running out. He was supposed to be in the States to get the Fay report and watch Fay's testimony before the Senate Armed Services Committee scheduled for September 9. After more frustrated wrangling and phone calls from Tate to personnel, Graveline received his orders on Tuesday, August 31.

During a normal, overseas Army move, a soldier receives his orders and has thirty to sixty days to sign out of all the Army facilities (hospital, personnel departments, equipment return), line up a moving date, ship a car, have his on-post apartment inspected for damage, and finalize flight arrangements. Graveline needed to leave within four days, so he could return to Washington, find a place to live, and be at work the next week. He started by taking his orders to the clearing station. The woman behind the desk laughed when he explained that he needed to leave on Saturday.

"There's no way that's going to happen," she said, shaking her head. "Not only is it impossible to accomplish everything in four days, Friday is a holiday because of Labor Day. Nobody will be around over the four-day weekend to review your checklist and sign off on you and your wife leaving the country."

If there was one lesson Graveline had learned from Tate in his first ninety days, it was that "no" is not an acceptable answer simply because "that's not the way we do it" or "no one had done that before." A solution had to be found. He explained that he was one of the prosecutors in the Abu Ghraib cases and that he needed to be back in Washington the next week. "I understand it might not happen, but I've got to try. Can you set up all the appointments I need?"

The woman did a double take. "You mean those pictures that are all over the news? Those are some big cases." She paused, thought for a minute, and then started scanning her computer database. "Well, it's not every day we get a celebrity in here," she said with a smile. "Let's see what we can do. And I guess I can come in Friday morning to make sure that you've got everything done." She printed off a list of the tasks and appointments for him. "Good luck."

The next three days were a whirlwind. Colleen prepped the apartment for the movers, who were scheduled for Friday. Graveline rushed around the Heidelberg area collecting medical records, signing out of more than a dozen different military sections, going to his headquarters company for all of his military records, packing up his office, selling one car to a young soldier, and dropping off their other car for shipment to America. The German movers packed up their small apartment in record time—boxes and wrapping material flying everywhere. As the movers pulled away, the Gravelines only had one task to complete —a thorough cleaning of the apartment. As the duo cleaned windows well into the night, Graveline grinned sheepishly at his wife: "At least, we can sleep on the plane tomorrow."

As he and Colleen slumped into their seats on the Lufthansa flight destined for the States, Colleen, being six months pregnant, tried to get as comfortable as she could. The baby kicked her in the ribs. *Don't kick me, kiddo. This is all your daddy's doing*, she thought with a wry smile on her face.

Next to her, her husband was lost in thought. *At the beginning of the summer, if somebody would have told me that we'd be moving out of Germany by September, I'd have told them that they were crazy. What have we gotten ourselves into?*

8

CASUALTIES OF WAR

After the hearings, Holley and Clemens mapped out an investigative plan. Since he first gained approval to bring Clemens on board, Holley had thought long and hard about how best to use him. There were many priorities for a freelance investigator, including: delving deeper into the details of what had happened at the prison, especially involving military intelligence; spending more time interviewing the soldiers of the 372d MP Company who were redeploying back to the States; and starting serious background investigations of the accused. As he contemplated his list, however, Holley determined that interviewing the soldiers of the 72d MP Company of the Nevada National Guard would be the ideal starting point. This company was the first MP unit to be assigned the task of establishing a detention center on the site of the former prison at Abu Ghraib during the summer of 2003. It had been replaced by the 372d in October of that year. Holley needed to know what the 72d had witnessed and heard about assisting interrogations at Abu Ghraib.

Utilizing his contacts in the MP Corps, Clemens learned the National Guard company's next weekend on duty would be September 10–12, 2004, in Henderson, Nevada, a suburb of Las Vegas. Before he knew it, the investigator was on a plane to Las Vegas, poring over the statements of some of the 72d soldiers who had already been interviewed by Brigadier General Taguba. As he made the short drive from Las Vegas to Henderson, Clemens could not help but notice the similarities between Nevada and Iraq. The arid air, stifling midday temperature, and brown-hued terrain seemed all too familiar to him.

Within moments, Clemens' thoughts turned back to the two men he had lost just a few months prior in a car bomb attack. At that time, Clemens had been the senior NCO for a detachment of Army Reserve MP soldiers in Mosul. It had also been a bright, hot day when Clemens received word over the radio of an explosion at an Iraqi police academy. He immediately realized that he had a team of his soldiers at that location providing identification cards to Iraqi police. He had to find out if everyone was safe. Unfortunately, they were not. There had actually been numerous explosions throughout Mosul that morning, and two of his soldiers, SSG Stephen Martin and SSG Charles Kiser, had gone up to the academy's roof to look for the smoke plumes and blast locations. As they reached the top, a truck crashed through the front gate and hurtled toward the building. One of the soldiers opened fire, and the truck exploded before reaching the academy. Kiser died that morning from shrapnel wounds; Martin died from his wounds a week later. Clemens took their deaths particularly hard. He had known both men for years, and as their senior NCO, he felt responsible for bringing them home safely.

Clemens snapped out of his thoughts and refocused on the task in Henderson. *Focus, Mike. You've got important interviews today.* As he walked into the unit's headquarters, 1SG Daryl Keithley and the company commander, CPT Troy Armstrong, greeted him. His first impression was that both men were exhausted. Since returning from Iraq, the entire unit had been inundated with media requests, investigators from Major General Fay's team, and the defense investigators. Despite their attention fatigue, Armstrong and Keithley related with Clemens, given their shared reserve military background. Armstrong, a tall man with a razor-clean bald head, seemed particularly eager to talk with Clemens and to set the record straight.

The company arrived in late May 2003 to find a completely gutted, hulking mess of a prison at Abu Ghraib. "The conditions were horrible when we arrived," Anderson began. "Trash was piled everywhere, my men received one hot meal per day, and we had one shower for five platoons of soldiers. But we didn't let the conditions deter us." The commander went on to explain that by the time the 372d arrived to relieve them, his unit had established generators to provide some consistent power, as well as water heaters, showers, a recreation room complete with pool and Ping-Pong tables, an Internet café. The soldiers were also getting hot meals two or three times a day.

Armstrong was very frank about his assessment of the 372d and its leadership. He had found practically the entire unit to be completely uninterested in the transition training his soldiers provided. Oftentimes, the 372d soldiers simply failed to show up for the training. "They just didn't give a fuck," Armstrong told Clemens.

One area of particular interest to Clemens was Major General Miller and his GTMO team's visit to Abu Ghraib in early September 2003. Armstrong explained that while there had been discussion of MPs helping MI with intelligence gathering, the only technique he remembered being briefed on was to passively listen to the detainees while transporting them or when they were in their cells. He confirmed receiving a standard operating procedure (SOP) manual from the GTMO team for detention operations, but there was no reference to MI in it that he could recall.

After thanking Armstrong for his time, Clemens sat down with Keithley, a large and mustached man. He related his recollection of the MI-MP relationship after Major General Miller's visit. "For the most part, they would request from us what they wanted done, like sleep deprivation plans, and they wanted to be responsible for when the detainees would wake up and when they could sleep. We were primarily there for security. We had an MP at one door, and we tried to have an MP in that wing to walk up and down and make sure that there were no problems or anything going on."

Clemens followed up. "In your opinion, who would you say 'owned' what went on in Tier 1A?"

"I would characterize it as co-ownership, but MI played a role in what actually happened there," the first sergeant stated. "But we took our role down there seriously. I went down there during the day, at night, checking on our people and the detainees. My soldiers were clear in our responsibility of protecting the detainees from harm. We even set up a complaint system for the detainees with forms written in Arabic that would allow them to lodge any complaints about their treatment."

As Clemens walked back out to his car, he could not help but think of the stark difference in officers and soldiers between the 72d and the 372d. *Anybody who doesn't think unit discipline and leadership matter only needs to compare these two units. These 72d guys found a bad situation and did everything they could to make it work. The 372d, meanwhile, found a tough situation and, because of a poor attitude and discipline, decided to use it as an excuse for failure.*

✦

As Holley returned to Baghdad from Germany his top priority was charging the first MI soldier thus far, SPC Armin Cruz. Holley wanted to ensure that the trial team followed Tate's advice to go wherever the evidence led them. This desire was especially true regarding any MI involvement in detainee abuse. Neither Holley nor Graveline was particularly pleased that the administration had described the Abu Ghraib events as the work of "seven bad apples" or that the prosecutors were perceived as trying to justify this characterization. Both prosecutors saw the scandal as far more complex and wanted to ferret out any criminal culpability beyond the soldiers initially charged.

It was during Specialist Harman's Article 32 investigation in June that the prosecutors had first heard from SPC Israel Rivera, an Army Reserve MI soldier. Rivera testified extensively concerning an incident of abuse that occurred on October 25, 2003. He described how three men, suspected of raping a juvenile male detainee, had been stripped, jeered at, and finally handcuffed together naked on the floor. Two other MI soldiers, Cruz and SPC Roman Krol, had joined in the taunting and physical abuse. Several photos taken that night clearly showed Cruz and Krol standing in a large group of soldiers over the detainees.

Rivera's testimony had piqued Holley's interest so much so that, throughout the months of July and August, he began studying the case he could mount against these two MI analysts. Holley also started exchanging e-mails with a defense attorney from Dallas, Stephen Karns, whom Cruz's family had retained to protect his interests. Despite these steps, a more pressing issue always seemed to demand his attention; however, he was now ready to take a set of charges to Tate.

"Sir, I'd like to talk to you about going after two military intelligence soldiers for their roles in some of the photographed abuse," Holley stated as he poked his head into Tate's office. He then gave Tate a thumbnail description of the evidence against Cruz and Krol. "If we're going after MPs like Harman and

Graner for their actions that night, then we've got to go after the MI soldiers there as well."

Tate listened intently and then asked, "Whose command do these two soldiers fall under?" Although the colonel had repeatedly told his young attorneys that he was interested in prosecuting whoever had been directly involved in any abuse, he did not want to interfere with prosecutorial decisions being made in other court-martial jurisdictions.

"Both of these soldiers are reservists. Cruz is still in Iraq assigned to the 502d MI Battalion. He had originally deployed with the 325th MI Battalion but was stopped here in country once CID identified him in the photo from this night. I'm not sure anyone in his current unit really knows who he is or what to do with him. Krol is back in the States and I believe deactivated," Holley informed Tate. "I've had a couple of conversations with Cruz's company commander and the civilian defense counsel he has retained in Texas. They're waiting on our recommendation."

"What charges are you thinking about?"

"I think we have a solid case for cruelty and maltreatment, dereliction of duty, conspiracy to maltreat, and simple assault against both soldiers," replied the major. "My initial talks with Cruz's defense counsel point to a pretty quick plea negotiation."

"All right, these charges look good," Tate stated as he examined the papers Holley had handed him. "Let's run them by the command and see how the defense wants to play this. Do you think Cruz might be able to help in any of the other prosecutions?"

"We'll definitely make that part of any deal. I think he could be particularly helpful with Harman and Graner."

"Let's make it happen."

✦

Finally. Graveline let out a tired sigh of relief. It was September 8, two days before Judge Pohl's discovery deadline, and the young captain had just received the long-awaited investigation prepared by Major General Fay and Lieutenant General Jones. Like Brigadier General Taguba's investigation, it was voluminous, containing eleven annexes filled with thousands of pages of reports and documents and close to 170 interviews of soldiers and civilians who had been present at Abu Ghraib. Graveline believed, however, that he could have it in the defense's hands in short order since Fay's team had properly classified the information and condensed it onto compact disks that he could readily copy.

He had been reading the investigation's report for a little over a week now. The 177-page document laid out the evidence that the investigation had unearthed and also stated the conclusions of both generals. They had identified forty-four incidents of reported detainee abuse, yet before delving into the details of what led to the abuse, Lieutenant General Jones prefaced the report with a cautionary note. He emphasized that the abuses could not be "understood in a vacuum" without taking into account how the units in Iraq, from CJTF-7 down to the units at Abu Ghraib, were woefully under resourced and lacked the personnel and equipment to complete the missions they had been given. This resource shortage, as well as the lack of oversight provided both at the facility and by higher headquarters, contributed to the squalid prison conditions. The generals' assessment rang true to Graveline. *It echoes almost every officer and soldier I've spoken to as part of this investigation. I don't think it's an excuse for the abuse, but it can explain the lack of supervision. There's no doubt our forces needed more troops in country.*

Against this backdrop, the officers grouped the abuses that occurred at the prison into two distinct categories: intentional violent or sexual abuses and acts based on misinterpretation or confusion about interrogation rules. They reviewed the acts underlying the infamous photographs and identified instances where interrogators abused detainees during discreet interrogations. More importantly to Graveline, however, they pinpointed two major areas that needed further work: the use of dogs during interrogations and the night known as the IP (Iraqi police) roundup. Fay pointed to the IP roundup as "a milestone event" at Abu Ghraib. On the night of November 24, 2003, a detainee who had openly admitted to traveling to Iraq simply to kill Americans had somehow obtained a pistol while in his cell. The guards had received word of the weapon on the tier and gunfire was exchanged. Fortunately, no American soldiers were injured. The detainee was wounded with buckshot to his leg. Suspecting that one of the Iraqi guards had smuggled the weapon to the detainee, the guards lined up all of the Iraqi police in the main hallway of the hard-site. The guards were stripped down to their underwear, or completely naked, and kept that way for several hours, and interrogators began questioning them very aggressively. Military working dogs, present at the facility to provide security and check for explosives, were brought in at this time to check for weapons, but they were also used on at least one occasion to scare a detainee. The entire prison building echoed with yelling, screaming, and barking. Utter chaos had ensued. Overseeing it all was the senior officer present, Lieutenant Colonel Jordan. Fay found that "the tone and the environment that occurred that night, with the tacit approval of Jordan, can be pointed to as the causative factor that set the stage for the abuses that followed for days afterward related to the shooting and the IP roundup."

Most of the soldiers Graveline had spoken with recalled the night of the IP roundup to be the first time military working dogs had been present in the hard-site. After that night, the two Army dog handlers, SGT Michael Smith and SSG Santos Cardona, became fixtures in the hard-site, using their dogs to frighten detainees for their own amusement and in conjunction with requests from a civilian interrogator. In Graveline's mind, the abuse photos with the dogs had been the most vivid and deserving of criminal prosecution. *As soon as I get a chance, I've got to get Clemens investigating those images.*

Beyond these acts, Fay's report emphasized the presence of other government agencies (OGA) or, as that term was used almost exclusively at Abu Ghraib, CIA interrogators as another problem area. Fay specified that at the prison, "CIA detention and interrogation practices led to a loss of accountability, abuse, reduced interagency cooperation, and an unhealthy mystique that further poisoned the atmosphere." The general pointed to the CIA's practice of not registering its detainees in the normal tracking system, or forming a class of "ghost detainees," which created both confusion on how to treat these detainees and a belief that OGA was above the law.

To underscore his position, Fay described the death of a detainee during a CIA interrogation conducted in the early morning hours of November 4, 2003. A Navy SEAL team captured a man suspected of attacking members of the International Committee of the Red Cross. According to reports, the man resisted, so the SEALs used force to restrain him that included a butt stroke of a rifle to his head. CIA interrogators then picked up the detainee and brought him to Abu Ghraib, where they took the man directly into a shower room in Tier 1B to begin their interrogation. After thirty to forty-five minutes, the CIA called an MP into the shower room to remove the detainee. The MP found the man, handcuffed and his face covered with a sandbag, unresponsive. The MP checked the man's pulse and found none.*

The leaders of the MI community, Lieutenant Colonel Jordan and Colonel Pappas, were notified and decided to place the deceased man in a body bag packed with ice until they could determine how to proceed. Closing off the room, they left instructions for the soldiers on the tier that no one was to enter. Later that evening, however, Graner and Harman sneaked in the room and took a series of photographs, smiling and giving thumbs-up in front of the deceased man's face. The next day Pappas and Jordan placed the deceased man on a litter with an IV in his arm, giving the impression the man was only sick, so as not to "draw the attention of the Iraqi guards and detainees." Fay concluded that this incident, coupled with creating "ghost detainees," fostered an atmosphere of little or no personal responsibility for the detainees' well-being.

This report is far more complete and detailed than Brigadier General Taguba's. This team dug deep and conducted some good interviews. I think their analysis of the systemic problems and general framework for classifying the abuses is correct, although the generals are very lenient on the MI community. They subscribe much of the abuse the MI soldiers were involved with to misinterpretations of the interrogation policy. I know that revisions of the policy were circulated, but that's not unusual in Army staff work. Every commander and staff officer knows what is official and what is a draft, and if they don't, it's their job to find out. From what I've seen, Lieutenant General Sanchez was clear. If interrogators wanted to go above and beyond the Army interrogation manual for techniques, they had to get his permission. What was so difficult to understand about that? For the top MI officers, like Colonel Pappas or Lieutenant Colonel Jordan, down to the interrogators to now claim they were "confused" or that they "misinterpreted" the policy is self-serving and fairly disingenuous.

---

* Military medical personnel in Iraq conducted an autopsy of the man, Manadel Jamadi, and found that a blood clot in his head, probably the result of an injury received during apprehension, was the cause of death. The Navy charged the SEAL team's leader, LT Andrew Ledford, for his actions surrounding Jamadi's death. Ledford was charged with assault, dereliction of duty, conduct unbecoming an officer, and false statements. The prosecution's theory was that Ledford and his team used excessive force to subdue Jamadi and then lied to investigators to cover their actions. A military jury acquitted Ledford of all charges on May 25, 2005.

✦

After his discussion with Tate, Holley called Steve Karns in Dallas. They worked out an agreement where Cruz would plead guilty to conspiracy to maltreat and maltreatment of detainees for his acts on the night of October 25, 2003, and provide information about any other abuse he had witnessed. In exchange, the convening authority would send his case to the military's equivalent of a misdemeanor court, a special court-martial, where his exposure to confinement would be limited to one year.

Holley, working with Cruz's new commanders in Iraq, formally charged Cruz on September 4, 2004. Cruz offered to plead guilty in writing that same day. The general accepted the offer the next day, and Judge Pohl set the guilty plea for the next Saturday, September 11. With such a short suspense, Kary, Neill, Toman, and Robinson frantically began working on the logistics necessary to hold a hearing in the Green Zone.

A few days prior to the plea, Kary walked into the team's small office. "You're not going to believe what's going on in the Green Zone this weekend," the young sergeant began. "The Iraqi Congress is meeting on one side of the convention center, where we're going to be, trying to work their constitution, and at the same time out on the streets there's a 'Million Man March' planned as a demonstration of solidarity."

Holley leaned back in his chair in disbelief. "So you're telling me that we're going to be holding a guilty plea for the Abu Ghraib abuse cases in downtown Baghdad with a million Iraqis demonstrating outside on the third anniversary of the attacks on our country. Talk about having a bull's-eye on your back."

Holley talked to Robinson about the developments. "It only gets better, Mike," Robinson added. "There's also a credible terrorist threat against the convention center this weekend." It was time to inform Tate of the dangerous situation.

"We could have a real security issue downtown this weekend," Holley stated, sitting across the desk from Tate in the senior officer's office. "Should we postpone the hearing for a day or two? Although the problem with that is the eleventh is the only date Judge Pohl is available on his trip through Iraq, which makes it very unlikely that we could get Cruz's guilty plea done before Frederick's," Holley said, answering his own question. "I'd prefer not to let that happen in case we would want to utilize some of Cruz's testimony during Frederick's hearing. Maybe move the hearing here to Victory Base?"

"It's General Metz's intent to keep these hearings as open to the Arab press and general population as possible. Let me talk to him and see how he wants to handle this," Tate replied.

Metz was determined to keep the trials as transparent to the Iraqis as possible and sent an e-mail to the team to that effect, stating that he would "surge the necessary combat power" to make it happen.

Holley read Metz's e-mail with a real sense of history. *That's the first, and hopefully last, time I'll ever see the words "surge the necessary combat power" in connection with a court-martial.*

✦

Midday, September 11, Holley listened intently as Cruz explained his background as an intelligence analyst to Judge Pohl. With a full battalion of infantry soldiers and attack helicopters lining the route between Camp Victory and the Green Zone, Lieutenant General Metz had indeed surged combat power to counteract any threat. Everyone arrived safely, without incident, and the guilty plea was under way.

After Pohl finished his preliminary questions, he looked at Cruz from behind the elevated bench. "Now, in your own words, just kind of tell me what happened that day [October 25, 2003]."

"I was on my cot," the soldier began.* "It was late. I was getting ready to rack out, or I was already racked out. Specialist Krol came to the hooch area that I was staying in." He then explained that Krol, an interrogator in his unit, had come in to see if he wanted to watch the MPs "disciplining three detainees that were alleged to have raped a teenager." Cruz agreed and the pair went down to Tier 1B. When they arrived, nothing was happening, but several MPs were present, including Graner, Frederick, Ambuhl, and another soldier dressed in a

---

* Unlike the majority of the abuse allegations, who was present and what their respective roles were for this particular episode are hotly contested. The MI soldiers have been adamant that what occurred that night was a matter of MPs disciplining prisoners who had misbehaved. The MP soldiers have been equally insistent that it was the MI soldiers who took the lead in abusing these men and ordered the MPs to take certain abusive actions that night. After evaluating all of the testimony and evidence available, the prosecution team came to the conclusion that the MI soldiers' story was more credible.

green camouflage uniform. Also there were Specialist Rivera and Adel Nakla, a civilian interpreter. Three detainees were taken out of their cells and stripped by the soldiers.

"So you walked up . . . you among others told them to take off all their clothes?" Pohl asked. "Why did you do that?"

"There's no real good reason why that would happen, sir. I didn't really see when I was looking at the three detainees that they were rapists," Cruz replied. "When I was looking at them, sir, it was shortly after a mortar attack, and frankly, I saw three guys that killed two soldiers and injured me, injured my bosses, and that's not a reason."

"No, it's an explanation though . . . the mortar attack that occurred about a month earlier where two soldiers died, including one who apparently you knew?"

"He was my boss for a while, sir. He was my NCOIC."

"So when you came on to this scene, you saw these three Iraqis, you associated them with the Iraqis who, or similar to the Iraqis, who had mortared your friends. Is that what you're telling me?" Pohl inquired.

Cruz agreed.

"Did you want then to take out on them what happened to your friends?"

"I believe that's correct," Cruz answered. He described how he and the others handcuffed the detainees together in various positions, yelled at them to confess to the rape, physically assaulted one detainee by slapping him, and forced the naked men to low crawl on the cold cement floor while he pushed them down with his foot so their genitals scraped against the ground. Krol stood on the second tier throwing a Nerf football down at the defenseless detainees. He followed Krol upstairs and tried to hit the prisoners himself with the Nerf ball.

Pohl wanted to know if there were ulterior motives for the soldiers' actions that night. "At the time . . . the MPs told you that these guys were suspected of raping a fifteen-year-old boy in another part of the prison, correct?"

"At the time, it went from being a solid 'they did it' to 'we think and suspect.' But at first, it was, 'These guys raped a kid.'"

"[Did] these guys, to your knowledge, have any type of intelligence value?" Pohl asked.

"No, sir. To my knowledge, they were never interrogated for any intelligence value whatsoever, sir."

"They were simply there [Abu Ghraib] for other types of criminal misconduct?"

"Most likely if they were in the hard-site, it was either there was some kind of criminal misconduct or they were a disciplinary problem, which was held on that side. I mean, just from the talks in the interrogation control room, you kind of have a feeling which guys are of intelligence value, and I never heard anything about these guys having any kind of intelligence value."

"Is it usual if someone is going to be . . . a detainee for which there may be some interrogation, I'm assuming there's some type of interrogation plan developed?" Cruz agreed with the judge's assessment, so Pohl continued. "It's not just, all of a sudden people show up and the MPs start interrogating these guys?"

"MPs don't run interrogations, sir. I mean, they can help with setting conditions, which is like where are they going to live, which camp . . . but the interrogation process itself is supposed to be done by interrogators."

Pohl followed up on this response. "Then what they were doing to these guys, do you believe that they were performing something of a military authorized function of interrogating them, or did they just want to take their chance to abuse detainees?"

"They wanted to take their chance, sir."

"Did anyone make any remarks that would indicate to you that that's what they were doing?"

Cruz responded that there were such statements. "At one point, when I asked Sergeant Frederick . . . 'Are we within our norms here?' I mean, I know what my IROE is, that's interrogation rules of engagement. You can't touch them except for handcuffing them, sir. 'What's your SOP, and what's your ROE?' and he [Frederick] said that he was 'in the green' and he was good. And then right after that in the same conversation . . . Sergeant Frederick said that 'well, the thing is, this kind of thing right here doesn't happen back home.' He works in a correctional facility somewhere . . . he said he worked in the jail. Then Corporal Graner said, 'He loves this shit. Hey, this is what he lives for.'"

"What was he referring to when he said that?" Pohl interjected.

"What's happening to the detainees, sir."

Pohl accepted Cruz's guilty plea, and the proceeding transitioned into the sentencing phase. The mortar attack Cruz referenced earlier was further detailed.

On September 20, 2003, Cruz had just started his evening shift at Abu Ghraib when a mortar exploded nearby. After waiting several minutes and hearing nothing, Cruz and a fellow soldier, SSG Mark Day, donned their Kevlar protective gear and ventured out. Several other MI soldiers were outside preparing to continue their nightly duty. Suddenly, another mortar hit only five to ten yards away. Both soldiers were wounded, but Cruz was able to triage some of the more seriously wounded soldiers. To his great consternation, he found SGT Travis Friedrich, his close friend, had been hit. Cruz worked as much as he could on the young soldier's injuries and helped carry his friend to the evacuation helicopter, reassuring him that he would make it, that he was going to survive. Cruz later learned that his friend had died on the helicopter flight to the military hospital.

Sergeant Friedrich's death hit Cruz hard. He related his attempts to seek help from his chain of command. "I asked to speak with a combat stress team. I asked to speak to a psychologist. I asked to speak to anyone to tell me that these things I was feeling, these dreams I was having, even things I was seeing when I was wide awake were normal. And I said to [his supervisor], 'I know where I'm going. This is not a good place. I want to talk to somebody.'"

"And did you ever get that help?" Pohl asked.

"I didn't, and in fact, the first couple times, he just laughed at me." Still, Cruz was not trying to avoid responsibility. "I accept full and total responsibility for my actions. As far as my actions are concerned, the buck will stop here. I clearly recognize the fact that I was in the wrong and have had since last October to think about it. I assure you that not one day has gone by that this tragedy has not haunted me . . . however, that night, I did not see three detainees. In honesty, I saw three people who tried to kill me and who killed my section leader and my friend. The amount of time I spent in the tier, in the hard-site that night was, without a doubt, the darkest hour of my life. I turned my back on my country and my Army and myself. I no longer fought for and upheld the values that I strived to uphold my entire life. I was a different person for that time. I assure you I'm not making any excuses, and I have said and continue to say that the events that transpired held no honor and were clearly wrong."

Judge Pohl exited the courtroom to contemplate his decision. After approximately thirty minutes, he reentered and took his seat. "SPC Armin Cruz, this court sentences you to be reduced to the grade of private (E1); to be confined for eight months; and to be discharged with a bad-conduct discharge."

✦

September 30, 2004, was the final day of what had been a very long month for Holley, and he was very much looking forward to a good night's sleep. But some time before 4:00 a.m., he was awakened by an earth-rattling explosion.

Mortars! The thought raced through his mind.

Holley shot up in his bed, unsure of the exact direction of the blast, but its intensity told him that it had happened nearby. His suspicions were confirmed when he saw flames flickering outside his window.

Holley's roommate rolled off his bed onto the floor and stuck his head out the door. His instincts told him to stay inside until he was sure the attack was over, but the flames dancing across the wall drew Holley toward the door. Sixty feet to the right of his trailer, he saw the source of the blaze—another sleep trailer was engulfed in fire, with wisps of flame shooting into the night sky. More than twenty soldiers circled around, watching.

Holley had a visceral reaction to the scene. *Why are all these people just standing there?* Earlier in his MP career, he had always hated the way passersby would gawk at a wreck. *If you're not helping, just keep moving. Let the MPs and medics do their job. And the mortar attack might not be over—you should be finding cover.* Frustrated, Holley returned to his trailer, sitting for some time to ensure that the attack had really ended. Finally, he laid back down and eventually fell back asleep.

In the morning, Holley walked by the burned-out trailer and was shocked by the devastation. He felt a mix of guilt and foreboding. He had overheard soldiers in the shower trailer that morning saying that numerous soldiers had been injured and one killed in the attack. *Maybe I should have tried to make it to the trailer, tried to do something,* Holley wondered. When he arrived at the palace, the attack was the talk of the office. Someone mentioned that an MP staff sergeant had been the soldier killed. Another person heard that the deceased solider had been close to retirement. Holley felt sick to his stomach as his thoughts turned to SSG Darren Cunningham.

Just three weeks prior, Holley had run into Cunningham, his most trusted NCO from his MP days at Fort Hood, in, of all places, a shower trailer on

Camp Victory. Holley had been showering when he had heard a familiar booming voice tinged with a Boston accent. Turning off the water, Holley poked his head out from behind the curtain to see Cunningham standing there wrapped in a towel.

"Sergeant Cunningham?!? What are you doing here?"

Cunningham's round face broke into an enormous grin. "Sir, I guess I could ask you the same thing. I'm here working with the Iraqi police. How 'bout yourself?"

Holley briefly filled his old sergeant in on his role in the prosecutions but quickly turned the conversation back to Cunningham's job.

"The Iraqis are not picking up the training as quick as we would like, but they're good men in a real tough spot," Cunningham explained.

Some things never change. Sergeant Cunningham is always tough on his subordinates, whether American or Iraqi, but tough because he loves them.

The grizzled NCO continued describing how he ended up in Iraq. "I was getting pretty close to retirement when this war kicked up. The guys back at Fort Hood tried to move me around in the battalion to keep me from deploying. But, as luck would have it, my old unit didn't deploy, and the one they moved me to did." Cunningham laughed. "Never could catch a break."*

"Hey, I've got to run right now, but let's get together and have lunch or dinner one of these days," Holley offered. "I work up in the palace on the third floor if you want to stop by."

"Sounds good. I can swing by there, but it'll have to be pretty soon. I hope to be out of here in a couple of weeks," Cunningham said with a wide smile.

Holley walked back to his trailer that morning with a thousand memories flooding into his head. He had first met Cunningham in January 1994.

Sixth platoon, 545th MP Company. Brand-new 2LT Mike Holley. Man, I had no idea what I was doing.

At the time of Holley's initial assignment at Fort Hood, second lieutenants, the newest of the new officers, were not assigned directly to the 545th MP Company. Instead, they normally started on the staff at battalion where they would

---

* It was only later that Holley discovered that there was more than a small element of volunteering in Cunningham's deployment to Iraq.

be closely supervised and mentored by more senior officers. The 545th expected too much self-sufficiency and autonomy to place a second lieutenant in the lead since its mission was to patrol the sprawling central Texas post with little supervision. However, for reasons unknown to Holley, he had been thrown right in as a platoon leader in the 545th.

I was at such a loss trying to figure out how to command respect and lead men and women who were either ten years older and far more experienced or the kids who could have been my younger siblings. Holley had seen other new second lieutenants typically try one of two different tacks to manage their precarious situations. First, fake competence and play arrogant. Bravado can go a long way. Second, adopt some humility and rely on your NCOs and soldiers. Holley chose the latter. And fortunately for him, he had Darren Cunningham, the heart and soul of the platoon, to rely on.

He was such a likable guy from the get-go. I really had to completely trust Sergeant Cunningham in those days, and he never let me down. Holley shook his head as he thought of his newness and naïveté at the time. *I can never thank him enough for his loyalty. He was the consummate squad leader, the most important position in the Army. I wonder how his wife and little girl are doing.* Holley knew that Cunningham, just as many soldiers who had sold out to the Army lifestyle, had experienced some marital problems in the past. He hoped that they had ironed themselves out.

Weeks had passed since their reunion in the shower trailer, and Holley had not found the time to meet up with Cunningham. He went immediately to the Joint Operations Center, fearing for some unknown reason that Cunningham had been the MP sergeant killed in the attack but hoping to find someone who would deny it. As he entered the multitiered operations center, Holley spied a fellow MP officer he had known from their lieutenant days together at Fort Hood.

"Did you hear about the attack?" Holley asked.

"Yeah, Staff Sergeant Cunningham was killed," the officer stated matter-of-factly. "The sole mortar round smashed directly into his sleep trailer."

A shiver ran down Holley's spine, and his entire body felt completely numb. *No!*

Holley wandered into the main foyer of the palace in a daze. Somehow he guided himself up the staircases and back into the main JAG office. Tate, seeing that something was wrong, guided Holley into his cubicle office and shut the door.

Holley broke down completely, shaking and violently weeping. As he gasped out the few words to let Tate know the news, Tate silently put his arm around his grieving soldier. He had known loss himself and knew that words had no effect at times like these. Tate suggested that Holley take some time away from work that day to clear his head. It pained the colonel to see this officer he had become particularly close with in this state.

Holley headed toward the chapel, a small one-story structure two hundred yards in front of the palace. Sitting alone, he replayed all the memorable times he had spent with Cunningham: the field exercises, the crazy police calls they had responded to, the personal ups and downs of daily life in the Army. Tate slipped in the back and sat down next Holley. Guilt was beginning to fill the young major.

"I should have done something. Maybe I could have pulled him out if I had gone down to that burning trailer," Holley poured out.

Tate caught his eye with a look, both firm and compassionate. "There'll be none of that. There was nothing you could have done to save Darren, and you can't do anything to bring him back. All you can do now is honor his memory by what you do in the future."

Tate's advice hit home for Holley. *Yes, what I do in the future will honor Darren, a true MP and soldier. Maybe I can help restore some of the honor of the MP Corps and the Army that has been squandered in the shameful acts at Abu Ghraib.*

In the days that followed, Holley drove to the other side of Victory Base to 545th MP Company headquarters. He found another NCO who had worked with him and Cunningham back in 1994. This sergeant filled in some previously unknown details. Cunningham had signed his retirement papers on the day he was killed and was set to fly out of Iraq within a few weeks. His marriage had failed, but he had planned to go back to Fort Hood to be with his daughter as much as he could. He had given his entire life to the Army. It had cost him his family, a lucrative job in Massachusetts, and ultimately his life.

As Holley sat at the memorial service for Cunningham, it was evident that he had been the same old Sergeant Cunningham. Everyone spoke highly of him, and the pain of his loss was clear on all the soldiers' faces. Holley was particularly struck by the ceremonial platoon of soldiers whose job was to stand stoically and present the American, Army, and unit flags.

Hardened soldiers, battle-tested warriors all, standing in rigid formation—crying.

9

"JUST DON'T KILL HIM"

Welcome back to Iraq, Graveline thought as the gray C-130 military cargo plane lurched violently back and forth in preparation for landing. Every so often, he caught a quick view of the sandy terrain from one of the few circular windows across the plane. Flying into Baghdad International Airport was an aerial experience like no other. Instead of smoothly gliding into a final descent, the hulking planes would spiral down in a steep descent once directly above the airport. This maneuver had the dual effect of reducing the airspeed enough to land and providing a more difficult target for any would-be missile-wielding insurgents. Looking around the cargo-filled airplane with passengers sitting in four rows of webbed seats, Graveline noticed many solemn faces as the other passengers concentrated on not throwing up. Looking especially displeased with the "death spiral" was Gary Myers, Frederick's counsel.

Graveline, Myers, and Clemens had flown together from Washington Dulles International Airport; through Frankfurt, Germany; into Kuwait; and now were approaching Baghdad for the court-martial of Staff Sergeant Frederick, scheduled to start October 20. Frederick still planned to plead guilty, but first he had to convince Judge Pohl that he knew he had committed a crime, present evidence on his own behalf, and receive his sentence.

The plane finally came to a bumpy halt on the asphalt tarmac, and the passengers were escorted out the large ramp at the rear of the plane. Once they could hear each other away from the roar of the jet engines, Myers turned to Graveline with a half smile.

"I'm getting way too old for that."

✦

The judge sat silently behind the bench, scanning the pages in front of him. He looked up, staring intently at the sullen man dressed in desert camouflage seated behind the table to his right.

"Sergeant Frederick, in your own words, tell me what happened on the fourth of November 2003 with the detainee and the Meals Ready to Eat box and the wires." Judge Pohl referred to what by then had become the iconic image of Abu Ghraib—a hooded man draped with a poncho standing on a cardboard box, wires dangling from his fingers.

"I had just started my shift, and the first thing I do when I take over is make rounds to all of the wings," the guard started in a low voice. He was clearly uncomfortable talking about his actions. "I started with 1 Alpha and 1 Bravo and went down there to make a security check. I looked in the shower and seen this detainee standing there holding a box. I asked Corporal Graner what was going on. He said that a CID agent Romero wanted him stressed out as much as possible because he needed him to talk tomorrow." Frederick paused.

"What happened next?"

"I, in turn, looked over on 1 Bravo side, and I seen Agent Romero over there. I went over and talked to him, and I asked him what was going on with this particular detainee, and he told me that he had some valuable intelligence about the remains of four American soldiers and who possibly killed them." Frederick picked up the pace of his account. "So I said, 'Well, what do you want done to him?' He said, 'I really don't give a fuck, just as long as you don't kill him.' I went over and I just stood there and looked at the detainee for a while. I seen these wires hanging from the wall inside the shower. I walked by them many times, so I just took one and wrapped it around his finger. Sergeant Davis put one on his other hand, and I think Sabrina . . . "

The judge cut him off mid-sentence. "This CID Agent Romero, what was he to you, duty-wise?"

"He was nothing. I guess he was just in charge of that certain detainee."

"And he said he wanted him stressed out, 'Do whatever the fuck you want as long as you don't kill him?'"

"Exactly, sir."

"So, you were just obeying his orders when you did this?"

"Yes, Your Honor."

It became very quiet in the courtroom, save the whispering between Frederick and Myers. They were just beginning Frederick's guilty plea, and the sergeant was already having problems accepting responsibility. Under military law, the accused soldier must first explain to the judge how his actions were wrong and convince the judge that there are no defenses for such acts. With his last answer, Frederick raised the defense of obedience to orders that, if valid, would provide him a complete defense against the crime to which he was pleading. If the defense had some basis in fact, the guilty plea would be over and Frederick would be headed for trial.

At their table, mere inches from the defense's in the tiny, oddly shaped courtroom, Holley and Graveline exchanged sideways glances. Neither prosecutor was surprised this issue had come up. It was, after all, Frederick and Myers who had delivered the photos to CBS, the *New Yorker*, and other media outlets to convince their audiences that these images depicted abuse committed at the behest of military interrogators. Frederick had already agreed in a signed stipulation of fact that had been presented to the court that no one had ordered him to act the way he did. But, as in many courts-martial, the accused soldier wanted to be only barely guilty and pass off as much of the blame to someone else as possible. It was now Judge Pohl's job to determine which was the truth: was this a case of Frederick merely shifting blame away from himself, or did he actually have a defense in that he was following what he believed to be lawful orders?

After a few moments of conversation with Myers, Frederick looked toward Pohl. "There was no lawful order from the agent. I just acted on my own."

"Did or did not the CID agent tell you to do, 'Whatever the fuck you wanted, just don't kill him'?"

"He didn't tell me specifically what to do."

"But as long as you didn't kill him, the detainee, you were within the range of the stuff he told you to do, true?"

"He didn't order me to do anything."

The judge knew that these simple conclusory statements were not doing anyone any good, so he broke his questioning down into smaller facts. "Do you know Romero's rank?"

"He was an E-5, I believe," responded Frederick, a higher-ranking E-6.

"Did he have any command relationship over you at all?"

"No, Your Honor."

"What do you think his role was in the prison to begin with? What was he doing there?"

"He was in charge of that particular detainee because he was a CID hold . . . " Frederick stated, seemingly becoming more confident.

Pohl asked Frederick if he assumed that Romero was the soldier responsible for interrogating this detainee; Frederick delivered an affirmative response. "So, when he told you to do that, and you didn't take it as an order, what did you take it as?"

"An opportunity just to scare him to help out his interrogation."

"So you did this thing with the wires and the hood and everything to help out the interrogation?"

"Yes, Your Honor . . . no, Your Honor."

"Well, that was a 'yes' and a 'no.' Which is it?"

"No, Your Honor."

"'No, Your Honor' what? You've confused me now. So, you didn't take it as an order from Sergeant Romero, but you knew that Sergeant Romero wanted to interrogate this guy the next day. So you were trying to 'set the conditions' for an interrogation?"

"Yes, Your Honor."

"Did you think what you were doing to the man on the box was right?"

"No, Your Honor."

Growing frustrated with Frederick talking in circles, Pohl tried another approach to clarify Frederick's position. Knowing that the defense counsel for the cases were contesting their clients' guilt based on the argument that the acts in question were merely "setting the conditions for interrogation," Pohl would not allow Frederick to plead guilty while still hedging on that defense. The judge wanted specifics about what the MPs were told by the interrogators or there would be no guilty plea.

"Let me back up. From the time you took over as the NCOIC of the hard-site in mid-October, what was your role and, more generally, the MP mission as far as how you worked with the interrogators?"

"They would tell us what conditions to set for them, whether they keep their clothes, give them cigarettes, things like that, what kind of foods they ate," replied Frederick.

"Did they tell you to do these things to specific detainees?"

"Yes, yes, Your Honor."

"Were these interrogators civilian, military, or some you just don't know what they were?"

"Exactly, some I didn't know."

"I suspect there were all sorts of people floating in and out . . . so they would tell you as the NCOIC of the night shift that detainee one, 'We want him to eat MREs instead of hot food,' or something like that?" Frederick agreed, so Pohl persisted. "You took this as your role as an MP to set conditions for a subsequent interrogation?"

"Yes, but nobody ever told me to do 'what the fuck I wanted to do,'" the sergeant stated strongly.

"Okay, that's what I was about to ask you. At any time, were you ever told to do anything like put this detainee on a box?"

"No, Your Honor."

"So when you were told to set conditions for a detainee by these intelligence folks, by that I mean anybody who may have played an intelligence role at the prison in terms of interrogation . . . CID, civilians, mystery people or whoever, did they always tell you what conditions they wanted you to set?"

"Yes, Your Honor."

"The examples you gave earlier were food change or sleep deprivation?"

"Yes, Your Honor, food change, sleep deprivation, loud music."

Pohl started to widen his inquiry. "At any time, did any of these people ever tell you to, for example, strip the detainees?"

"No, Your Honor."

"At any time, did they say anything about putting a hood on a detainee's head . . . well, were detainees regularly hooded?"

Frederick described that the MPs used the green sandbag hoods as a security measure, placing the bags over the detainees' heads so they could not identify their surroundings as they were moved throughout the facility. He stated that there was no need for the hoods when the detainees were inside.

"Had anybody, on these prior occasions when they asked you to help set the conditions, given you blanket instructions like 'I don't care what you do, just don't kill him'?" Pohl asked.

"Nobody told me specifically what to do, but I did see military intelligence soldiers involved in some activity that was sexual." Frederick went on to detail the events to which Cruz had already pled guilty.

"So, when Romero told you, 'Just don't kill him,' and you've seen in previous instances where the MI folks were physically handling the detainees, why would you think what you did with the hood and the wires and anything, because you weren't even . . . I mean, this wasn't hurting the guy, was it?"

"I never saw the MI soldiers doing things to make the detainees believe that they were about to be killed by electricity or anything like that."

The judge attempted to ensure that the soldier omitted no facts. "Sergeant Frederick, you can't plead guilty unless you believe you are guilty. Go through with me exactly . . . you walked in, step-by-step, you saw the guy holding the box. What happened next?"

"That's when the wires were placed on him. I put one on, Sergeant Davis put one on, and Specialist Harman put one on."

"When and who took the pictures?"

"I took one and Specialist Harman took one."

Pohl then asked the question the world had been waiting to hear since the abuse photos surfaced. "Why did you take photos?"

"No reason, Your Honor."

"Sergeant Frederick, people do things for some reason." Pohl seemed to have had enough of his equivocations. "Why did you take the photos?"

"Just to take back home," Frederick answered, indicating that as the reason behind the photographs he had taken during his time at the prison.

"Were you going to use them to show other detainees that if they don't cooperate what will happen to them?"

"No, Your Honor."

"All your previous dealings with the MI folks, or any intelligence folks, was taking photographs of the detainees designed to use as an interrogation technique with other detainees?" Pohl inquired.

"Not to my knowledge, Your Honor."

"The detainee on the box with the wires attached to him, what do you think he was thinking at the time?"

"I guess he thought he was going to be electrocuted or shocked."

"Do you believe all this activity . . . putting him on the box, telling him he's going to be electrocuted, and photographing him in this pose . . . was abusive to this detainee? Despite what Romero said or that on different occasions you were allowed to set certain conditions?"

"Yes, Your Honor."

"No doubt in your mind?"

"No doubt, Your Honor."

Frederick then described his misconduct in the prison during the fall of 2003. He had known that the seven men brought in on the night of the human pyramid were common criminals accused of initiating a riot in Camp Ganci, the large detention camp at Abu Ghraib. He confessed to punching one of the unsuspecting, hooded men square in the chest. By way of explanation, Frederick stated that he had been informed that this particular detainee had thrown a rock at a female soldier earlier during the riot. The sullen guard continued with how he took photographs of the human pyramid that Graner had put together. He had been the senior soldier there that night, both silently allowing and actively joining his fellow soldiers in mocking, assaulting, and tormenting the seven men. Finally, Frederick admitted to Pohl that he had been the person to start the men masturbating that night.

"They stood them against the wall, and I told one of them to masturbate and he did. I grabbed a hold of his arm by the elbow, put it on his genitals, and moved it back and forth, gave him the hand motion."

After finding out that this sexual abuse had taken place in the public corridor of Tier 1A, and a number of photographs and video segments captured the incident, Pohl asked Frederick why he forced the first man to masturbate.

"Just to humiliate him."

After completing his questioning into that night of abuse, Pohl proceeded to look at the big picture of how the prison was run. "Now during any time . . . did you ever report how these detainees were being treated to others?"

"No, Your Honor."

"Prior to October, or prior to any of these instances, did you ever get any briefing or anything to indicate that because of the problems getting intelligence from detainees that they could be treated harshly?"

"No, Your Honor."

"At any time, did any of these detainees ever assault any of you or your guards?"

"No, Your Honor."

"And, other than the time with Romero when he says, 'I don't care what you do, just don't kill him,' did you ever receive directions from anybody that were that general that Romero told you?"

This question from the judge made both Clemens and Simril lean forward in their seats a few feet behind the prosecution table. Prior to this hearing, Holley had told the investigators that once this plea was over they were to begin a thorough debriefing of the prison guard. This debriefing would be the team's chance to finally obtain complete information from the inside circle of MPs at the heart of this scandal, and Holley wanted the interview started as soon as possible. Clemens, for his part, had already spent hours thinking ahead to the best way of establishing a good interview relationship with Frederick and the numerous topics he wanted to cover. The most important issue in Clemens' mind was the answer to this very question: who, if anyone, told you to abuse detainees?

Frederick singled out a civilian contract interrogator by the name of Johnson. He told the judge that on one night a detainee received a gun in one of the tiers and began a shoot-out with the guards. During the subsequent questioning of Iraqi guards to determine their involvement in securing the weapon, Johnson had asked Frederick to physically coerce the men who were not supplying information by applying stress to certain pressure points of the body with his hands. Frederick also mentioned a young female intelligence soldier, Specialist Spencer, as another person who would use him to assist in interrogations. Pohl followed up on the information Frederick provided.

"But each time, except again Romero, I want to put him to the side, but each time somebody, whether it was a CACI employee or Specialist Spencer or whomever, when they told you to do something to a detainee, did they specify what to do?"

"Yes, Your Honor."

"And you cooperated with them in doing what they told, but did they ever tell you to do anything like you did on the eighth of November?"

"No, Your Honor."

"On the fourth of November?"

"No, Your Honor."

"Do you think what you did on those dates that we've talked about, the fourth and the eighth, was okay because it was consistent with that military intelligence mission?"

"No, Your Honor."

At this point the hearing had been going on for more than two hours, but Pohl had one last item he wanted to cover with Frederick before breaking.

"Not that it's been raised here today, and it's something you may have said a long time ago, but I want to go over it with you, and that deals with what you told CBS News. Now, according to the stipulation of fact, you told them on May 6, 2004, that the command was responsible for the problems at the facility, that you had no support and no training whatsoever, and you had basically . . . the command wouldn't provide you rules and regulations. Now that's not necessarily inconsistent with your guilty plea, and so I'm not saying it is. But I want to make sure that it's explained . . . you explain to me. Now, do you still stand by those words that you told on *60 Minutes*?"

"I do stand by those comments."

"Okay, I'm not saying they're inconsistent with your guilty plea, but I want you to give me the context of those comments with what you've just told me. But just . . . give me the context of where you see the command responsibility stops and your culpability starts. Do you understand what I'm saying?"

Frederick nodded. "It's just that I had no support. When I would bring certain things up to my chain of command, they would tell me to do what military intelligence said. They wouldn't offer me any type of rules and regulations, where I could find them, how I could find the AR [Army Regulation] 190-8. They provided me with nothing." He then added that he had asked numerous people in both the unit the 372d had replaced and his own chain of command for any standard operating procedures or written guidance about how to actually perform his job at this prison. He received only promises from his command that they were working on it, but he never saw any such guidance.

Pohl looked intently at Frederick. "All you got was, 'Check is in the mail. It may be coming,' but you weren't holding your breath for it to come is what you're telling me."

"Exactly, sir."

"Was that true of some resources, too?"

"Yes, Your Honor."

"All that being said, not having rules and regulations, do you feel your chain of command just wasn't supporting you?"

"Yes, Your Honor."

Pohl had now arrived at the point he had been driving toward. "You may have been frustrated with your chain of command, but . . . I just want to put it in the context, and you may have had a very unsupportive chain of command, and you're telling me you thought you did. All that being said, does that in any way excuse your actions on the fourth and the eighth of November?"

"No, Your Honor."

"You knew they were wrong at the time?"

"Yes, Your Honor."

"You know they're wrong now."

"Yes, Your Honor."

✦

As the sentencing phase began, Holley rose to his feet and called Hussein Mohssein Mata Al-Zayiadi to the witness stand. Tension ran thick in the courtroom as the other accused guards and defense counsel sat in the fifteen-by-eight-foot area cordoned off for spectators awaiting the entrance of the witness. The wooden door in the back of the courtroom swung open, and a short, round-shouldered man walked in tentatively. His eyes were fixed on the floor, seemingly unable to look up. This was one of the seven men from the night of November 7, 2003—a man arrested by the Iraqi police and held at Abu Ghraib while awaiting a court hearing on suspicion of robbery.

Now sitting less than five feet from his tormentor for the first time in months, it was his turn to describe what had occurred in the dark prison hallway. Testifying with the aid of an interpreter, the Iraqi stated that he and the other detainees were thrown in a pile on the floor where a soldier stood with his full body weight on Al-Zayiadi's head and legs. The witness motioned frantically with his hands as he explained how the soldier had pressed down. Al-Zayiadi then related how they were stripped naked.

Holley interjected, "Were you ever punched or kicked at this point?"

"They then put the bags over our heads, and someone held me from behind, twisting my hand while another person came and thrusted a punch to my chest," the witness answered, showing once again with his hands and upper body a twisting motion and then putting his right hand in the center of his chest.

"How hard were you struck with this punch?"

"It was a strong punch, and I fell down and I lost my breath, then I simulated that I needed help because I was out of breath. I was afraid of being hit again, and I wanted to see who was hitting me." Al-Zayiadi went on to the forced masturbation. "I noticed that one of my acquaintances was placed standing, or was placed in front of another fellow who was underneath, and they were . . . he was being forced to masturbate on top of the other person."

"How exactly did they force this man to masturbate?" asked Holley.

Al-Zayiadi described what he witnessed, using his hands. "They hit him a few times, and they took his hand and put it over his groin area and motioned to masturbate."

"Did they make you masturbate, as well?"

The witness's eyes returned to the floor. "They grabbed me and placed one of my acquaintances under me and placed my right hand on my privates and pushed me to masturbate over my acquaintance. I was crying, and I wished I would kill myself at that point." He became visibly shaken as he recalled the events of that night.

Realizing that Al-Zayiadi would have difficulty answering many more questions, Holley asked him to describe what followed the masturbation incident. Al-Zayiadi collected himself and replied that he and the others had been placed naked, with sandbags over their heads, into prison cells with water on the floor—the unceremonious end to a night of mockery.

An uneasy pall settled over the courtroom at the Iraqi man's retelling of the events. Myers attempted a cross-examination to highlight the fact that Al-Zayiadi was an accused criminal, a thief, and therefore of dubious reliability. However, since his client had already admitted to beating and abusing Al-Zayiadi, these efforts fell flat after the Iraqi's powerful testimony.

As Al-Zayiadi left the witness stand, Myers and Shuck began their case in mitigation on Frederick's behalf. They wanted to drive home two essential points to the judge: the confinement facility at Abu Ghraib was complete chaos, and

Frederick was a caring, psychologically normal person who had been caught up in a situation beyond his control. To lay the foundation for both points, the defense team put Frederick on the stand.

Frederick recounted his upbringing in rural western Maryland, how he had joined the Maryland National Guard during his senior year in high school, facts about his family life, and how he came to be a correctional officer in Virginia in 1996. Myers began to paint a picture of a small-town, American husband and father who liked to hunt and fish on the weekends and spend time with his children. Additionally, Myers asked questions to juxtapose the orderly, strict environment of the prison where Frederick worked in Virginia with the chaotic environment of Abu Ghraib in 2003. He particularly stressed that, prior to these abuses, the worst thing Frederick had ever been reprimanded for, either at work or in the military, was being five minutes late one day to a shift at the Virginia prison.

Myers focused Frederick's attention on his impressions when he had arrived at Abu Ghraib. Frederick described an environment that seemed out of control with naked detainees handcuffed to cell doors at MI's request, OGA agents dropping off detainees without documentation (i.e., "ghost detainees," lazy and corrupt Iraqi guards), and a wild shoot-out between the guards and a detainee in Tier 1A.

The stoic guard summed up his experience at Abu Ghraib: "I didn't think anybody cared what happened. I knew it was wrong to do, but I just didn't think anybody cared what happened to the detainees, as long as they didn't die."

Myers buttressed Frederick's bleak assessment of Abu Ghraib with his next witness, Frederick's company commander, Captain Reese. Testifying from the Pentagon via video-teleconference,* Reese admitted that his initial reactions of

---

* Setting up these video-teleconferences was no small task. In order to ensure that no one could hack into the video feed, this testimony had to be taken over a secure bandwidth. There was also the issue of finding secure video-teleconference space where witnesses were testifying from (Washington, D.C.; Germany; and Italy) and getting civilian witnesses clearance and access to these VTC locations. Underlying these moving parts was the not-so-simple task of making the technology work from the middle of a combat zone and reconfiguring the courtroom to handle teleconferences. Any number of people spread over three continents were instrumental in completing this enormous task, including SGT Jared Kary, CWO Robert Kelly, LTC Matthew Stern, MAJ Kenneth Patterson, SFC Tony Merriweather, SGT Travis Gibson, Scott Wheeler, Chief Warrant Officer Phillip Kraemer, MAJ Tim MacDonnell, CPT Jeff Phillips, Romona Parker, SGT Keoki Suerth, and Legal Spc. Gloria Boykin, U.S. Navy.

shock and disgust to the abuses had been replaced by a feeling of victimization for himself and his soldiers. He was now in the mood to blame everyone but them. The commander was followed by some of Frederick's coworkers and his wife, all of whom testified from the Pentagon.

However, Myers' ace in the hole was Philip Zimbardo, the famous Stanford University psychology professor. Myers and Graveline had spent weeks figuring out the best way to present the doctor's testimony. By late September, Myers settled on having Zimbardo live by video feed, but Zimbardo's schedule put him in northern Italy during the court-martial. Graveline arranged for Zimbardo to testify via video-teleconference from the naval base in Naples, Italy, where the doctor was vacationing and guest lecturing.

"I believe that you have done a study at Stanford that gained significant scientific recognition," Myers began. "Could you describe to the military judge what that study was?"

"This was the study conducted thirty-two years ago in which I created a prison-like environment at the university in which we put ordinary young men, college students from all over the United States who were in the San Francisco area that summer. We made half of them be guards and half prisoners based on a random assignment that we employed. And before putting them in those two conditions, we gave a battery of psychological tests and interviews, because at the beginning of the study, we wanted to be sure that every one of those young men, whether they were guard or prisoner, were normal, healthy young men.

"The study then followed the psychology of imprisonment to create in that prison-like setting similar psychological phenomena that occurred in those prisons that I had studied in depth. What happened was surprising to us, because the study was supposed to go for two weeks and I had to end it after only six days because the guards got out of control. They were abusing the prisoners verbally and physically. They began to abuse the prisoners in sexual ways, stripping them naked, putting bags over their head, putting them in solitary confinement for extended periods of time, depriving them of food, so that I, as the superintendent of the prison, I no longer had control over the guards."

Myers interjected with a question. "Were you able to identify any causative factors which made these normal, average people do the abhorrent things that they did?"

"Yes, we did that because we observed day and night throughout the experiment the change in the behavior of these young men who at the beginning were ordinary, average citizens to the point at the end where they were behaving in these abusive, sadistic ways . . . the first is something called 'deindividuation,' that if you make people feel anonymous, that nobody really knows who they are, nobody really cares . . . the second process is called 'dehumanization,' where you begin to think of the other people, in this case, the prisoners, as not comparable to you, as not morally equal. That is, you begin to think in the extreme as animals, and you begin to treat them that way. The third thing is related . . . the third process called 'moral disengagement' where ordinarily moral people disengage their sense of morality for a short period of time in order to dominate control over other people in the situation or in order to do sometimes illegal, slightly immoral things."

"Other things like groupthink . . . that the guards begin to think in similar ways. Social facilitation where one guard behaving in an extreme way began to influence other guards to do the same thing. And then, there were also new standards that emerged, called 'emergent norms,' that in that setting, abusing the prisoners became acceptable. And in fact, on each day of the study, or in fact, the worst things happened each night of the study, that became a platform for escalating abuse from day to day to day."

Pohl interjected at this point. "I have a question. On your prison, these college students, did they have any training whatsoever in being a prison guard before they got that job?"

"No, not at all. There was no training."

Pohl continued, "Are you trying to extrapolate that study with every prison situation in the United States?" Graveline sensed from the judge's voice that Pohl was not willing to make the same connections the doctor was advocating.

"In some ways, yes. In fact, in most prisons that I have studied, there's minimal training, certainly psychological training for prison guards . . . in the particular case at the Abu Ghraib prison, as far as I know, there was almost no training of any of the guards in the Abu Ghraib prison, certainly not in Tier 1A, much like in our own study."

After this interruption by the judge, Myers asked how Zimbardo had prepared for his testimony. Zimbardo detailed how he had spent some time with

Frederick and his wife,* reviewed psychological testing of the guard, and read all of the military-produced reports on Abu Ghraib. The defense counsel followed by asking if the doctor had found elements within his investigation that would have fostered the results Zimbardo had witnessed in his college study.

Zimbardo nodded in agreement. "My sense was that the military created inhumane working conditions for the guards who worked in that prison, specifically, high levels of exhaustion. Sergeant Frederick worked twelve-hour shifts, from 4:00 p.m. to 4:00 a.m. seven days a week with not a single break for forty days. That's unheard of in any occupation. He got a day off and worked twelve days before another break. When he was off, when he was not in Tier 1A, he slept in a small cell, six by nine with no toilet, in a different part of the prison. And he missed breakfast and lunch regularly, so he was . . . some level of food deprivation. He didn't sleep well because, in addition, there was a great fear that the prison was under mortar and grenade attacks. Several soldiers died. Many Iraqi prisoners died. There was enormous stress.

"The other thing was, it was a situation of total chaos . . . there was some confusion as to the relationship of the military police Army Reservists to the civilian contractors doing interrogation, to the military intelligence and to the general system of interrogation in which they were encouraged to prepare prisoners—detainees—for interrogation. And again, in all the reports, I'm not saying this, but each of the reports I had mentioned indicated that there was confusion, lack of coordination between each of these units. There was approval of what could be called 'soft torture' stress deprivation . . . stress positions, use of dogs, use of nakedness, use of sleep deprivation.

"The Fay report begins by saying, 'Behavior does not occur in a vacuum,' that when we list all of the acts that Sergeant Frederick stipulated to, the terrible acts, sadistic acts, clearly abhorrent behavior, that the question is, what is the context in which those behaviors occurred? I want to argue that the things you just mentioned essentially create a scaffolding on which his behavior was played out, was amplified, was supported, so that he was in a setting where there was chaos, confusion, and he saw a social model. He saw these terrible things hap-

---

* The Army had flown Frederick back to the States in early September to meet with Dr. Zimbardo in San Francisco.

pening. He didn't make the prisoners naked. He didn't make the dogs frighten the prisoners. He didn't have the prisoners put women's underwear over their heads. He didn't have prisoners chain themselves for long periods of time. This is what he found. Some of this was with the 72d Battalion [Company]. That setting was continued. This was the foundation on which he had to somehow maintain discipline.

"One of the interesting things is that on one hand you say, 'Well, he was a corrections officer in civilian life so he had some training.' I think paradoxically his experience made it even worse because he had been in a setting where he had control, there was low stress, no fear. In this situation, he really had almost no control. Things were out of control. Everything was filthy. Things were chaotic, and his psychological report, one of the main factors in his personality, is he's somebody who is obsessive about order, about cleanliness, about discipline. And so, when he went out of control, I want to argue that it was because he was put in a situation that was totally out of control."

Myers moved on to his next point. "When you look at the totality of the circumstances that were created at Abu Ghraib by those individuals superior in rank to Staff Sergeant Frederick . . . when you look at the failings of that group, do you conclude that part of the responsibility for what Sergeant Frederick did can be laid at the corporate feet of those individuals?"

"Yes. It's a very unusual case, because in all the research I have done, we create an entity from abnormal behavior, abhorrent behavior, violent behavior. How much comes from within the person, sadistic personality traits, paranoia, things of that kind? And how much does the situation, the kinds of things I described, the dogs and the fear, wanting revenge, stress, the anonymity? But in this case, there's a third level of analysis that has to be included, and that's the systemic, that is, that situation in Tier 1A. We have to include all the failures of leadership. In every single report that I read, the Jones report, the Taguba report, the Fay report, all point to that there was a failure of leadership, the lack of leadership, no oversight, no accountability, no training, inadequate resources, that my sense is that Sergeant Frederick is guilty of the acts that he stipulated to, but he is not responsible for it. The responsibility clearly has to be shared by all of those in the chain of command slightly above him."

Myers ended with one last question. "Given the actual circumstances that existed at Abu Ghraib, that irrespective of who occupied the role of night shift guard, was there a certain inevitability to abuse, given all the factors that existed?"

"Yeah, I guess I would be drawn to that, is that not every single individual in a setting like that gets out of control. What we have found not only in my prison study, but many other studies, is that the majority . . . the typical reaction of someone in that study is to give in to the situational forces. It's the exceptional person, the heroic person who can somehow resist. But it's impossible to do so when you're encouraged to soften up the detainees for interrogation."

These final comments from Zimbardo struck Graveline profoundly. *Guilty, but not responsible? Impossible to resist the situational forces? What does that say about the human condition that we are essentially fated to immoral, abhorrent behavior based on the situation in which we find ourselves?*

Graveline had spent considerable time over the previous two months preparing to cross-examine Dr. Zimbardo. Clemens had researched him thoroughly, finding congressional testimony that Zimbardo had given back in the early 1970s and multiple other articles written by the doctor or about his experiment. The young attorney had also spent hours discussing Zimbardo's prison experiment with a psychologist he knew well. *Clearly, the situation a person faces plays a significant role in his actions, but to say that bad action becomes inevitable negates the responsibility, free will, conscience, and character of the person. I think Zimbardo's playing fast and loose with the facts of what happened at Abu Ghraib to bolster his previous experiments. I mean, he lists the use of dogs during interrogations as one of the things that lead Frederick to abuse, and the dog handlers did not even arrive at the prison until late November after all of the crimes he pleaded to were committed.*

Graveline wanted to focus on Zimbardo's positions on individual responsibility and the inevitability of evil that is attributable to a person's surroundings. "Dr. Zimbardo, you subscribe to a situationist perspective in understanding abhorrent behavior, correct?"

"Yes."

"If I could be so bold as to attempt to summarize that line of thinking in just a few sentences. When clearly evil behavior is committed by an otherwise psychologically normal person, you must look to the situational circumstances surrounding the event rather than those of personal choice, character, or free will to explain the conduct, right?"

"No. That's too simple an explanation. People always have free choice. Ultimately, individuals are always responsible for their actions. A situationist approach simply says that when trying to understand any behavior, we have to take into account various factors in the situation."

"I apologize. I must have misunderstood. When you testified before Congress, did you say the following, 'Individual behavior is largely under the control of social forces and environmental contingencies, things that occur, rather than some vague notions of personality traits, character, willpower, or other empirically invalidated constructs'? You said that, correct?"

"Correct, yes."

"You went on to say, 'We create an illusion of freedom by attributing more internal control to ourselves . . . to the individual than what actually exists.' Did you say that, as well?"

"Yes, I did."

"You went on one more time and said, 'We put too much stock in some notions of character, free will, or personality traits to which there's no evidence, psychologically, that they even exist.' You said that, as well?"

"Yes."

"Is it your testimony today that SSG Ivan Frederick, because of the situation he found himself in [in] Abu Ghraib last fall, was essentially guaranteed to commit the heinous crimes?"

"You're misconstruing what I said in my position. I didn't say people do not have free will. I said, those are vague constructs, that we use them in a vague sense. You don't measure free will. You don't measure character. It doesn't mean they don't exist, but they are vague constructs in comparison to the very specific things of . . . we can measure the level of exhaustion. We can measure the level of stress. We can measure specific event situations. So, I don't want you to . . . it sounds to me like you're trying to twist my position, that he had free will to act in the way he did or not, but that free will got undercut, that free will gets distorted the more situational factors you have that pushed behavior in this negative direction."

Graveline pressed on. "Now, you listed a number of ways that you believe the situation at Abu Ghraib paralleled the experiment you conducted at Stanford. Is that correct?"

"Yes, I did."

"One of those parallels would be hooding, the chaining, and sexual humiliation. Is that correct?"

"Yes, it is."

"The guards in your experiment were young college students, right?"

"Yes, they were all between eighteen and twenty-three or -four."

"And Staff Sergeant Frederick is thirty-eight-years-old, right?"

"Correct, yes."

"With seven years of experience as a correctional officer?"

"Yes."

"With the hooding of the inmates in your experiment, that was not the idea of the guards. That was actually yours and your staff's idea, correct?"

"Yes. It was our idea when the prisoners left the yard to go to the toilet, the guards then escalated using the hoods on their own to increase the confusion of the prisoners at various other times."

"Now, likewise, it was not the guards who originally chained the inmates in your experiments, right? That was once again your and your staff's idea."

"No, the idea of chaining the prisoners to each other was the guards' idea. The idea of wearing a chain on one's foot as a symbol of your powerlessness . . . that was part of the psychology of imprisonment we were studying."

"And it was yours and your staff who picked smocks and insisted that the inmates not wear any underclothes in order to sexually humiliate and emasculate them, correct?"

"Correct."

"So, the parallels you see between Abu Ghraib and your experiment, specifically hooding and chaining and sexual humiliating, were not abuse that your guards originally came up with, but were actually research controls of your own experiment?"

"No, not completely, because what the guards did was use the prisoners as playthings. They had prisoners bend over and had other prisoners simulate sodomy. That's not anything that we encouraged, anything that we allowed. All we did was put prisoners in smocks because we wanted to emasculate them, essentially, so you would want to minimize their masculinity. And this is what happens in many, many prisons. But the guards went way beyond that simple fact of having prisoners leapfrog over one another so their testicles would bang on their other prisoners' heads, to have them, again, simulate sodomy. That has nothing to do with me or the staff. This was the invention of the guards on the night shift."

"So when the guards did start taking the sexual humiliation that was built into the experiment to a new level, that was on the night shift. Is that correct?"

"Yes, it was on the night shift."

"And that's because they didn't believe anybody was watching them at that time."

"Correct."

"And they did it during the night shift because they knew their conduct was wrong and they didn't want to be caught doing it if you were watching them. Isn't that correct?"

"It's not clear that they thought it was wrong. I don't know if they thought it was wrong. I can't read into their minds. All I knew was, even in that setting, they didn't want me to intervene."

As the prosecutor closed his questioning, Myers was already on his feet to ask his witness another question. "You're not here to excuse his conduct, are you?"

"Oh, I don't excuse his conduct. Again, the situational approach is not excuseology. It's not saying, 'Oh, we're going to blame the situation and take the person off the hook.' It simply says in trying to understand why Sergeant Frederick suddenly did these terrible things to which he has nothing in his history, nothing in his personal background, nothing in any psychological test that would have predicted that he did these terrible things, that what we have to put on trial is both the situation and also the system of . . . on trial has to be all of the officers who should have prevented it. Abu Ghraib was treated with indifference. It had no priority, the same low priority in security as the archaeological museum in Baghdad. These are both low-priority items, and this one happened to end with these unfortunate circumstances.

"So, I think that the military is on trial, particularly all of the officers who are above Sergeant Frederick who should have known what was going on, should have prevented it, should have stopped it, should have challenged it. They are the ones who should be on trial. Or if Sergeant Frederick is responsible to some extent, whatever his sentence is has to be, I think, mitigated by the responsibility of the whole chain of command."

The defense rested with these last words from Dr. Zimbardo. Now, it was in Judge Pohl's discretion as to what Frederick's sentence would be. Pohl went into his small office inside the courthouse to read over some of the defense submissions.

He returned after an hour.

"Accused and counsel, please rise. SSG Ivan L. Frederick II, this court sentences you to be reduced to the grade of E-1, to forfeit all pay and allowances, to be discharged with a dishonorable discharge, and to be confined for ten years."

✦

With the close of the court-martial, the lawyers were now arguing over who would get a chance to speak with Frederick first, with Womack demanding an opportunity to interview him before he left Iraq the next day. Pohl agreed that Womack would be first in line. Clemens and Simril would have to wait another day to debrief Frederick.

Over breakfast the next morning, the two investigators worked on their strategy for the interview. Both men strongly sensed that the future direction of the prosecution hinged significantly upon this interview. They wanted to build a good rapport with Frederick, make him comfortable with the two of them, cover areas that Frederick had already covered in his guilty plea, and then begin to pry into the details of the photographs.

Simril had arranged to have exclusive use of the CID trailer on Camp Victory for the day; no interruptions would be imperative in order to set a good climate for conversation. Frederick was ushered in, and the three men began to talk about their backgrounds: their common police training, their time in Iraq, and their plans for leaving Iraq.

This interview's going really well, Clemens mused.

As if on cue, mortars began to impact around the trailer. All three men knew the telltale whistle, swoosh, and impact of the mortars. With their protective training kicking in, Clemens and Simril instinctively pulled Frederick to the trailer floor and covered him with their own bodies. *This guy might not be the president, but he needs protecting,* Clemens thought. The next mortar impacted incredibly close to the trailer, rocking the building . . . and with that, silence. Seconds of calm passed with the men lying on the floor, braced for the next mortar shell. Suddenly, Clemens broke into laughter. As the three soldiers picked themselves up from the floor, he couldn't help but laugh at Simril's new camouflage pattern. The front of Simril's uniform was covered in the chicken, rice, and gravy they had been eating for lunch. *I guess it's really not that funny,* Clemens thought, *but sometimes laughter's the only way get through days like this.*

Frederick, however, was visibly shaken. "I just know I'm going to die here. I've got to get out of Iraq."

"We're working on it," Simril reassured him. "You should be on a flight to Kuwait by tomorrow."

"They didn't get us that time, and they're not going to get us before we get you safe and sound to Kuwait," Clemens added.

Even with Simril's and Clemens' attempts to calm his nerves, Frederick needed to take several minutes to calm himself. He was literally shaking like a leaf.

Clemens tried to get his mind off of the attack. "Let's start at the beginning. When did you first meet Charles Graner?"

Frederick took a deep breath. "I met Graner when we were both activated after September 11. We were in two separate reserve units but were both sent to help guard Carlisle Barracks in Pennsylvania. I really didn't get to know him there, but I definitely remember seeing him there. The next time I saw him was in February 2003 when we were mobilized for Iraq. Graner had been transferred into the 372d from his old company."

"We didn't really hang out or anything like that. We talked about work and getting ready to deploy," Frederick continued. "My first impression of Graner was that he was an arrogant, loud, and obnoxious-type person."

"What gave you that impression?" Simril asked.

"His tone of voice, the stories he talked about, stuff like that," Frederick answered. "Like he told one story about putting OC spray in a fellow correctional officer's coffee while working at a prison in Pennsylvania.

"It was at Fort Lee that Graner and England really started hanging out together. I remember Graner talking about going to Virginia Beach with England

and another soldier, Specialist Strothers. Graner talked about the water still being cold, taking pictures of England with her top off, and skinny-dipping in the ocean. From my understanding, it was him and England doing this. You could tell he and England were becoming a topic because they hung out together and the way they talked to each other."

Frederick was feeling comfortable with the agents now and began to fill out their understanding of the 372d MP Company, how it ran, and its various personalities. "Even at Fort Lee, Graner could be testy at times with our superiors. The best way I can explain it is that he knew the rules, but he would always look for a way around them. This only continued when we deployed. While in Kuwait, I recalled our leaders talking about a verbal reprimand for Graner and England for having sex together in another tent. This was the first time I noticed that First Sergeant Lipinski was on both Graner and England about their relationship. It didn't stop once we got to Al-Hillah in Iraq. Graner started contesting orders and doing whatever he wanted. For example, he put barbed wire on the front brush guard of his Humvee to keep the kids off and wrote on the back 'Po White Trash.' First sergeant and the commander didn't care for that too much. I thought they just got tired of him always challenging them."

This topic seemed to trigger a sudden memory in Frederick. "One time when we first got to Al-Hillah, we lost power so everybody started using chem-lights. There were a lot of people there. Graner made a comment about it being 'naked chem-light Tuesday.' Then he pulled his shorts out, broke a chem-light, poured the liquid into his shorts on his penis and everything, and paraded himself around. It was dark, so you could see the illumination, like glow in the dark. I didn't think he took his shorts all the way off, but I believe he had them down. First Sergeant Lipinski was there, and pretty much everybody was laughing and relaxing."

Wow, thought Clemens as he stared intently at Frederick. *This 372d MP Company was one messed up unit. Soldiers prancing around naked and glowing in the dark? The first sergeant watching it all and laughing? This is not the Army that I know.*

However, Clemens' disbelief was only beginning. Frederick related yet another story about the unit as it left Al-Hillah to assume duties at Abu Ghraib. "In July 2003, parts of the company returned to Kuwait to regroup, get more supplies, and then move to Abu Ghraib. We filled one trailer with alcohol, but as we started driving, the trailer tipped over and some cases of beer spilled over the road."*

Where were the officers and senior noncommissioned officers in this outfit? Clemens wondered to himself. Clemens had been in any number of active duty and reserve units over the years, with varying degrees of quality, but he had never encountered a unit as poorly run and chaotic as the 372d. *And this is before they even got to Abu Ghraib!*

Frederick moved to detailing the unit's first few days at Abu Ghraib. He picked up where he had left off in his guilty plea regarding the lack of training. "We barely had any time with the 72d MP Company. Our right seat ride was about two days and very brief. I wasn't told anything about the detainees or how to treat them. The whole place was messed up. I went down to Tier 1A and saw naked detainees handcuffed to the bars of their cells. I also saw some wearing women's underwear, not on their heads, but actually wearing them."

"I was made night shift NCOIC of the hard-site in mid-October. Graner also worked the night shift. I knew he was a civilian correctional officer so I put him in charge of Tier 1A."

"How was Graner around the detainees?" Clemens asked.

"Graner could be rough with the detainees. The first time I remember Graner abusing detainees was when I saw him push a detainee into a pole. I was called over to the wood site [a small wood booth used for interrogations] to pick up a detainee and return him to his cell. As I was heading out there, I saw Graner walking toward me with the detainee who was hooded, with his hands cuffed behind him. I saw a six- to eight-foot pole sticking out of the ground and told Graner to watch out for it. Graner just let the detainee run right into the pole, then yelled at him for hitting it. The detainee was hooded and couldn't have seen it."

Simril and Clemens pulled out some of the pictures CID had seized from the accused soldiers' cameras and hard drives. They started with the various photos from the night of the human pyramid and forced masturbation. Frederick confirmed that the entire night was pure entertainment for the MPs.

---

* No Army soldier had been allowed alcohol in theater since the beginning of the invasion.

This explanation rang true to Clemens given all the sexually themed photos from the 372d soldiers that he had seen taken. There had been speculation of widespread sex going on in the hard-site, possibly even with detainees. He showed Frederick a photo of Graner and England engaging in fellatio in a prison cell with England giving a thumbs-up to the camera.

"Can you explain this picture?"

"We were in the supply cell over in Tier 1B, and Graner asked if I would take a picture of England giving him a blow job. So I agreed to take the picture, and they went into the supply room. I gave them a couple minutes, then I leaned in, took the picture, and left. It took about ten seconds. Graner told me later that he and England had sex in the cells."

Since it was getting late, the two agents decided to end the interview for the night. The arrangement was already in place to fly Frederick to Kuwait with his attorney the next morning. Clemens and Simril could see the relief on the staff sergeant's face as they told him of the plan. The investigators, however, would not be able to fly to Kuwait until the following day.

"Get down to Kuwait, relax, and we'll pick up where we left off in two days," Clemens told Frederick. He could already sense that they were building a good rapport with Frederick and thought that they were in a position going forward to answer many of the lingering questions about who, if anyone, ordered the abuse.

With their gear packed for the flight the following morning, the two agents awoke later that night to the sound of explosions and impacting mortars. *Those were really close,* Clemens thought. As he and Simril scrambled out of their trailer, smoke and dust hung in the air. Looking to their right, they saw that the shower trailer a few down from them was ablaze. The area buzzed with soldiers providing medical and security response. *I am going to be happy to get out of this place, too.*

Clemens learned the next day that Special Agent Edward Seitz of the U.S. State Department's Diplomatic Security Service (DSS) had been in the shower trailer when the mortar hit. Clemens could not believe the news. For a couple of weeks, he had been trying to set up a meeting with Seitz, who was a friend of a friend back in the States. Clemens had heard so many good things about Seitz, and now he would never get a chance to meet him. He slowly shook his head as he reflected on all the unexpected pain this conflict had caused him and remembered the soldiers he lost on June 24. *You never get used to the losses of war.*

✦

Frederick's interview resumed in the much more relaxed setting of the CID trailers at Camp Arifjan, Kuwait, the afternoon of October 25, 2004. Simril and Clemens went through the pictures with Frederick one by one. They started with the images relating to Cruz's guilty plea. Frederick confirmed Cruz's account that the three detainees were being questioned about a rape and not any intelligence matter impacting the war. He also agreed that both MI and MP participated in the abuse and that it had been Graner's idea to treat the detainees as they had. Frederick did not know, however, who took the photographs that night.

"Did you know it was wrong at the time you and the other soldiers were taking these actions?" asked Simril.

"Yes, we knew it was wrong. As far as making them do PT [physical training like jumping jacks, push-ups], I didn't think that was bad; but everything else, the crawling on the floor naked, handcuffing, and making them touch each other, yes, I knew it was wrong, and so did everybody else. They were piled on top of each other, handcuffed together, so their genitals were touching each other."

"Who ordered that the detainees be put in this position on the floor?" Clemens inquired.

Frederick credited Graner with the sexual pose. He reiterated that no one had ordered the abuse of these three detainees as he was shown each photo of that night.

Sliding the photo of the human pyramid across the table to Frederick, Simril asked, "Who ordered that the detainees be treated like this?"

"No one ordered us to treat them that way." As they went through over thirty photographs of that night, Frederick's answer remained the same. No one ordered them to do, or even knew, what they were doing to the seven detainees the night of November 7.

Frederick is reinforcing practically everything we already know. For the most infamous photos, there were simply no orders and no reason for these soldiers to do these things to the detainees other than for their own entertainment, Clemens thought as the agents ended the interview for the night.

Frederick was being held at a prison camp set up in the desert away from the main body of the U.S. camp. As the two agents drove to the camp the next morning through the seemingly endless white sands, Clemens, at the wheel of the SUV, intentionally gave a very wide berth to any random piece of sandbag and assorted debris.

"What's the deal, Mike?" Simril asked after a particularly broad veer that took the SUV off the road.

"I don't want to run over anything that could be an IED."

"We're in Kuwait, man. There are no IEDs here."

"I know that, but I can't help but be on edge. I've seen too much damage and injuries come from them."

Simril came up with an idea to help Clemens break out of this mental block. "How about this? Try running over every piece of trash out here, so you get over that fear."

That is the craziest idea that I've ever heard, Clemens thought to himself. *But if it will make Art feel better I'll try it.*

Clemens started driving over every piece of trash he could find—it worked. *Who knew that Art is a pretty good psychologist as well?*

Arriving at the prison camp, Clemens and Simril sat down with Frederick again. Clemens showed the staff sergeant a picture of a detainee exposing her breast. "Who took this picture and why?"

"This is one of two female detainees who were brought into the hard-site," Frederick stated. "I think they were there for prostitution. I don't know who actually took this photo, but I did see it on Graner's camera. When he showed it to me, he said that he had tried to get a picture of her pubic area, but she wouldn't let him. I think it was taken the first night they were brought in since they were only there for a few days."

"Were there any other incidents that involved this female detainee?" Simril asked.

Frederick's face suddenly became ashen, and he refused to answer the question.

The instant change in Frederick's demeanor took Clemens by surprise. *What just happened?!? We're going on day three of the interview, and there've been no subjects off-limits. Whatever it is, we'd better resolve it, or this interview is coming to a halt.*

"I want to talk to my lawyer," Frederick abruptly announced. He was visibly shaken.

Simril quickly set about locating a satellite telephone and Gary Myers. After establishing contact with Myers, Frederick was on the phone alone with him for what seemed like an eternity to the investigators. As Simril and Clemens discussed the situation, the only thing they could think of that would have provoked that reaction was some sort of marital infidelity. But they would just have to wait to find out.

Frederick finally ended the call with Myers and agreed to continue the interview. "The female in the photo was being very forward with me. She kept asking me, 'Fiki, fiki?' which in Arabic means sex or something to do with sex. I told the female MPs to take all three of the females down and give them a shower. As they were getting dressed, the female in the photo met me at the door of the shower.

"Where we were standing, in the shower entrance, nobody could really see me. She started saying, 'Fiki, fiki,' and I asked her where. She pointed to her cell. My pants were pretty loose because I had lost weight, and she reached over, stuck her hand down my pants, and touched my penis. It was less than five seconds, and she was saying 'Fiki, fiki' and trying to get me to go in her cell. She stepped closer and let me put my hand down her sweatpants. Then she tried to get me to hug and kiss her, but I wouldn't, so we left the shower."

"Why did you put your hand down her pants?" Clemens pressed.

"I was just curious," Frederick responded sheepishly.

To Clemens and Simril, this revelation was a turning point. It was not necessarily what they had learned about this particular incident, but that Frederick told them at all. Frederick had clearly not wished them to know, and he was heartbroken that his wife would find out. The two investigators would have never discovered it, as there were no other witnesses to the event. But he had told them about it nonetheless. While he was still minimizing his behavior as much as possible, the interview continued in a new light, with the agents confident Frederick was not going to hide anything that happened, no matter the cost.

The agents turned the conversation to particular officers and their level of knowledge of what had happened in the hard-site.

"How about Colonel Pappas?" Clemens asked. It was now time in his mind to figure out where the military intelligence leadership stood in this mess.

"He was in the tier once that I can recall and saw the naked detainees handcuffed to the bars. He was also down there during the two Red Cross visits."

"Did he say anything about the naked detainees?"

"He didn't say anything. He didn't have time for me, but nobody ever came back and said anything to me about it being wrong."

"Lieutenant Colonel Jordan, what did he see?" Simril inquired.

"He was in the tier a few times, making rounds. He saw them nude and handcuffed to the doors. I spoke with him a couple of times, and he never said anything to me about how we were treating detainees. The first time I heard he was down in Tier 1A, I ran down to meet him. I asked him about rules and regulations, and he said he would check into it. But I didn't get anything from him."

Frederick went on to relate that his chain of command, Captain Reese and Captain Brinson—his company commander and platoon leader, respectively—also saw naked detainees handcuffed to cells in Tier 1A and said nothing to him about it. He also related that he rarely saw any of these officers during his shift but that he saw Colonel Jordan the most. Frederick was adamant that, at least to his knowledge, none of these officers were aware of the abuse that he and his fellow soldiers had committed.

10

SMOKING GUNS

At the same time the team prepared for Frederick's guilty plea, Holley was also negotiating a deal with SPC Megan Ambuhl and her attorneys, Harvey Volzer and CPT Jennifer Crawford. From his first days on this investigation, Holley did not know what to make of Ambuhl or the case against her. She was older than the other female guards, England and Harman, and a bright college graduate who worked in biomedics in Virginia. Ambuhl had been the guard in charge of Tier 1B, the tier of females and juveniles, on the night shift and shared the office between Tier 1A and 1B with Graner. She only appeared in two photos of abuse (those with England and the man on the leash), and her name had rarely appeared in statements given by the other accused soldiers.

To make matters worse, Holley hated the charges against her. She was charged with four crimes: conspiracy to maltreat detainees, maltreatment of detainees, indecent acts, and dereliction of duty. All of her alleged misconduct, however, was framed in terms of "watching" or "observing" abuse or "participating in a photograph." *She's facing charges that could bring her nine and a half years, and we have nothing showing her active participation in any of these acts. Still, how could she have seen everything going on in Tier 1A on the night shift and not either be part of it or report it?* Holley stared at her charge sheet for what seemed like the hundredth time. In contrast, both Neill and Graveline voiced their opposition to offering Ambuhl a deal. Neill, in particular, argued that Ambuhl was an intelligent woman, intelligent enough to stay out of the pictures and stay quiet after the investigation broke. Neill and Graveline were convinced that as their investigation developed, their case against Ambuhl would only strengthen. *Well, one thing is clear—she's a minor player when compared with Graner and Frederick,* Holley thought. *If we can get her to plead guilty to a lesser charge, with her presence in the tiers every night, she could make a valuable witness. There's at least one charge against Graner, the leash incident, in which Ambuhl's testimony could be critical.*

Holley slowly brought Tate, Graveline, and Neill around to his reasoning. So, with Tate's permission, Holley e-mailed Volzer and Crawford with a proposal. Ambuhl could plead guilty to dereliction of duty, the crime that seemed to best fit her actions, and they would drop the other three charges. If she agreed to cooperate and testify truthfully at any future abuse trials, she could plead to this essentially misdemeanor charge at a summary court-martial.* A summary court-martial is the least serious court-martial possible where the punishment for a soldier of Ambuhl's rank is limited to thirty days of confinement, forty-five days of hard labor, sixty days of restriction, demotion to the lowest rank of private, and/or the loss of up to two-thirds of one month's pay. It is a free-flowing hearing, used mostly as a means of military discipline rather than to address serious criminal misconduct, where the formal rules of evidence do not apply and the presiding official is an officer as opposed to a military judge. Although the proposal was a significant drop in the severity of the charges, Holley believed it was appropriate given the evidence.

As September rolled into October, Holley and Volzer, a Virginia attorney and former JAG officer with whom Holley had formed an amicable relationship almost immediately, negotiated the exact terms of the deal. Ambuhl would tell investigators everything she knew about the abuses and admit to witnessing and failing to stop or report three occurrences of abuse: the incident with England holding the man on the end of the leash; the night involving the three alleged rapists with Cruz, Graner, Krol, Harman, and Frederick; and the abuses surrounding the seven rioters and the human pyramid. Ambuhl agreed and pled guilty in front of the summary court-martial officer on October 30, 2004, ten days after Frederick's guilty plea. Volzer and Crawford put together an extensive packet, over a hundred pages long, of letters on her behalf from friends, family,

---

* In the military justice system, there are three types of court-martial: general, special, and summary. The courts-martial vary in the severity of the charges and the potential range of punishments.

and coworkers and the statements of the other accused soldiers minimizing her involvement. The presiding officer took all of these materials into account and sentenced her to forfeit a half of month's pay for one month and the loss of two military ranks, making her a private.*

✦

Simril and Clemens shielded their eyes from the midday sun as they waited for Ambuhl to arrive in Camp Arifjan, Kuwait. They were fresh off their debriefing with Frederick and feeling comfortable with their combined interview skills and plan. Frederick had provided a lengthy statement, more than 120-typed pages, which the two investigators were still analyzing and prioritizing for investigative leads. Now was a perfect opportunity to speak with another insider who could further bring into focus the overall picture of Abu Ghraib.

Sitting across the table from her, Clemens initially found Ambuhl to be very apprehensive. He and Simril attempted casual banter but were met with one- or two-word responses from Ambuhl, her eyes remained firmly fixed on the table.

"Why don't we talk about England and the leash incident with 'Gus'?" Simril asked.

Ambuhl explained that Gus had been brought into the hard-site earlier the same day as the photographs and was placed in the "hole," or the solitary cell with the solid metal door. She stated that she, Graner, and England went to bring him to a different cell in Tier 1B but found him uncooperative.

"Did Gus physically resist Graner?" Simril inquired.

"It was all verbal. Graner would tell Gus to stand up, and Gus would refuse and start threatening him," Ambuhl replied.

The soldier went on to describe how Graner shut the solid metal door, found a strap from somewhere (she did not know where), reentered the cell, placed the strap around the man's neck, and led him out of the cell as Gus crawled behind him. Graner then handed the strap to England, stepped back, and snapped the pictures. Ambuhl was leaning up against the wall, watching. She acknowledged that other techniques could have been used to move Gus.

"Why was the leash used?" Simril pressed.

"I think it was because he wouldn't move and to embarrass him," Ambuhl

---

* Ambuhl was subsequently administratively discharged from the Army on November 20, 2004.

stated, her eyes returning again to the table. "It was more to humiliate him." She then admitted that no one had ordered them to do this to Gus; in fact, it had been just the three of them down in the tier. She also stated that Graner had tried to electronically black her out of these photos once CID started investigating.

Ambuhl went on to support Frederick on a number of incidents he had related (the night of the seven rioters' human pyramid and when the prostitute was photographed exposing her breast) and that MI soldiers, specifically Specialists Spencer and Cruz, had asked Frederick and Graner to assist in one interrogation by yelling at a detainee. She was very detailed about the use of dogs. She remembered two military dog handlers in particular, Smith and Cardona, and that the dogs became a familiar sight in the hard-site after the IP roundup on November 24, 2003, the incident where a detainee smuggled the weapon into his cell. She stated how a civilian interrogator, Steve, would have the handlers scare a particular detainee, nicknamed "al Qaeda" or "AQ," before or during interrogations. AQ was apparently incredibly afraid of dogs and would react intensely to them. Steve also encouraged her and other guards to manhandle AQ, or treat him roughly, when bringing him to and from interrogations. *Both Taguba and Fay have mentioned this Steve guy,* Clemens thought. *We need to look into his use of dogs more closely.*

✦

Clemens had grown accustomed to making cold calls. It was never easy gaining the confidence of a complete stranger, especially after you identify yourself as a police officer, but it was part of the job and Clemens had developed a knack for the friendly banter that usually got him a foot in the door. Despite all the training and experience, there is always an uncomfortable silence on the line before the other person decides to talk to you. That silence could not have been more deafening to Clemens as he waited for Staci Morris, Graner's ex-wife, to respond to his initial introduction over the phone.

Clemens had returned to the JAG offices in Virginia ready to begin background work on Graner, the next investigatory priority. He intended to visit the guard's hometown in order to see what he could turn up. By cold calling now, he was laying the groundwork for such a visit, hoping to establish a rapport with potential witnesses prior to showing up at their door. Still, he could tell

SPC Megan Ambuhl (far left) and PFC Lynndie England stand above "Gus" during the "cell extraction" designed by CPL Charles Graner on October 20, 2003.

SSG Ivan Frederick checks his digital camera after placing a Iraqi detainee on a box and attaching wires to his hands with SPC Sabrina Harman on the night of November 3, 2003. The pictures taken this night would soon become emblematic of the abuses committed at Abu Ghraib.

CPL Charles Graner posing for the cameras early on the night of the seven rioters, November 7, 2003. Graner attached this photograph to an e-mail he sent to family back in the United States with the message "hey buddy here is a pic of me at work and they had a riot at one of the outside camps and when they brought the bad guys in to where i work. we gave them a reason not to ever come see me or my friends again."

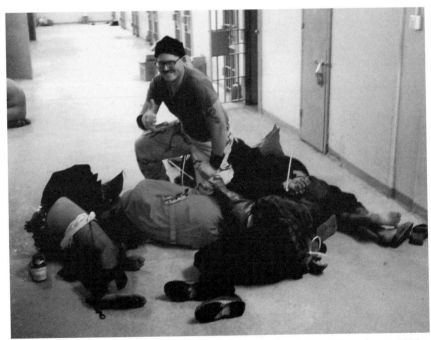

Corporal Graner posing for the cameras again early on the night of November 7, 2003. Graner attached this photograph to an e-mail he sent to family back in the United States with the message "a good upper body workout but hard on the hands."

CPL Charles Graner and SPC Sabrina Harman pose behind the pyramid of naked men placed in this position by Graner on the night of November 7, 2003.

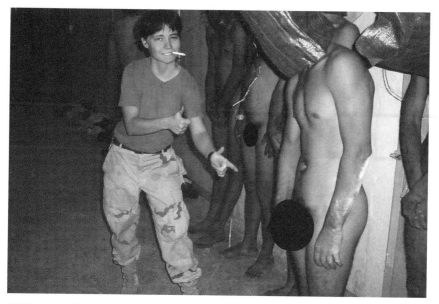

PFC Lynndie England poses in the now infamous thumbs-up position toward the end of the night of abuse on November 7, 2003.

SSG Ivan Frederick (dressed in a black jacket, on the far right) watches as the two Army dog handlers, SGT Michael Smith (with the black dog) and SGT Santos Cardona (with the brown dog), pin a detainee against the wall. According to several witnesses, this photo was taken during a "cell search." Every time the detainee attempted to lie on the ground, he would immediately retreat, owing to his fear of the dogs. He eventually jumped on Graner and was bitten in the leg by the dogs.

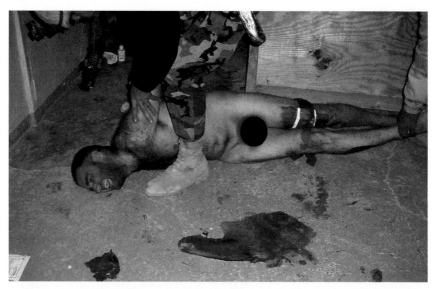

A detainee bitten by a dog on the night of December 16, 2003. Corporal Graner attached this photograph to an e-mail he sent to family back in the United States with the message "inmate from iran tries to escape to kill more americans . . . i find out . . . i punish inmate . . . i bring in dogs . . . i get assaulted . . . dogs bite inmate. then the guys give me hell for not getting any pictures while i was fighting this guy. i ended up getting kicked in the left calf, which is still pretty sore, and punched a couple of time on the metal plate of my vest before the dogs got him. i think he was more trying to get away from the dogs than really wanting to assault me but he did and he paid."

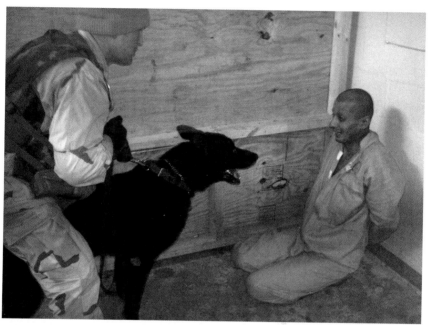

SGT Michael Smith stands with his military working dog inches away from the face of "AQ," the detainee initially thought to be al Qaeda but later determined to be the salesman he had claimed to be from the beginning. According to several witnesses, Sergeant Smith used his dog in this way at the request of a civilian military interrogator in order to strike fear into the detainee.

A view of the Al Faw Palace on Victory Base, Baghdad, Iraq, at night.

Courtroom sketch of MAJ Michael Holley during the court-martial of SPC Armin Cruz. (Specialist Cruz is pictured on the left.)

Courtroom sketch of MAJ Michael Holley (on right) and CPT Christopher Graveline during SSG Ivan Frederick's plea hearing in Iraq.

Courtroom sketch of CPT Christopher Graveline delivering the closing argument in the *United States v. CPL Charles Graner* court-martial. Seated in the foreground is Corporal Graner (in uniform) and Guy Womack (in the gray suit). Judge James Pohl is pictured seated behind the raised bench.

MSG Michael Clemens, CPT Christopher Graveline, and MAJ Michael Holley (from left to right) outside of the Camp Victory Courthouse after Staff Sergeant Frederick's court-martial, October 2004.

Several members of the trial team at Fort Hood, Texas. Pictured from left to right: CPT Cullen Sheppard, COL Butch Tate, SGT Jared Kary, CPT Chuck Neill, and MAJ Michael Holley.

by the tone in her voice that Morris was unenthused with the idea of talking with anyone about her ex-husband. She explained that since the abuse photos had been made public, she had been inundated with media requests but had decided to keep a low profile. Clemens reiterated that he was not from the media but rather with the Army, investigating what had occurred at the prison. Morris continued to refuse. As far as she was concerned, Graner was no longer a part of her life, and she did not want his actions to affect her or their two children.

"I completely understand," Clemens replied. "But I would really like to sit down and speak with you. I'm going be to up in your area in a few days . . . it really won't take but a few minutes . . . "

Morris relented and directed Clemens to her home in Uniontown, Pennsylvania. Clemens wasted no time arranging his schedule in order to start the four-hour drive as soon as possible. He pulled up in front of the two-story house on the evening of November 17.

Noticing that there were no stairs leading to the front door, Clemens went around to the back door and was greeted by Morris. As he entered the home, Clemens was taken aback by its condition. Morris must have seen the look on Clemens's face because she immediately told him, "That is Charles' handiwork." Apologizing for the mess, Morris explained that when she and Graner were going through their divorce, he had ripped plumbing and electrical wires out of some of the walls. The repairs had never been done.

"I don't grade for neatness," Clemens reassured her. Morris ushered Clemens into the front room. She offered a seat on the couch as she sat across the room from the investigator.

Clemens started by asking a series of background questions. Graner and Morris had married in 1990, and she became pregnant soon after, just as Graner was being called up as a Marine Corps Reservist in support of Operation Desert Storm. Morris recalled that Graner was so concerned about what he might encounter in Iraq the first time that he told her he was taking a copy of the Geneva Conventions with him. She remembered seeing him pack the green military-issued manual.

During his deployment, Graner and others were caught stealing Humvees in the desert. *Caught stealing?* This news piqued Clemens' interest. Morris then began to list other things he had stolen. The family dinner plates and glasses were from a Chi-Chi's restaurant. He had taken plenty of military equipment: helmets, camouflage clothing, a case of MREs, and ammunition—lots of ammunition. She described several green cans of magazines filled with red- and yellow-tipped bullets. Clemens immediately recognized this to be military-issued ammunition. The detailed description enhanced her credibility, as did her offer to show Clemens the cans out in her garage. The wheels in Clemens' mind were turning.

Morris shared that after seven years of a hard marriage, she finally filed for divorce in 1997. Clemens had already pulled the divorce papers. They told a story of physical abuse and threats by Graner. In addition to the divorce, Morris also obtained a protection-from-abuse order against Graner. "It seemed as though he loved to see me being terrorized," she told Clemens. The investigator tried to connect Graner's apparently abusive family life with his work by asking Morris whether she knew anything about rumors of Graner abusing inmates at his job as a prison guard in the Pennsylvania correctional system. While he worked at the Fayette County Prison, Morris recalled, Graner told her about duct-taping prisoners to a chair and beating them with a phonebook so as not to leave any marks. She didn't know if Graner had been reprimanded for this behavior or if he had simply exaggerated to impress her with his bravado.

After several more minutes of conversation, Morris mentioned that she was truly disgusted by the e-mails her ex-husband had sent to her and their children during his time at Abu Ghraib—with photos of the prisoners attached. *What?!?* Clemens could barely contain his excitement upon hearing this revelation. He could only imagine what Graner could have said about the photos in these e-mails.

"Do you still have those e-mails?"

"I don't think I deleted them," Morris responded. She walked to the computer and opened them. Clemens could not believe that he was staring at e-mails complete with attached photos and comments provided by Graner. One e-mail sent to his son was titled "a great workout" and included a photograph of Graner kneeling on the pile of the seven hooded detainees with his fist cocked over one of them. The e-mail read, "they brought the bad guys in to where i worked. We gave them a reason not to ever come and see me or my friends again."

Holly and Graveline aren't going to believe this! At Clemens' request, Morris printed out copies of the e-mails and said she would get other e-mails Graner had sent her family members. While this trip already proved more profitable than he had imagined, Clemens asked Morris if any of the stolen military property was in the house. Concerned for her own safety, she was unwilling to cooperate any further. Clemens reassured her that he only wanted to look and would not take anything from the house. She reluctantly told him that Graner had left military gear in both the attic and garage.

Clemens climbed the wooden stairs to the attic, finding it to be no cleaner than the rest of the house. Years of clutter filled the small space: old military uniforms, toys, and boxes—lots of boxes. His eye spied a milk crate in the corner overflowing with military manuals and training materials. He began to flip through the manuals. It was all there—a copy of the Geneva Conventions, prisoner-handling protocol, and worksheets that detailed the rights of detainees. *So much for the "I haven't received any training in how to treat prisoners" argument,* Clemens thought. That particular defense argument had never sat well with the veteran MP who knew the extensive schooling military police receive about the correct way to treat detained individuals. Clemens separated out the relevant material, but per his agreement with Morris, he left all of the materials in the attic. Out in the garage, Clemens found numerous cans with thousands of military ammunition and tracer rounds sitting on the floor.

Morris was not about to let Clemens leave with anything he had found; she was too afraid of how Graner would react. The investigator eased her fears by explaining that he would go through the more official route of obtaining a search warrant to seize the property.

As Clemens pulled away from the house, he was already dialing Graveline's number. "Chris, do you want to know what I just found . . . "

✦

Before leaving Pennsylvania, Clemens drove out to the correctional facility where Graner last worked. An interview with Michael Muccino, one of Graner's superiors at the Pennsylvania prison, in the *Pittsburgh Tribune-Review* had caught his attention:

> "First thing I thought was they gave the Army a black eye, gave the military
> police a black eye," Muccino said. "Looking at the pictures I can't believe

military intelligence or anyone would tell other soldiers to stack people up in a pyramid naked and take pictures behind them with thumbs up. There wouldn't be a reason for that." . . . "I wouldn't say I'm surprised," Muccino said. "I just think they were bad MPs. I feel they should be charged and prosecuted, discharged from the service and if it's deemed they should get jail time, then so be it."

Clemens decided this person was someone he should meet.

Muccino, a small man with a wiry frame and firm handshake, met Clemens at State Correctional Institution–Greene, the prison where he and Graner had worked together. Clemens immediately identified with Muccino as the guard related how he, too, was a Army Reserve MP, having recently returned from serving at Baghdad's Camp Victory. He was an experienced man in both the military and corrections; he knew Graner personally, having worked with him. In fact, Muccino said he had been contacted by Graner to be a character witness for him during the upcoming trial, a request Muccino refused since, in his words, "I never thought Graner was a productive member of society."

The guard stated that he first met Graner in 1994 when Graner had been hired into the prison. Graner was often "sick" or late to work and frequently used the prison's employee assistance program "to his advantage." Graner was a "know-it-all guy" who would do things "his way, regardless of the right way." Muccino said that Graner's time at SCI-Greene was marked with a number of prisoner complaints against him. Inmates reported to Muccino that Graner would flicker their cell lights on and off to irritate them, intentionally flood their cells by controlling the water and air pressure, and play the radio over the intercom just to drive them crazy. Graner was also known in the prison as a guard to hold grudges and be vindictive to inmates. Muccino shook his head, "The union is so strong . . . firing these guys is next to impossible."

He told Clemens that Graner had sent him some questionable e-mails and photo attachments earlier that year. The e-mails caused Muccino to worry about what Graner was doing at Abu Ghraib. *We've got to round up as many of these e-mails as we can that Graner was sending to family and friends,* Clemens thought to himself. *They are going to be critical in understanding what he was thinking.*

Muccino was very concerned about the impact the abuses at Abu Ghraib were having. "Graner doesn't understand the negative impact of what he did to the Army, MP Corps, SCI-Greene, and the country. Graner made a lot of people look bad. He destroys every one of the Army and MP values. Every American soldier has to worry about what will happen to them if captured, thanks to him."

As Clemens wrapped up the interview, Muccino had one final thought. "Graner will never plead guilty, because he has never accepted responsibility in any proceeding before. You could catch him red-handed, and he would deny it when confronted."

✦

As Clemens returned to Arlington, he knew exactly what his first task would be: obtain a search warrant for Graner's Army e-mail account. The entire drive back from Pennsylvania, all Clemens could think about were the e-mails Morris and Muccino had either shown him or referenced. *If Graner had sent the e-mails I've already seen with the abuse photos, I can only imagine how many other times he e-mailed photos with thoughts about "what a good job he was doing."*

He went directly to Graveline's office the next morning. He fully briefed the JAG about what he had learned. "Why don't we have all of these e-mails already?" he asked.

Graveline explained that CID had thus far been unsuccessful in obtaining enough information to establish the probable cause necessary for a search warrant. Clemens was now on a mission. He contacted CID headquarters. After several rounds of "why don't you talk to this person?" he was finally told outright that CID had tried but had not developed enough evidence in its mind to obtain a warrant.

Clemens went back to Graveline, "If there is one thing I can't stand, it's being told that something can't be done."

Graveline shrugged his shoulders with a mischievous grin. "They said that they tried really hard . . ." Clemens understood immediately what Graveline meant, went back to his office, and began to type up an affidavit to support his search warrant request.

Graveline came to the door late that night. "I've got to get home. You almost ready to call it quits?" Clemens handed Graveline his affidavit. "Shoot, if I was the judge, I would sign it," the prosecutor offered.

Clemens faxed the affidavit to a military judge, COL Mark Toole. After clarifying some information with the investigator, the judge was satisfied that the evidence Clemens had collected established probable cause, allowing Clemens to obtain the contents of Graner's Army e-mail account.

"I need you to raise your right hand," Toole announced over the phone.

Clemens stood up in the silence of the empty JAG office, looked out the window at the city lights and empty streets, and raised his right hand. After taking the oath affirming the information in the warrant application, Clemens lingered at the window, contemplating the significant evidence this could unveil.

✦

With the Frederick and Ambuhl guilty pleas complete, Holley and Graveline assessed that the remaining defendants—Graner, Harman, and Davis—were going to trial. While they had been able to present civilian witness testimony during the Frederick plea via VTC, that means would not be an option during a trial since the U.S. Constitution's Sixth Amendment provides a defendant with the right to confront his accusers face-to-face. This right is relaxed during sentencing but is fiercely guarded by U.S. courts during an actual trial. As such, if the trials were to be held in Iraq, both government and defense witnesses would have to be flown and housed there. Holding trials in a combat zone is not uncommon for the military, since typically most witnesses to the misconduct are fellow soldiers colocated with the accused soldier. But these cases had stretched on for close to a year, and all the witnesses, other than the victims, were now redeployed back in the United States or Germany. The safety and logistical concerns of moving and caring for an anticipated forty or more witnesses in a combat zone, while also attempting to put on the best case they could before a jury, made trial in Iraq untenable for both of the prosecutors. Additionally, the time of trial was anticipated to be a very challenging time operationally as the January 2005 Iraqi election was looming and combat resources would be at a premium. Since Graveline had returned to the United States shortly after Frederick's guilty plea, it was up to Holley to now convince Tate that moving the trials back to the States was in everyone's best interest.

The young prosecutor found Tate receptive to the idea. However, the senior JAG reminded Holley that while the logistical problems enunciated by the team were true, there was also the important consideration of the Iraqi people seeing justice being served. Still, upon considering all facets of the problem, including the interests and requests of the defense, Tate agreed that moving the cases was the best possible solution.

"Where do you suggest we send them?" Tate inquired. "General Metz has started as the convening authority for these cases, and he's going to want to keep them under his supervision."

"We can the send them back to Fort Hood. Since General Metz is normally the commander there, he can keep the cases under his supervision here in Iraq and order that the place of trial be back in Texas." Holley suggested that the team had a perfect opportunity to make the move since the remaining defense counsel had all filed motions to move the trials out of Iraq, and the government's response was due the first week of November. They could simply inform Judge Pohl that the issue would be moot and that they would be moving the place of trial to Fort Hood.

"Sounds like a plan," Tate responded. "But, given all of the considerations, this is a decision that's going to be made well above our pay grades. I'll take it to General Metz to see what he has to say."

Graveline and Holley had been hoping for a quick decision with the motion deadline approaching; however, none was forthcoming. Tate told Holley that the general wanted some time to consider all of the possibilities.

Graveline, in particular, was becoming exasperated with the slow process. He needed to respond to the motions for moving the trials and had already asked Pohl for an extra week. He expressed his frustrations repeatedly to Holley over the phone. Holley, who was no less annoyed, tried to calm his partner.

"We're just going to have to stall the court for a few more days," he assured Graveline.

Shaking his head, Graveline typed an e-mail to Pohl and the defense counsel. "The government requests more time to fully consider its response to the defense's change of venue motion." Pohl agreed, but the team still had no idea when the decision would be made. Finally, on Tuesday, November 9, 2004 (election day back in the States), Tate received word—the trials were going to Fort Hood.

✦

On some of the e-mails Clemens had received from Morris, he noticed an e-mail address with an Army domain, belonging to one Andrew Beerman. Using the Army locator databases, he learned that Andrew Beerman was a sergeant stationed with the 1079th Garrison Support Unit, Fort Dix, New Jersey. *It might just be worth my while to get up to Fort Dix and see Beerman.* He decided not to call ahead, figuring an element of surprise might help in getting the sergeant to talk.

Clemens sat in the company commander's office, waiting for the soldier to arrive. As he entered, Beerman did not appear surprised to see an investigator at his unit. Sitting across from Clemens, he stated that he wanted to cooperate fully and immediately began to explain how he had first met Graner in 2001. Beerman was responsible for all of the ammunition used in training at Fort Dix, and Graner had been assigned to him for a little over a year. *So that's how he got his hands on all of that ammo in his garage,* Clemens thought. Beerman related how he and Graner had become quite close and that he had actually written a reference letter for Graner.

As Beerman talked, Clemens sensed that the soldier was holding back. He could not figure out exactly what made him think that, but years of experience had fine-tuned his intuition. He decided to push Beerman a bit, sliding a few of the e-mails and photos across the table to him. Noticing Beerman's eyes fixate on the e-mails, Clemens seized the moment and requested to see Beerman's e-mail account, sliding a consent to search form across the table. Beerman asked for a moment and stepped out of the room. He returned shortly, saying that he thought it would probably be in his best interest to show Clemens his e-mail account.

The two men sat down at Beerman's computer as the sergeant brought his e-mail up on the screen. Clemens identified five e-mails from Beerman to Graner and twenty-one e-mails from Graner to Beerman. As he read through them, Clemens saw that Graner had made it a habit to take pictures of the detainees and e-mail them to friends with captions and little sayings that apparently he thought were funny. He began to take notes.

December 1, 2003—from Graner to Beerman and several family members with the caption "pic of the day." Attached to this e-mail was a photo of Graner with a syringe and forceps, appearing to insert stitches into the forehead of an Iraqi prisoner. The body of the message read, "I now give stitches without the aid of medics anymore. This was one of the ip's [Iraqi Police] who brought things into the prison . . . things may have gone a little bad when we were asking him a couple of questions. O well." Another e-mail that same day from Graner to the same group read, "the gash." It included a close-up of Graner with the syringe and forceps. The message stated, "It didn't seem that bad but he made a bunch of noise."

December 2, 2003—from Graner to the same group titled, "a good upper body workout." The message read, "but hard on the hands." Attached was a photo of Graner kneeling on a detainee with a big smile, thumbs up, and several other detainees lying still on the floor. Clemens recognized it as one of the early pictures from the night of the human pyramid.

December 5, 2003—from Graner to the same group containing part of the text, "sometime you need to have a little fun with them." This e-mail included a photo of a detainee that had a "smiley face" drawn on his nipple.

December 12, 2003—from Graner to the same group titled "just another dull night at work." Attached to this e-mail were photos of two dog handlers with their dogs barking at a naked detainee and of a detainee lying on the ground with a bloody bandage on his thighs.

December 26, 2003—from Graner to the same group attaching pictures of his steak and shrimp dinner and another of several soldiers smiling with an inflatable snowman.

December 29, 2003—from Graner to the same group describing his duty day: "yesterday and today we did nothing but sit around our room playing xbox [sic] . . . "

May 3, 2004—from Graner to Beerman with the message, "If you have watched the news you may have seen good ole fathead. Well for doing what the army wanted us to do now the army wants to burn us for it. O well I can live with myself." The e-mail also asked for a character reference letter from Beerman.

Beerman had responded to that e-mail by writing a letter in which he lauded Graner's work ethic and his "attention to detail" in ammunition accountability. Beerman also offered to fly to Iraq to testify on Graner's behalf. After reading this e-mail exchange, Clemens turned to Beerman. "Do you know anything about the cache of stolen ammunition in Graner's garage?"

A look of shock appeared on Beerman's face. He seemed devastated. In Clemens' estimation, Beerman had no idea that the man he called "brother" had actually taken advantage of their relationship.

✦

Walking into his cubicle back in Arlington, Clemens found even more e-mails waiting for him. The search of Graner's Army e-mail account had returned. Clemens plopped down in his chair, eagerly opening up e-mail after e-mail. He quickly began to find the e-mails shown to him previously by Graner's family and friends. Some new ones also caught his attention, however. The investigator found a message from November 1, 2003, where Graner ordered a collapsible baton, or asp. This e-mail immediately piqued Clemens' interest as it could be a good piece of corroboration since a detainee had accused Graner of beating his fresh wounds with a collapsible baton during the December time frame. However, Clemens' attention was drawn to several e-mails between Graner and his partner on the night shift, Megan Ambuhl. These e-mails had nothing to do with their jobs. They were overtly playful and detailed a sexual relationship between the two in late 2003. Clemens leaned back in his chair. *It appears Lynndie is not the only woman Graner seduced at Abu Ghraib.*

11

"WE'RE GOING TO FIND OUT WHAT
KIND OF A MONSTER I AM"

On the busy Saturday afternoon of November 13, 2004, Washington Dulles International Airport was abuzz with activity. People waiting for family, friends, and business acquaintances packed the long hallway that abutted the baggage carousels. Arrival information flashed across electronic boards for a dozen or more flights. In the midst of this chaotic weekend tumult stood Renee Holley with her four children and other close family members nervously awaiting their loved one's return from Iraq. They had not seen Holley for more than five months, save the few days back in August when Renee was able to see him in Germany. Their excitement and impatience only escalated as the connecting flight was delayed from Frankfurt, Germany.

Shouts of joy arose from the small group when Holley and Tate appeared from the exit doors. Holley exchanged long embraces with his family; there could be no denying that the separation had been very difficult. For his part, Holley had found it incredibly hard to be separated from Renee, especially while he grieved the death of Sergeant Cunningham. As Holley hugged his family, he thought about his time in Iraq and how precious life is.

From the moment he had boots on the ground in Iraq, Tate had been ensnared in one international legal issue after another, on top of these Abu Ghraib cases. Beyond legal work, Tate took his duty to watch out for the safety and well-being of more than seventy-five lawyers and paralegals very seriously. This responsibility only exacerbated his strong feelings about missing his only child's high school graduation, not seeing her move away to college, and leaving his wife with the burden of moving their home to an unknown post. With his wife, Lynn, in Texas, Tate was headed from Dulles to see his daughter, Sarah, at James Madison University, then off the next day to the Pentagon for briefings. After those briefings, he would take his trial team to Fort Hood, get them settled in, and have a few days to visit his wife. He would then depart Hood in time to return to Iraq to serve Thanksgiving dinner in the Camp Victory dining facility.

Still, the joy of the homecoming was tempered by the reality that these reunions would be short lived. Tate would only be home for a week in order to pave the way for his young charges as the cases moved to Fort Hood. It was then back to Iraq until III Corps' deployment ended in early February. Similarly for Holley, this landing was only a quick stop en route to Fort Hood, where there was much work to be accomplished and very little time before Graner's trial.

✦

The first item on Monday morning's agenda was a meeting with the Army's two-star Judge Advocate General, MG Thomas Romig. Tate, Graveline, and Holley convened outside Romig's Pentagon office, which was a sizable, gray-tinted room, its walls lined with military flags and placards commemorating the general's past accomplishments and assignments. Awaiting the men inside were three of the five general officers of the Army JAG Corps: Romig, MG Michael Marchand (the assistant JAG), and BG Daniel Wright.

After discussing the current situation in Iraq, Tate turned his attention to the team's prosecution plans. The generals sat poker faced around the table, listening intently. Holley and Graveline had both been somewhat surprised by the generals' hands-off approach thus far to the prosecutions. These senior officers continued in the same manner during the meeting as they were circumspect in their advice and put forth very general guidance along the lines of "keep up the good work." It was obvious that they had a great deal of confidence in Tate and his ability to shepherd the various investigations toward tangible in-court results.

As Holley and Graveline exited the room, the one-star general stopped them in the hallway.

"I just want to say that we all think you two are doing a great job. Keep up the good work." The general paused and leaned in toward the two men and delivered the only direct "guidance" the two officers had heard from the JAG general officers to date.

"I'm sure I don't have to tell you this, but . . . this is a fuckin' no-fail mission."

He looked them both in the eye and slapped them on the back. Holley and Graveline started out of the Pentagon through an interior hallway overlooking the courtyard.

"No pressure, eh, sir," Graveline said with a half-smile.

"None whatsoever, my friend . . . none whatsoever."

✦

The next evening Tate and Graveline set off for Killeen, Texas, home of Fort Hood. This trip was somewhat of an odd one for Tate since he was heading to a "home" that he had yet to lay eyes on. In August, Lynn had moved all their belongings to Texas without him. Despite being in the Army for more than twenty-five years, he had yet to spend any significant time at Fort Hood.

As the pair's plane began its descent into Dallas–Fort Worth International Airport, a flight attendant announced over the intercom, "There's quite a bit of fog in the Dallas area. Please check the desk at our arrival gate to see if your connecting flight will be delayed."

As Tate and Graveline walked off the plane, the scene in the airport confirmed the flight attendant's report. Several dozen people were already lined up at the ticket counter, and by the looks on their faces, it did not appear that any flights would be leaving that night. As the two men contemplated how to rescue their checked luggage, Sergeant Kary came up behind them. The young sergeant had flown into the States with Holley and Tate but had proceeded to North Carolina to visit his wife.

"No flights out?" Kary inquired as he set his large, overloaded backpack down.

"The airline is offering a bus ride to Killeen, but we have to figure out where our luggage is first unless we don't want to see our bags for a few days," Graveline replied.

Always up for a challenge, Kary went to work. Within minutes, he had tracked down their bags and located the rental car office. After a brief negotiation between Kary and the rental agent, the three men were driving south on I-35 in a full-sized van, the last vehicle available that night.

Both Tate and Kary dozed off while Graveline zipped through Waco. Red and blue patrol lights lit up the van's rearview mirror. Graveline looked down quickly at the speedometer. He was going seventy miles per hour in a fifty-five zone. *I can't believe this . . . and with my boss in the car,* Graveline thought. *Maybe I can talk myself out of it.*

The Texas state trooper asked Graveline to step out of the van. "Do you know how fast you were going?"

Graveline sheepishly admitted that he was going fifteen over the speed limit. Before the trooper could get a word in edgewise, Graveline rattled off anything he could think of that might trigger sympathy: he was in the Army, a lawyer working on the Abu Ghraib cases, this was his first time in Texas, and he was driving a colonel back to Fort Hood after his return from Iraq.

"Well, welcome to Texas," the trooper nodded as he handed Graveline a speeding ticket, "and slow down."

✦

The remainder of November and December found the trial team in frenzied preparation for Graner's trial. Captain Neill and CPT Cullen Sheppard, a young JAG officer who possessed the deep southern drawl of his native Georgia and a quick sense of humor, returned home from Iraq to help in the preparations. Neill was designated the media liaison and Sheppard was assigned to do legal research. Clemens continued to aggressively investigate Graner's background, looking for any detail that might give Holley and Graveline an edge. Simril compiled the evidence and interviewed last-minute witnesses. Kary was joined by SFC Tiffany Noel and Staff Sergeant Brann, arranging flights and lodgings for the roughly forty anticipated witnesses, preparing the photographic evidence, and readying the courtroom and Officers' Club for the surge of attorneys and reporters. Holley led the effort while he and Graveline sharpened the questions they would be asking the witnesses and responded to legal motions.

As another round of hearings approached in December so did the expected arrival of Graveline's second child. The hearings were December 3–6, and the baby was due December 6. Graveline hoped to finish the hearing the morning of the sixth, then immediately head home to D.C. After her doctor's appointment on Friday, December 3, Colleen called with a status update.

She was three centimeters dilated and 75 percent effaced. "I don't think the baby's coming this weekend," Colleen speculated, "and my mom's here. Just finish up on Monday, and we'll go from there."

Holley was on the phone with Renee a few hours later and related Colleen's condition.

"Tell Chris that he needs to get home to his wife now," Renee stated. "You can handle these motions by yourself; she could deliver any time." The firmness in Renee's voice convinced Holley that despite Colleen's bravado, his young partner should leave.

Holley spun around in his chair with the phone still up to his ear. "You're flying out of here on the first available flight tomorrow. I can handle what's left here."

Graveline was on a plane within a few hours—and was with his wife when their second child was born four days later.

✦

Jury selection began first thing in the morning on Friday, January 7, 2005. In the military justice system, the convening authority, in this case Lieutenant General Metz, with the input of his subordinate commanders, selects a pool of officers and soldiers to serve on court-martial duty. Service members are chosen for this duty based on certain factors: age, experience, education, training, length of service, and judicial temperament.* From there, the convening authority selects certain members to act as primary jurors, and the remaining selectees serve as replacements. Once in court, the prosecutors and defense counsel can excuse jurors either for being biased or for no reason other than trying to populate the jury with individuals who may be receptive to the arguments either side is about to make.

Usually, only about a dozen soldiers are chosen as replacements. However, given the amount of international publicity and sensationalism that surrounded these abuse cases, Metz had selected twelve primary jurors and a hundred alternate jurors. The prosecution was sure jurors would fall off quickly when asked if they had already formed fixed opinions about Abu Ghraib. Still, they remained optimistic that a jury could be picked by the end of the day or early on the second.

The initial jury consisted of three colonels, three lieutenant colonels, five sergeant majors, and one first sergeant. The majority were combat veterans

---

* These factors are congressionally mandated by Article 25 of the Uniform Code of Military Justice. Rank, race, sex, and duty positions cannot be used as discriminating factors.

having returned from either Iraq or Afghanistan. Their service proved to be beneficial in insulating them from most of the media hype. All answered that they had seen the various photographs and had heard some commentary from the media, the administration, or the defense. Still, the jurors, save one, affirmed that they could set what they had heard aside and base their verdict strictly on the evidence presented in court. Judge Pohl pressed each juror individually to ensure that soldier understood that no matter who was interested in the case's outcome (e.g., the president, Congress, the secretary of defense, their chain of command), the juror's only job was to listen to the evidence and give Graner a fair and impartial hearing.

After excusing one juror for his admitted bias against Graner, Pohl asked both sides whom they wanted to remove. Holley selected a lieutenant colonel whose responses had not sat well with him. Womack, however, surprised the prosecutors by not eliminating any of the jurors. For all of the prosecutors' concerns of finding untainted jurors, they had selected their jury within an hour and a half.

During an impromptu press conference outside the courthouse, Womack revealed his strategy to the media.

"This case involves terrorists and insurgents and the war on terrorism. We could not pick a truer jury of peers than to have a combat veteran tried by combat veterans."

✦

The following Monday, a slight chill hung in the air under the gray Texas sky as Holley and Graveline arrived for the first day of trial. Photographers and cameramen congregated on a small patch of grass near the courthouse's front doors. It had been easy for the two Army prosecutors to put the international scope of this trial out of their minds as they sat up late at night, talking to witnesses, going over strategy, or preparing their questioning in the quiet of the III Corps' headquarters building. But now, there was no avoiding how much scrutiny would be surrounding them over the next week, especially with the scores of satellite trucks in the parking lot preparing to broadcast trial updates to the world.

Graveline, however, was surprisingly calm. *The defense has been doing all the talking for the last six months. Now, we get our turn.* He believed that their case was strong and the evidence would have a powerful effect on the jury. Still, Graveline expected to be more nervous—then again, he did not have to deliver the opening statement for the government that morning.

That honor belonged to Holley. Holley's goal in these first remarks was to give the jury an understanding of the facts. *Confusion over the facts is a prosecutor's worst enemy and a defense attorney's best friend. Now was the time for clarity,* he thought as he went over his prepared statement in his mind.

As the trial team assembled before the hearing in their "office" (the courthouse's utility room, now outfitted with two desks, chairs, a computer, and a printer), Clemens burst excitedly through the door. "The Graner entourage just showed up, and you're not going to believe what he just said outside. As they were walking up, Graner leaned over right into one of the cameras and said, 'We're going to find out what kind of a monster I am today.' No joke, it was one of the weirdest things I've ever seen." This statement by Graner only confirmed in Clemens' mind what a loose cannon Graner could be.

Within moments of this episode, all of the trial participants were seated in the courtroom and listening to Judge Pohl's opening remarks to the jury. After the judge finished, Holley started off the trial with a graphic description of the human pyramid and forced masturbation. He then familiarized the jury with the "who, what, and when" of Abu Ghraib. Using a PowerPoint presentation, he explained the prison's general layout, the chain of command, and the time line of events. However, Holley's main objective was to preview the theme of the prosecution's case.

"You will see that there was a lot wrong at Abu Ghraib. There were training problems. There were logistics problems. There were certainly leadership problems. It was a very chaotic environment, much like you'd expect in a combat area. But there were certainly acts of misconduct by a wide variety of individuals. The system is that we resolve those one at a time, so we would ask you that, while other appropriate and responsible commanders resolve those other cases, we are resolving Specialist Graner's case today.

"We're not asking you to be Sunday morning quarterbacks with regard to even the accused's behavior . . . no, what we're presenting to you during the course of this trial is the serious misconduct that . . . where anyone would say, 'That's illegal. That's beyond the pale. There's no way that's right.'"

Womack then took his turn to address the jury. His opening statement concentrated on the two themes of the defense's case. "It's been said that success has many fathers, but failure is an orphan. A form of failure is embarrassment. In our careers, each one of us has had the potential to be embarrassed . . . we have had subordinates, superiors, or peers who have been embarrassed, and we know how bad that feels. People commit suicide because of embarrassment. The embarrassment in this case came when these pictures were leaked to the public . . . we all know, from common sense, that there are things that we have had to do in our professional life, perfectly legitimate, that we would not want the press airing, especially the things that we do that are done in private.

"Well, embarrassment causes pressure. This case is about pressure. Pressure on the intelligence community to come up with actionable intelligence that we could use to target the enemy or to avoid IEDs that were going off every day. Pressure to do our jobs in the profession of arms to save American, coalition, and Iraqi lives. There was a tremendous pressure on the intel community, as there always is and should be. Pressure on the intelligence gatherers, those tactical HUMINT [human intelligence] teams, those individuals who are tasked with going out and collecting information so that it can be analyzed and turned into intelligence, so that it can be used by us to save American and other lives.

"Embarrassment puts pressure on the government. How do we mollify the world and make them like us again, when they've seen pictures that, if taken out of context or even if taken in context, can be embarrassing? There was tremendous pressure."

As the court took its first break, the prosecution team piled back into its office. Neill complimented Holley on the opening statement. "I thought it set up the case really well."

"I've only got one question," Graveline inquired with mischief in his eyes. "Was I the only one wondering, 'What the hell is a Sunday morning quarterback?'"

Sheppard, Clemens, Simril, and Kary burst out laughing. "Sir, the phrase is 'Monday morning quarterback,'" Sheppard said in between chuckles.

Holley shrugged sheepishly. "You're sure that's not the right phrase? I mean college football is played on Saturdays . . . ," he trailed off amid his friends' laughter.

✦

Holley called the first government witness to the stand, SPC Matthew Wisdom. Wisdom was the twenty-one-year-old soldier who witnessed the extensive abuse on the night of November 7 and immediately reported it to his team leader. Prior to trial, the entire trial team had discussed the best way to present the government's case with the strongest order of witnesses. Holley wanted to lead with Wisdom and Jones to show how the atmosphere of Abu Ghraib was not so warped that regular soldiers could not distinguish right from wrong. Holley liked Wisdom's straightforward character most of all. His slight frame made him appear several years younger, but Wisdom's clarity about proper soldier behavior gave him a maturity beyond his years.

The slender soldier's uniform hung on him loosely as he recounted seeing his fellow soldiers running the detainees into walls, SGT Javal Davis jumping on the pile of men as well as stomping on their hands and feet, and Graner punching one of the hooded men in the face. Wisdom further testified that he remembered SPC Sabrina Harman taking photographs despite the fact that the unit had been briefed that no photos were to be taken in the hard-site. The last straw for Wisdom was witnessing Frederick punch a man in the rib cage, then turn to the young soldier, and say, "You've got to get some of this."

"What was your reaction when you witnessed these things?" Holley asked.

"I was very upset. I didn't know what to do with it, so I went straight out to tell my team leader what had happened . . . it made me kind of sick almost."

Wisdom went on to relate that another sergeant sent him back down to Tier 1A later that evening to get Frederick. Upon his arrival, he witnessed two naked detainees: one kneeling directly in front of the other while the latter masturbated. Frederick walked toward him, smiling and saying, "Look what these animals do when you leave them alone for two seconds." Although out of his line of sight, Wisdom distinctly heard Lynndie England yell, "He's getting hard." Wisdom immediately exited the tier and reported the scene to SGT Robert Jones, his team leader, who was manning one of the guard towers that encircled the prison. Wisdom testified that Jones left him alone in the tower as the sergeant went to find Frederick. Jones later told Wisdom that the matter had been handled and that he would not have to work in the hard-site again.

On cross-examination, Wisdom admitted that he was not assigned to Tier 1A and could not speak to the tier's normal operating procedures. However, he ended his testimony by summarizing his experience that night. "When you're brought up through the MP Corps, you're taught every day in basic training about values, and you're supposed to be in big situations . . . that you're supposed to be better than the average soldier, and there's a lot of pride that's supposed to go along with that. Basically, when I came onto the tier, I just saw what I saw, and it didn't look right. It didn't look normal. It didn't look like something an MP would do."

Sergeant Jones followed Wisdom on the witness stand. A short, broad-shouldered, and muscular man, Jones presented a stern appearance that reinforced his prior service as a Marine and his current job in Maryland as a Baltimore city police officer. In response to Holley's questioning, he confirmed Wisdom's two trips to the guard post the night of November 7. After Wisdom recounted the masturbation scene, Jones left his tower to find Frederick. During an angry confrontation, where Jones was "borderline disrespectful and aggressive," he demanded Frederick confirm or deny whether Wisdom's allegations were true. Jones described a stoic Frederick who simply looked at him and replied, "What do you want?" The sergeant said that he told Frederick he wanted Wisdom out of the hard-site and away from Frederick.

Jones testified that he then reported the matter to another staff sergeant, Robert Elliot, who stated that the report sounded fairly fantastic to him and, without more proof, would let the matter drop. Since his request to remove Wisdom from the hard-site was granted by Frederick, Jones opted not to follow up on the incident or report it further.

"In retrospect, do you wish that you'd handled that situation a little bit better?" Holley asked.

Sergeant Jones did not hesitate. "Yes."

✦

Building on Wisdom's and Jones' testimonies, the prosecution was ready to call its first coconspirator, SPC Jeremy Sivits. A generator mechanic with the 372d MP Company, Sivits had been the first to take responsibility for his actions at Abu Ghraib by pleading guilty on May 19, 2004, to conspiracy to commit maltreatment, cruelty and maltreatment against the detainees, and dereliction of duty. Judge Pohl sentenced Sivits to the maximum punishment allowable under his guilty plea: one year in jail, a bad-conduct discharge, reduction to the lowest rank, and total forfeiture of any military pay. He was serving his time at a military prison in Fort Knox, Kentucky.

Holley had briefly visited with Sivits while the convicted soldier was held in Kuwait pending his transfer to the States. Holley had assessed that Sivits was not a malevolent instigator of abuse but rather a young soldier who had simply been caught up in a very bad situation. Since that initial encounter, neither prosecutor had spent any time with Sivits, so they flew him out a week before trial. Because Graveline would be examining Sivits on the stand, the two men sat down in the spacious Fort Hood courtroom a few days before trial to get acquainted.

"How's everything going for you, Private Sivits?"

"Fine, sir. Just a few more months and I'll be home with my wife," Sivits stated with a smile on his round face. Sivits was slightly overweight with a shock of black hair that jutted off his shaved head. "It's been close to two years since I've seen her. I just want to serve my punishment, do what I've got to do here, and go home."

The soldiers continued talking about family and home for several more minutes. The more they spoke, the more Graveline began to empathize with the young soldier. *This young man is really a gentle guy. He's repentant about his role, which was really not much more than taking a couple of the photos the night of the human pyramid, and really understands how wrong all the actions were that night and the negative impact they have had.*

Now on the witness stand, Sivits described for the jury the abuse of the seven rioters, documenting in detail what was happening in the twenty-three pictures and three videos taken that night. Each picture was flashed on the large projection screen for the jury and on a series of monitors for the judge, witness, and attorneys.

"What was the general demeanor of the soldiers at this point in the night?" Graveline inquired, as he showed a picture of Graner kneeling over a hooded detainee with his fist cocked.

"Pretty much just laughing . . . seemed to be just having a good time with it. Just like they were enjoying what was going on, sir," Sivits replied.

Graveline focused specifically on Graner positioning the seven men into the human pyramid. "Did any of the soldiers object to what was going on at this point of the night?"

"No, sir."

"Did anyone say, 'Stop. We shouldn't be doing this to these people'?"

"Not that I can recall, sir."

"Who was still present at this point?"

"At that point, Private First Class England, Corporal Graner, myself, Specialist Harman, and Staff Sergeant Frederick, sir."

"Did the detainees do this pyramid willingly?"

"No, sir."

After Sivits finished describing the forced masturbation that followed, Graveline asked him if Graner had said anything to him that night as he left Tier 1A. "At some point in time, Corporal Graner said, 'Hey, we're just following orders, doing what we were told,'" the soldier answered. "I can't remember exactly when he had said it, but it was sometime that night."

Graveline then asked Sivits why he had never reported the abuse. "Because I'm a man of my word, and I just tried to be friends with everybody in my company . . . and I didn't want anybody to think that I was a snitch or anything of that nature, sir."

Sivits' testimony finally turned to one more incident he witnessed. "It was some time around mid- or early December [2003], right after I had come back from leave. I went down to 1A and Corporal Graner had the detainee . . . as far as I knew, he was called 'Buckshot' because he had tried to shoot Sergeant Cathcart and he had gotten shot with some buckshot.* Corporal Graner had him handcuffed to the bed and was telling him to take off his shorts, and he was hitting him with an asp . . . a collapsible nightstick that police officers carry. He was hitting him on the gunshot wound that was on his leg, sir."

"What was the detainee saying at that point?"

"He was asking, kind of like crying, 'Please, mister . . . please, please, stop. That hurts. That hurts. Please stop.'"

---

* This detainee was the one who had been successful in obtaining a pistol from one of the Iraqi correctional officers and started a shoot-out in Tier 1A toward the end of November 2003.

"And what was the accused's response to that?"

"Just kind of like, 'Oh, does that hurt? Does that hurt?' and he would . . . he hit him two more times after that, sir."

Womack's cross-examination homed in on Sivits' lack of experience with handling prisoners at Abu Ghraib. "Your training and your experience is as a mechanic, isn't it?"

"Correct, sir."

"As such, you wouldn't have known what the SOP was for Tier 1A, would you?"

"No, sir."

"You wouldn't have known what duties the guards at Tier 1A had towards their prisoners, would you?"

"No, sir."

As Womack continued to show Sivits' general lack of knowledge about Tier 1A operations, he asked how often the generator mechanic was actually in that particular tier.

"I was in probably about a dozen times totally, sir," Sivits responded. "Pretty much the evening shift, sir, when Corporal Graner was working."

"And would you agree that, often, when you came to Tier 1A, you'd see detainees who were naked?"

"The only time that I saw them naked was that night, sir."

"Didn't you notice that, occasionally, some of them were actually naked?"

But Sivits remained firm that it was uncommon to see naked detainees in Tier 1A. "The nights that I was down there, sir, it was just that one night and that was it that I can remember, that I can actually recall seeing anybody naked."

Despite this momentary setback, Womack began to establish a theme for the charges stemming from the night of November 7: Graner and his fellow soldiers were responsible for dangerous thugs who presented a constant danger to the guards, and Graner had performed the best he could with the measures available. But while he made some inroads through his questioning of Sivits, the young soldier would not relent on the major points: neither the seven men stacked in the pyramid nor the wounded man whom Graner beat posed any threat to Graner or the other soldiers. Womack would have to develop his defense through some other witness, possibly SSG Ivan Frederick.

✦

Ever since Neill had sat down with Frederick the night he had appeared outside the prosecutors' door in June, the team had been both optimistic and concerned. Given his insider status, Frederick would be a strong witness for the prosecution, and as the senior soldier charged, he would be in the best position to know if anyone had ordered the abuse. On the flip side, Frederick was simply not a talkative person. Any detail past yes or no was like pulling teeth. He was also prone to spouting generalities that did not stand up to close questioning. These traits could lend themselves to making an ineffective, or inaccurate, witness.

Consequently, Clemens, Simril, and Graveline had spent considerable time with Frederick since his guilty plea. They concentrated on focusing Frederick on the details. When did a particular event happen? What was said? By whom? What guidance had the chain of command given upon arrival? As their time at the prison wore on? The task was equal parts tedious and painful for both Frederick and the investigators.

Now, moments prior to Frederick taking the stand, Graveline stepped into the small witness room to see the staff sergeant. Frederick sat in his dark green Army uniform stripped of any medals and ribbons with handcuffs around his wrists and an MP sitting across from him.* He was clearly nervous.

"You ready?" Graveline asked.

"Sure, I can't wait to get this done," Frederick replied, his hands shaking. He was very worried about Womack and Graner, especially Womack, who he was sure would rip into him on the witness stand.

"It'll all be over soon," Graveline offered feebly. He knew that Frederick was in for some tough questioning over the next few hours. The team had war-gamed how Womack might cross-examine Frederick. One option could be to attack him as a liar fabricating his entire story to curry favor with the government and receive a lower sentence. Another method might be to paint a picture where Graner was merely following the lead of Frederick, his supervisor, and that the abuse had been approved by Frederick. Womack could also try to get Frederick talking about the prison's deplorable conditions and the lack of guidance they

---

* After a soldier is convicted and confined, he is no longer authorized to wear any awards that he has previously earned.

had received. In addition, Frederick's propensity to gloss over details could help the defense cloud the facts of the events. The team concluded that the cross-examination would probably include elements of each approach. Regardless of which one Womack chose, it would not be easy for Frederick.

Opening the questioning, Graveline ran through Frederick's background and the abuses that Frederick had participated in or witnessed. The guard's answers supported Sivits' testimony as he described the night of November 7. Frederick elaborated on a litany of other abuses Graner inflicted on the detainees that began almost immediately after the 372d arrived at the prison: walking a hooded man into a pole; delivering a sharp elbow to a detainee's face; forcing Said Mohammed, a.k.a. Shitboy, to roll through the mud on a cold winter night and then photographing him; videotaping that same man ramming his head into a steel door and doing nothing to stop him; and photographing the female detainee exposing her breasts. Finally, the guard detailed how Graner showed him the picture of Lynndie England holding the naked man by what appeared to be a leash around his neck and told him, "Look what I had Lynndie do."

Graveline was surprised by how well Frederick presented himself on direct examination. For as nervous as he had been, Frederick did not show those nerves on the stand. He maintained steady eye contact with the jury and explained the abuses in good detail. However, now it was Womack's turn to push Frederick.

The former Marine assumed a fairly friendly demeanor toward this key witness. It soon became clear that he intended to use Frederick to make his point about MI running Abu Ghraib.

"As far as taking daily orders and directions, you took those from the MI, didn't you?"

"We never really took orders from them, just other than to house them, separate them, and things like that."

"Do you recall telling me [during pretrial interviews] that you were given orders by the MIs all of the time?"

"We were given orders to separate them, punish them for talking back and forth, to handcuff them to the doors, and things of that nature."

"You were ordered to strike them from time to time?"

"No, sir."

"You were ordered to deprive them of sleep from time to time?"

"Yes, sir."

"You were ordered to undress them?"

"Yes, sir."

"And to keep them undressed, even in cold cells?"

"Yes, sir."

"You were ordered to manipulate their diet?"

"Yes, sir."

"Correct me if I'm wrong, but wasn't there a list of approaches or tactics to be used by interrogators?"

"Not that I seen."

"Okay, but you were told that these things that you were doing were part of these approaches, weren't you?"

"Yes, sir."

"And the people who told you that were military intelligence?"

"Yes, sir."

"And civilian intelligence?"

"Yes, sir."

"Did you ever, as you recall, take orders from other government agencies?"

"No, sir."

The prosecution decided to follow Frederick's testimony with the trial's most reluctant witness, Megan Ambuhl. Graner's night shift partner and lover, it was an understatement to say she did not want to be on the witness stand. Her reluctance and unpredictability were major concerns for Holley.

Even after talking with her, I'm still not sure what she's going to say when she gets up there, Holley thought. *She's so close to the defense she could be planning to sabotage our case and help her boyfriend. But she's also the only witness to some of the abuse . . . we'll just have to keep her very focused on those events.* It was actually one particular instance of abuse that drove Holley's decision to call Ambuhl—the infamous "leash" photographs.

Dressed in a black pantsuit and with curly, sandy blond hair to her shoulders, Ambuhl walked timidly through the courtroom's double doors. Holley ushered her to the witness stand and handed her the pictures of Lynndie England holding the naked man by a strap tied around his neck. Ambuhl admitted that she was there in the tier that night and identified the detainee by his nickname "Gus."

"Can you tell the members of the panel how Gus came to be in that position?"

"Well, Gus wouldn't leave the hole that he was in. He was threatening us, and Corporal Graner got a 'tether' . . . I think it's called . . . and placed it around his neck, and then he handed that to Private England."

Holley looked down at his notes on the podium. *So, this is how she is going to try to help Graner. She's never referred to that strap being a tether before; in fact, no one ever had prior to Womack's opening statement.* "Had you ever seen Gus before this evening?" he continued.

"No, sir."

"Where was Gus prior to being pulled out into the hallway?"

"It's called the 'hole.' It's not the same as the other cells in that area. There's no bars that you can see out of, which the other cells have."

"When you opened that door the first time, what did you see?"

"Gus . . . I believe he was laying down. He wouldn't follow any commands to come out of the hole, and he was threatening . . . " The young prison guard then explained that Gus used his limited English to say that he would kill the guards.

"Did he ever take a swing at you?"

"Not on that time, sir," Ambuhl replied.

"On this particular occasion, did he ever use any violent actions towards you or Corporal Graner?"

"I was . . . I'm not sure what . . . Corporal Graner went into the hole, but he didn't swing at me, sir."

Holley was not about to allow her to equivocate about the threat posed by the naked detainee lying in the cell. "And, Ms. Ambuhl, you didn't see him swing at Corporal Graner either, did you?"

Ambuhl, who, up to this point, had delivered her testimony in a very soft voice, looked down at the floor and answered just above a whisper, "I didn't see that, sir."

"What did Corporal Graner do next?"

"He put the tether around Gus' neck."

"Did Gus fight him when he put the tether around his neck?"

"I don't remember that happening, sir."

"But you were watching?"

"Yes, sir."

Ambuhl then said that Graner handed the strap to England, stepped back, and took the pictures of the petite soldier holding the naked man by the strap as he crawled along the floor. As he finished taking three photos of the scene, Graner took the tether off the detainee's neck and walked him unassisted to a cell at the other end of the tier about fifty feet away.

CPT Jay Heath, Graner's military defense counsel, proceeded to reinforce the idea that using a tether was nothing more than a cell extraction method. "So your purpose in going down there was to get Gus out of his cell, correct?"

"Yes, sir."

"You weren't going down there for any other reason?"

"No, sir."

"You weren't going down there to harass Gus?"

"No, sir."

"You weren't going down there to interrogate Gus?"

"No, sir."

"This was a cell extraction and movement?"

"Yes, sir."

Heath pointed out that Graner was the only one of the three soldiers who had significant experience in prison operations. Through his questions, Heath argued that Graner's sole purpose that day was to remove Gus from the cell with the least amount of force. Ambuhl was more than willing to help Heath paint Graner's actions in the best light possible. Heath went a step further and suggested that Graner had used Gus' cultural tendencies to gain his compliance.

"Were you familiar, at that time, with sort of the cultural differences between the sexes of men and women and their relations in Arab culture? Is it a fair statement that Arab men would not like to be in a position of subordination to women?"

"Yes, sir," Ambuhl answered.

"Gus was combative or stubborn with Graner, correct?"

"Yes, sir."

"And yet, when England was put in a position of authority over Gus, Gus became compliant?"

Ambuhl agreed.

"Cell extraction complete, with one trained MP, correct?" Heath summed up.

"Yes, sir."

Holley was quick on his feet in response. He had Ambuhl's previous statement to Simril and Clemens in his hand. He directed Ambuhl's attention to her previous answers regarding this incident. "Please read the highlighted question to the jury."

"'Why was the leash used?'" the witness recited.

"And read your answer, please."

"'I think it was because he wouldn't move and to embarrass him.'"

"Read the next question, please."

"'So, the purpose was never to drag him from the cell?'"

"And read the answer."

"'No, it was more to humiliate him because he wouldn't cooperate.'"

"And then, finally, what's the next question?"

"'Was this done at anybody's direction?'"

"And your answer?"

"'No, it was just the three of us. At that time, I didn't know that England was not an MP,'" Ambuhl read quietly.

✦

It was then SGT Joseph Darby's turn to take the stand. Darby was one of the most intriguing characters in the Abu Ghraib scandal. He had been the soldier who had anonymously slid the abuse photographs under a door to CID in January 2004. Since that time, Darby had been hailed as a hero by the president, members of Congress, and media outlets around the world but had become reviled in his own hometown of Cumberland, Maryland, even to the point of receiving death threats. To many people in western Maryland and Pennsylvania, especially the relatives of the other soldiers in the 372d MP Company, Darby was a traitor—someone who had turned his back on his fellow soldiers. To protect Darby, the Army kept him on active duty, doing personnel work in an undisclosed location around Washington, D.C. It was now his time to tell his side of the story.

Darby, a heavyset young man with his head shaved bald, began by testifying that he had been assigned as a reserve MP to the 372d since 1996, having deployed once to Bosnia prior to his time in Iraq. He had first met Graner in early 2003 as the unit was preparing for its Iraq mission at Fort Lee, Virginia. Darby testified that while he worked and hung out with Graner during this period, Graner spent most of his time with Lynndie England.

"How would you characterize his personality?" Graveline inquired.

"Corporal Graner had a personality . . . it was kind of like an overpowering personality. Everybody wanted to be . . . most people wanted to be around him and be associated with him."

Graveline wanted to move Darby's testimony along into the incidents that happened in Iraq. "At a certain point in October, did the accused approach you, after his shift was done one night?"

"It was early morning, around 3:30 or 4:00 a.m. I was just getting ready to go to work. We had one vehicle to transport us from work to the living area and back, so we had to wait for the outgoing shift to come pick us up. I was sitting on a stack of lumber, which was out front. We had the engineers improving our building, and Corporal Graner came up to me with his camera and showed me a picture of a man. He said, 'Hey, Darby, check this out.' It was a man chained to a cell, handcuffed with his arms open, and he was naked except for a bag on his head. There was a puddle of water at his feet. He looked at me and he said, 'The Christian in me knows this is wrong, but the corrections officer in me can't help but love making a grown man piss himself.'"

Graveline asked Darby why he had not reported Graner to his command after seeing that photograph and hearing Graner's statement.

"Well, other than the comment, the fact of a prisoner being chained to a cell . . . if a prisoner got out of control and had to be handcuffed to a cell to be held or something, or not having clothes on, that was not out of place from what I had seen during the walk-through, when we went through the prison with the 72d."

The prosecutor inquired as to when Darby actually received the abuse photos. Darby explained that he had gone home to the United States during mid-November 2003 and returned to Abu Ghraib shortly after Thanksgiving. Once back, he had heard about the shooting and asked around to see if anyone had pictures of the incident or its aftermath. Someone suggested that he ask one of the guards down in Tier 1A.

Darby continued, "I approached him [Graner] in the cyber café one evening, and I asked him if he had any pictures of the hard-site from the shooting. I had just gotten my laptop, and I had no pictures, and he said, 'Sure, hold on a second.' He handed me two CDs, and I dumped the CDs onto my computer that evening, and the next day I returned the CDs to him. I didn't . . . the first part of my shift is pretty hectic, so I don't get to get onto my computer until later in the day. So I gave them back to him at the beginning of his shift, and later that evening, that's when I finally looked at what was on the CD. The first CD was pictures of places we'd been, things that we'd done, people posing for the camera and what not. The second set, in a separate file, were pictures of the accused in the hard-site with prisoners in different positions, a pyramid . . . the accused on top of a prisoner punching him."

Graveline asked why Darby had waited so long to turn over the pictures if he had received them at the beginning of December.

"Some of these people were friends, people who I had been in combat with and been in Iraq with. It was hard for me to turn in people who I had such a camaraderie with," Darby explained. "At the time that I had the CD, between the time that I had gotten it and the time I turned it in, Corporal Graner had been working the road, doing escorts from our station to BIA [Baghdad International Airport] and back. At that time, Sergeant Cathcart was in the hard-site and Sergeant Cathcart was my team leader, so I knew him well enough to know that nothing was going on while he was there. But at the end of that month, in the beginning of January, Graner was returning to the hard-site, because they were on a one-month rotation, and I was concerned that the things would start over again."

Graveline continued to push Darby, pointing out that Frederick was still in the hard-site at this time, and he was clearly in the pictures abusing detainees.

"It was in this little clique. You had Sergeant Frederick, Corporal Graner, and the other accuseds, who were up there most of the time. But, in my opinion, Sergeant Frederick isn't really mentally astute enough to think of some of the things that I saw in the CD," the young MP rationalized. "I mean, I've known Sergeant Frederick for years and . . ."

Graveline interrupted. "Who did you think was astute enough to do that?"

"Corporal Graner."

Womack took over the questioning. He continued to emphasize his core defense. "You . . . learned that it was actually the military intelligence community that was running Abu Ghraib, wasn't it?"

"To a point, sir. The majority of the hard-site was under the jurisdiction of the CPA. It was where we kept normal Iraqi-on-Iraqi detainees, people who were tried by the Iraqi government."

"Good point. Let's focus down to Tier 1A. That was actually run by MI, wasn't it?"

"Roger, sir, military intelligence folks were there," agreed Darby. "We had their prisoners, sir, but there were never any military intelligence personnel who worked the site. To my knowledge, they came and picked their people up and dropped the people off, and we were only responsible for the holding of the people when they weren't using them for intelligence questioning." Darby also concurred that the guards in Tier 1A would have him call MI interrogators to ask if they could allow certain detainees to sleep.

"You were there when the 72d MP Company turned over the running of Abu Ghraib to the 372d?" Womack continued after Darby stated that he had been, "During that time frame that the 72d was still there at Abu Ghraib, you saw detainees wearing women's underwear?"

"Yes, sir."

Darby had witnessed another guard forcing naked detainees to do jumping jacks and yell in English, "I eat pussy." Womack asked why he had never reported that particular incident.

Darby tried to explain. "Well, PTing [physical training] a prisoner was common. The lack of clothes was . . . well, when we first got there, we were told by the 72d that the clothes were taken as a disciplinary measure. So seeing him naked and doing PT wasn't something that struck me as odd, sir. The only thing that struck me as odd was the comments that he was making, sir."

Graveline ended the questioning of Darby by asking, "Why didn't you go to your chain of command with these photos?"

"We'd had incidents in the past where my chain of command had covered up things, disciplinary problems . . . we had one soldier who had a drug-abuse problem, and I didn't think that the chain of command would do anything about it, sir."

Next on the stand were two CID agents, Brent Pack and Rusty Higgason, who had spent the most amount of time studying the abuse photos and computer evidence. Specializing in computer forensics, Pack had been tasked with determining the exact times and dates the photos were taken by utilizing the computer data embedded inside the digital images.

"The files that the photographs are on contain metadata," Pack described. "This is information inside the picture file that tells us the date and time, the camera make and model, and several other pieces of information. If you look at the picture in text view, these dates and the camera makes and models become pretty evident." The agent went on to explain that each photograph has a unique hash value, a 128-bit value similar to a digital fingerprint.

"What happens if someone tries to alter one of these photographs? What happens to the metadata?" inquired Graveline.

"The metadata is destroyed during that process, and you're not able to see that information in the file anymore."

"Did any of the photographs that you reviewed have the metadata taken out of it in this case?"

"I dealt strictly with the files that still had the metadata in it. There were a few of them that had been altered, but I didn't even put those in my examination because there's no way that I could tell exactly when that picture was taken." Pack continued to elaborate on the evidence he had found. "During the examination, I identified five cameras that were used to take the photographs that I was looking at. Each of those five cameras was set to a different date and time. So I had to go through a visual examination of the pictures themselves and compare them with the metadata and attempt to time-sync the five cameras. In order to do this, I had to find instances where the cameras were used to take photographs of the same incident. Once I found those, and I found about eight of them, I was able to establish a theoretical time line."

Pack produced time lines of the photos that he believed to be accurate, plus or minus one hour. He showed the jury that the leash incident occurred on October 24, 2003, between 8:16 and 8:17 p.m.*; the photographs of the prostitute lifting her shirt happened on October 29, 2003, at 3:44 a.m.; the photographs including the human pyramid and masturbation started at 10:15 p.m. and ended at 12:22 a.m. on the night of November 7, 2003; the photographs of Said Mohammed naked and covered in mud were taken on November 12, 2003, at 11:25 p.m.; and the photographs of the detainee receiving stitches to his forehead on December 1, 2003, at 12:48 a.m.

Pack finished by stating that since the videos taken by the digital cameras did not contain the metadata found in the photos, he used the metadata behind photos taken of the same incident to accurately judge the time and date. Using this method, he determined that the video of Said Mohammed slamming his head into the steel door was taken just before or after midnight the night of December 1–2, 2003. In total, Pack examined and placed in order 281 photos of abuse.

When Pack finished, Agent Higgason took the stand. In Graveline's mind, he would deliver the final blow to the defense's "MI made us do it" argument.

Higgason explained that as the investigation into the abuses developed, he was tasked with reviewing the various MI computer databases from Abu Ghraib. He zeroed in on detainee interrogation dossiers, personally looking at more than 3,300 interrogation reports in approximately 2,200 dossiers. These files also contained photographs of the detainee, interrogation notes, and various other documents related to the individual. He described for the jury how detainees were accounted for in the prison: detainees being held on behalf of the Iraqi government received a five-digit magistrate number while coalition force captures, be they enemy prisoners of war or civilian internees, received a six-digit internment serial number.

Graveline directed Higgason's attention to the detainees depicted in the abuse photographs. Higgason began to tick off the information that he had uncovered:

Gus (the man on the end of the leash)—held for simple assault, only identified with a magistrate number, never interrogated

---

* To help set a reference point, this event occurred nine days after Graner and England arrived at Abu Ghraib.

the seven men in the human pyramid—held on charges ranging from rape to burglary, all seven only identified with magistrate numbers; none were ever interrogated

Noor Kareem (woman photographed exposing her chest)—held on prostitution charge, only identified with a magistrate number, never interrogated, held at Abu Ghraib for three days

Said Mohammed (photograph and video of man hitting his head into the metal door and photos of him naked and covered in mud or feces)—held on charge of home invasion, only identified with a magistrate number, never interrogated

The prosecution rounded out its case by presenting three final witnesses. Clemens and Staci Morris, Graner's ex-wife, each took the stand to enter into evidence the e-mails and training manuals Clemens had found in Graner's Pennsylvania house. One could sense the tension and animosity between Graner and Morris as they sat feet apart from each other. *I'd hate to see what it would be like in here if she were testifying to more than just recognizing his handwriting in the manuals,* Graveline mused.

Finally, Holley played a video deposition of Al-Zayiadi, the same detainee who had testified about the human pyramid during Frederick's guilty plea. As the video ended, Holley rose and said the words that he and the rest of the trial team had been awaiting for months.

"Your Honor, the United States rests."

12

JUST FOLLOWING ORDERS

After fourteen prosecution witnesses and more than sixty exhibits, it was time for the defense to bring its case before the jury. Womack tailored it around two central theories: Graner had simply followed orders from MI to assist in collecting information, and Graner's actions had been nothing more than attempts to run a prison tier in a combat zone with little to no support or equipment. Up to this point in the trial, he had tried to establish these themes through cross-examination of government witnesses, but now it was time to put on his own evidence. Along these lines, the defense began with Graner's first sergeant, Brian Lipinski.

Periodically, soldiers receive written counseling statements from their superior officers or noncommissioned officers. These counselings serve a variety of purposes. As part of a career development plan, they act as status reports highlighting specific performance or individual development. In contrast, they can act also as reprimands, documenting an undesirable pattern of behavior. Graner had received a written counseling statement from CPT Christopher Brinson, his platoon leader, in November 2003, and the defense was intent on drawing the jury's attention to it. Brinson refused to testify without immunity, and since the government was unwilling to grant that protection, the defense wanted to utilize Lipinski, who had worked with Brinson on this counseling. The defense believed a statement within the two-page document was illustrative of the situation at Abu Ghraib.

"Lieutenant Colonel Jordan says that you're doing a good job. Keep up the good work." To Womack and Heath, this statement reinforced their claim that MI was directing Graner's actions on Tier 1A. Heath fleshed out this theory to Judge Pohl as he argued for its inclusion in evidence. "This is the OIC [Brinson] of the hard-site passing on that Corporal Graner, that they knew he worked for MI, that he was dealing with high-value security detainees, that he had received accolades from the MI unit and from Colonel Jordan, and . . . he was given in-structions, 'Continue to perform at this level.'"

The prosecutors had a completely different view of this counseling. *This counseling shows just how myopic the defense has become in their obsession with MI,* Holley thought. *Just because this counseling mentions Colonel Jordan doesn't mean that MI had complete oversight over everything going down in Tier 1A.* Holley be-lieved that context mattered with this counseling, and he was ready to provide it.

"Sergeant Lipinski, it's my understanding that you have personal knowledge of this counseling statement and the contents of it. Is that true?" Holley began.

"That's correct, sir," the squarely built sergeant answered.

"Well, let's take this through. You were down at the hard-site and saw blood on the wall . . . and you saw a detainee who'd been injured, right?

"Correct, sir."

"He had a cut up above his eye, he had a cut on his chin, and he also had a cut on his neck or under his chin, correct?"

"There were approximately four points of contact. It wasn't conducive with one fall."

"When you asked Sergeant Frederick or Corporal Graner, one of the two told you, 'Oh, this guy fell down.'"

"On a little . . . small pile of rubble in the corner."

"And so you and Captain Brinson investigated these events, true?"

"Yes, sir."

Holley pressed on. "And Corporal Graner then said, 'Well, actually, I slammed him into a wall because he resisted.' Is that true?"

"That's correct."

"So the story changed?"

"That's correct, sir."

"And so you were suspicious, you and Captain Brinson, were suspicious about these events?"

"Yes, sir."

"So, ultimately . . . fundamentally, this is a warning to Corporal Graner, true?"

"Absolutely, sir," Lipiniski confirmed.

Holley was not finished. "All right, let's get to this. There are comments about accolades from Colonel Jordan. Now, you've never heard Colonel Jordan give accolades to the accused, did you?"

"In the battalion meeting that I was in, he mentioned Sergeant Joyner frequently."

"But never Corporal Graner?"

"As to the unit as a whole, he would mention the unit as a whole, but he specifically praised Sergeant Joyner."

"And your MPs were, in fact, helping the MIs on Tier 1, true?"

"That's correct."

The first time he had seen the defense witness list, Holley knew he could utilize Lipinski in order to debunk the defense's assertions that Graner was nothing more than an exemplary soldier who was just doing the best he could.

"Now, the second bullet concerning matters about your performance . . . 'We've got some problems with your maintaining standards,' true?"

"That's correct."

"And that's exactly consistent with your experience with the accused as well, isn't it?"

"Absolutely."

"Constantly pushing the edge?"

"Yes, sir."

"And, again, in understanding your personal knowledge of this counseling session, it was essentially saying to Graner, 'We've checked this out and we can't disprove your story, but you need to know that we're watching you.' Is that a fair assessment of this counseling session?"

"That's correct, sir."

"Now, if you can turn the counseling statement over on the back . . . you told the accused, 'Look, we'll provide you with the ROE [rules of engagement],' true?"

"Correct, sir."

"'We'll make an SJA [staff judge advocate] officer available to explain it. If you have any question about the ROE, we'll make that SJA officer available,' true?"

"Yes, sir, they were available on-site," the first sergeant replied.

"And you said in the counseling, essentially, that the accused was told, 'We will work to rotate you out. If you've got some problems with stress, we'll work to help you on that,' true?"

Once again, Lipinski agreed.

"The chain of command essentially tells the accused, 'Hey, we'll make the chaplain available to you or other options, counseling options for stress management,' true?"

"Yes, sir."

"And Sergeant Frederick was also counseled similarly?"

"Yes, he was, sir."

After some back-and-forth questioning from both the prosecution and defense, Holley finished with two questions for Lipinski.

"In fact, first sergeant, your experience with the accused was that he continued to push the limits with regard to following orders?"

"That's correct, sir."

"And wants to do his own thing?"

"That's correct, sir."

As Holley returned to the prosecution table, he was pleased with how the first defense witness had played out. *For a witness whom the defense wanted to establish that Graner was working at the behest of military intelligence, we were able to get that his chain of command was concerned about how rough he was treating detainees and that he was willfully belligerent when it came to following orders. Not a bad way to start the defense case for us.*

✦

The defense continued to buttress its argument that military intelligence was behind the abuses with SPC Chi Yu Liang, a young female soldier from the 372d MP Company. She had worked in the hard-site during the day with SGT Hydrue Joyner, Graner's counterpart for the day shift.

Heath focused Liang on what MI wanted her to do with the detainees in Tier 1A. "Did MI or OGA personnel ever make suggestions that you play loud music?"

"Yes, there was a written request on the sleep management program."

"What about taking blankets away?"

"That's usually verbal. It's not directed to me though."*

"How about what kind of food they could eat?"

"Mostly MREs, but the MI usually tells us which ones get catered food."

"What's 'catered food'?"

"Iraqi food."

"And why would, to your knowledge, why would a detainee get one over the other?"

"I guess because they were cooperating."

"Did you ever hear the term 'special treatment' being used, and what was 'special treatment' to you? What did that phrase mean?"

"Cold showers and that kind of thing."

"And who would tell you . . . were you ever directed to give someone 'special treatment'?"

"No, sir, not to me. It was directed towards Sergeant Joyner, not directed to me."

Heath had her relate an instance where she saw civilian intelligence personnel, identified by Liang as OGA, bring three men into Tier 1A, yell at them, kick and slap them, and strip them of their clothing. She could not remember when exactly this event had occurred, only that it had happened.

Prior to trial, Holley and Clemens had spoken at length with Liang and found her to be sincere but imprecise with facts, dates, and particulars about her time in Iraq. They believed that the defense was exaggerating the young soldier's experiences by using her imprecision to their advantage. Consequently, Holley intended to focus her testimony with details. In response to his questioning, Liang confirmed that the majority of her work-related time was spent in the prison clinic with a couple of six-hour shifts in Tier 1B per week. She went on to relate that the hard-site teemed with activity during the day, with many people (i.e., officers, noncommissioned officers, civilians, the Red Cross, medics, and VIPs) coming in and out.

* Liang added, however, the MPs on the day shift would also punish misbehaving detainees by taking away blankets and clothes.

"Now, I want to talk about directions from MI. When I say, 'MI', Specialist Liang, I also mean OGAs and civilian contractors as well. Basically, those non-MPs. Does that make sense?"

"Yes."

"Now, the directions that the MI gave, they gave to Sergeant Joyner and not to you, true?"

"True."

"And that includes the sleep management system." Liang agreed. "The sleep management system is generally a written plan, right?"

"Yes."

"It limited the sleep of detainees to a certain number of hours within a two . . . a one- or two- or three-day period, right?"

Liang concurred and stated that the sleep management plan would sometimes call for loud music in order to keep the detainee awake or to give the detainees food or showers at certain times, so the detainee would not know if it were day or night.

"And the showers, they're just the normal showers that everybody else gets, right? Whether it was a hot or cold shower, it would depend on whether you had hot or cold water that day, correct?"

"Yes."

"And this was a written plan, generally?"

"Yes."

"And if there was a problem with the detainee's health, you would call a medic, and they would come and address that?

"Yes."

"And if a detainee on the sleep management plan tried to lay down, you would come by and might yell at them to get back up?" Once again, the MP soldier assented.

Holley then turned Liang's attention to the phrase "special treatment." To Liang, special treatment meant anything essentially out of the ordinary. It could be yelling at detainees to keep them awake, having detainees do physical exercise, taking their blankets, or giving them cigarettes or Iraqi food for cooperating. However, it did not mean physical assaults or beatings.

Finally, Holley turned to the incident Liang had testified about concerning

OGA interrogators abusing detainees. While she could not remember exactly when this event had occurred, she surmised that it had been after the detainee smuggled a weapon into the hard-site, or late November.

"The OGA folks didn't kick these detainees with enough force to hurt them; in your assessment, is that true? They used their feet to kind of push the detainees around as they were pulling their clothes off?"

"Yes."

"When they're slapping them around, it was to get them to move, so that they could pull their clothes off, is that true? None of these slaps, to you, Specialist Liang, looked like they were hurting them?"

The young soldier agreed.

The defense is trying to paint what happened at that prison with a broad brush, Holley mused as he ended his questioning. *They are presenting incidents that occurred at random times over the entire four-month period the 372d was at Abu Ghraib and using them to justify events such as the naked human pyramid that occurred weeks prior. There were clearly abuses and bad practices going on with the intelligence gathering, but to say that these events allowed Graner and company carte blanche to do whatever they wanted to the detainees is ridiculous.*

✦

Turning their focus away from MI, the defense called Thomas Archambault, a retired Massachusetts state trooper and now self-proclaimed use-of-force expert. Womack sought to elicit from Archambault opinion testimony that Graner's actions in removing Gus from his cell and constructing the naked human pyramid were proper inmate control techniques. Holley and Clemens, trained MPs themselves, could not believe that any law enforcement officer would justify these actions and were very skeptical of Archambault's underlying assumptions. So, prior to Archambault testifying in front of the jury, Holley asked Pohl to exclude from evidence his opinions as being far outside the mainstream of conventional correctional theory so as to make them unhelpful to the jury.* Pohl agreed that he should hear Archambault's theories before he testified.

---

* In American jurisprudence, an expert is only allowed to give his or her opinion before the jury if that person can demonstrate that this opinion is accepted within the scientific/professional community, has some support in research or experience, and will prove helpful to the jury in deliberating a disputed fact.

A short, barrel-chested man with graying temples, Archambault sported a leather coat, open-collared shirt, and large gold chain as he took the witness stand. Womack started by asking Archambault whether the use of a tether device, referring to the strap in the photo of England and Gus, was an authorized means of extracting a prisoner from his cell.

Archambault shifted in his chair. "I wouldn't say that it was necessarily an authorized means, but based on the circumstances that he was faced with, it was a reasonable means of removing him from the cell."

Judge Pohl tried to cut to the core of the issue. "Let me ask you this: is there any empirical, anecdotal, or any other evidence that would say that this was a recognized cell extraction technique?

"I would not say that it was recognized, but the attempts were, when you look at the whole picture and the circumstances that he was confronted with, and when you review the sequence of pictures as to how he was removed from the cell, I would say that, while it wasn't necessarily recognized or authorized, it was a reasonable method of trying to remove him from a cell, adhering to the factor of safety."

Holley jumped to his feet in the now free-flowing hearing. "Sir, if I could just ask one question . . . a tether around the neck . . . is that authorized under any circumstances?"

"No," Archambault replied.

After some more back-and-forth questioning, Pohl tried to bring the discussion of the leash incident to an end. "If you had a noncompliant prisoner that you needed to extract, and you're concerned about the possible safety issues, and you have insufficient personnel to do a normal cell extraction, you would use a leash to extract the individual? And, in this case, you have a female pulling it, what's to prevent the prisoner from just, the prisoner that you're worried about being so dangerous, coming out and attacking the person pulling it?"

"In looking at this, based on the circumstances with the feces and the urine, his verbal combative threat that 'I'll kill you,' the lack of sufficient personnel to do an extraction . . . I found that it was very reasonable what he did, especially the end result being that nobody was injured."

"This threat was so high, why would the biggest guy, the only male present, not do the extraction instead of standing back and taking pictures?" Archambault had no explanation for that question. "But you say that it's reasonable. Do you think that's . . . "

Archambault cut the judge off. "He was standing by, obviously, in case something might happen."

Pohl stated that he understood Archambault's opinion and asked if he could turn to the night of the seven rioters. From the evidence he had reviewed, the witness stated that he believed the pyramid was an appropriate, although not authorized, use of force to control a considerable number of detainees.

Standing at the podium, Womack interjected. "What's a cheerleader stack?"

"A cheerleader stack, or what I call a 'clown stack,' is basically putting people on their hands and knees and putting them at a point where, if one person moves, they all will move. The only reason we would do it is if people were not restrained. It would be a way to control and contain them. My understanding is that the restraints were removed from these individuals, and they had no restraints at all. My understanding is that there was a lot of yelling and screaming going on, obviously in Arabic, where you wouldn't know if they were planning to do an attack, knowing that all the restraints were off of these people and they were probably more dangerous." Archambault went on to say that the fact the naked men were on their hands and knees was significant because it reduced the potential for positional asphyxia or suffocation.

Holley picked up after Womack. "Now, sir, if I wanted to go to a training manual or call a professional association, where would I go to find this method of putting people one on top of another as an authorized technique to control inmates?" he asked, using one of the points Clemens had identified as an issue worth pressing. The ex-trooper conceded that Holley would not find it anywhere.

Womack jumped in, undaunted. "But is this something that would come under the bailiwick of officer discretion?"

"Yes, it was very creative," Archambault responded. "Honestly, in my professional opinion, Mr. Graner used good foresight in keeping these people under control." Snickering rippled through the section in the back of the courtroom where the reporters sat.

Holley then followed up on Archambault's threat assessment. "Given your assessment that this is reasonable because of the threat, how do you characterize the accused standing behind these individuals with a female posing for photographs?"

The witness demurred. "I look strictly at the use of force . . ."

"Sir, could you answer that question?" Holley pressed.

"I consider that a stress photo . . . a picture that's based on the high stress that these soldiers had gone through, what it's like to work in a corrections environment, in a filthy, soiled environment with prisoners that have killed American soldiers, I think that I would have done the same thing." This time, Graveline heard an audible gasp come from the reporter sitting behind him.

"Interesting. Do you think that's indicative of the level of threat that Graner felt that he faced by posing in front of these detainees? In other words, if he's very afraid of them, why did he stand in front of them and pose for a photograph?"

"They were in a position where he had a safe means of escape. If they had started to react, if anyone had tried to react, others would have had to have fallen as well. So he kept them in a controlled condition and . . . now, don't get me wrong, I am not in favor of pictures and things like that. Why he did that, that's his thing. But if you look at the whole picture, the fact is that he had a way to get away from him should they have reacted."

"Isn't it possible then, sir, that he put them in that position so that he could take the photos?" Archambault conceded that scenario was possible.

Since Archambault could not point to any accepted professional authority or training manual that permitted the leash or pyramid incident, Pohl refused to let him present to the jury what amounted to be his own personal opinion. But he did agree to allow Archambault's explanation that Graner, by putting the men on their hands and knees, had reduced the risk of positional asphyxia.

✦

Wrapping up their presentation of evidence, the defense recalled Megan Ambuhl to the stand. Her demeanor for this second turn on the witness stand was markedly different. This time she was testifying on behalf of Graner, a position she clearly preferred. Her reluctance and timidity had disappeared as she stated that, at least to her understanding, MI was completely in charge of Tiers 1A and 1B. Heath focused her attention on one particular civilian interrogator, Steve, the person Ambuhl claimed had encouraged her to "soften up" or "break" a particular detainee. Steve was responsible for interrogating the detainee nicknamed al Qaeda, and according to Ambuhl, Steve told the guards that "breaking" this detainee would have global implications. Prior to trial, Ambuhl had given the prosecution team specific tactics Steve had asked the guards to use, but on the stand, she testified only in generalities. Now, as Heath began asking her about the night of the seven rioters, her testimony took a turn toward the bizarre.

"What were you doing while the detainees were brought into 1A?" Heath inquired.

"Prior to that, I was sitting in the office, sir."

"And what were you doing up in the office?"

"Just sitting there, sir." She then testified that as the detainees were in Tier 1A, she went downstairs, closed the big cell door leading into the tier, went upstairs again, and stood along the railing. From that vantage point, she saw SGT Javal Davis stepping on the men's hands and toes, but instead of doing anything, she went back into the office. After a few minutes, someone requested an inhaler for one of the detainees, which she brought down. She stated that the strip search had started, but in the couple of minutes that she was there, she did not see any abusive conduct. After returning back upstairs to the office, she was joined, within mere moments, by Harman and Graner. The female guard testified that Graner stayed with her for the next ten to thirty minutes discussing where to place these detainees on the tiers. They then both decided to go use the phones in a separate recreation area. It was at this point that she and Graner were shocked to find Sergeant Frederick alone in the hallway with naked detainees posed in a simulated fellatio position. Ambuhl said she just shook her head and left to use the phones with Graner and Harman.

Heath directed her to his client. "Did you see what Specialist Graner's reaction was?"

"I believe that he was as surprised as I was, sir."

"I mean, do you remember seeing an expression on his face or a reaction?"

"Just that he was surprised, sir," she said, her eyes firmly planted on the floor.

"Okay, would you characterize your response to this as kind of muted?"

"Yes, I guess so."

Holley sat staring at Ambuhl. He could only guess what was running through the witness's mind. She was clearly caught in a moral dilemma. Any observer could tell that she had strong feelings for Graner, but it was difficult to come up with a story that would fully exonerate him. She was trying the best she could to do just that. Still, her discomfort on the stand was obvious. *Does she truly think anyone believes this story? It doesn't take into account any of the photos that clearly show Graner and Harman by the pyramid. She basically states that she sees some detainees starting to be strip searched, Graner comes upstairs a few minutes later and stays with her the rest of the time. They also talk about where they should put the detainees but then leave without putting any of the men into cells. Instead, they left seven unrestrained detainees alone with Frederick as they went to use the phones?!?* Holley had tried to show empathy toward Ambuhl's situation, a person he believed to be one of the least culpable individuals in this entire mess. Yet, he could not allow this testimony to go uncontested.

An exceedingly uncomfortable cross-examination ensued, highlighting Ambuhl's romantic relationship with Graner and the glaring inconsistencies in her account.

✦

Prior to the morning of January 14, Graveline had successfully pushed aside most of the pressure associated with conducting a trial in the full glare of the international media. He now sat alone in his hotel room, and the fact that he was a thirty-two-year-old attorney about to give a closing argument in a case of such import finally hit him. The clock read 3:00 a.m., and Graveline was going over these final arguments. It was normal for him to rise early and work out the details of an impending argument, but this one was different. The jurors would not be the only people he would be addressing this morning. He was well aware of the high probability that any one of the words or phrases he chose would be broadcast around the world within minutes by the assembled media. He furiously jotted, scribbled, and edited his arguments, attempting to omit any flippant remarks or unnecessary commentary.

Before he knew it, the morning hours had melted away, and Graveline found himself positioned a few feet from the jury box.

"Mr. President and members of the panel, 'The Christian in me says it's wrong, but the correctional officer in me loves to make a grown man piss himself.'"

Graveline motioned to the picture displayed on the courtroom monitors—Graner kneeling on top of a pile of detainees. "'They brought the bad guys in to where I worked. We gave them a reason not to ever come and see me or my friends again.'"

He turned to a photograph on an easel to his left—Lynndie England holding the leash. "'Look what I made Lynndie do.'"

"These are the words of the accused, SPC Charles Graner. These are the words that give you insight and context into his actions during the fall of 2003 at Abu Ghraib. These are the words that give a frame to the photos taken at Abu Ghraib."

Combining the computer projection system and blown-up photographs to emphasize particular points of evidence, Graveline pieced together the witnesses' testimony, the photographs, and Graner's own e-mails to show how the abuses occurred and the general mood in Tier 1A on the pivotal night of November 7. As he wrapped up his presentation, he argued that only one conclusion could be drawn from these events.

"What we have here is plain abuse. No doubt about it. There's no justification."

Graveline paused as if considering his last statement. "Now, the defense, in their opening statement, gave a possible justification: 'This isn't really abuse. This is like a cheerleader pose. We've seen cheerleaders do this all of the time.' Well, if we're going to take that analogy, we have to take that analogy all of the way. You have to take the analogy that you take a cheerleading team and you strip them naked, and then you assault them, and then you pile them against their will, hooded, in a pile on the floor and then take pictures around it, as you laugh and goof and give thumbs-up. No one would doubt that that would be abuse. There is no doubt that that is abuse, no matter how many pyramids cheerleaders do.

"Furthermore, you've also heard the testimony that this would be 'a control technique' . . . [but] none of those detainees were assaulting the guards. None of the detainees were resisting the guards. In fact, by their own visual . . . by what you see, they were cowering, cowering as they get pushed into the pyramid. The testimony of Private Sivits: not one of those detainees assaulted or made an aggressive movement towards any of the guards that night. The testimony of Private Frederick: he said the exact same thing. Furthermore, if you were that afraid of these dangerous men and of what could happen, why would you take off all of their zipcuffs at the exact same time? Why wouldn't you do it one at a time and then put that person into a cell? They're not afraid of these men. No, this is all about degradation."

Graveline continued to tick through the evidence underlying the twenty-five distinct acts of dereliction Graner was accused of committing. He finished with a quote that the detainee "Shooter" ascribed to Graner as the guard hit his wounded legs with the asp . . . "'Thank Jesus that you're alive.'"

"Once again, the words of the accused. Once again, the insight as to why he's doing these things. But, fortunately, the accused does not have the final word on the abuse at Abu Ghraib. The final word comes from you, the members of the panel. It comes in the form of your verdict . . . that word will speak volumes to this accused, it will speak volumes to our Army, it will speak volumes to our country, and it will speak volumes to the world. The true words about the abuses that occurred at Abu Ghraib are 'guilty as charged.'"

Womack was ready to respond. "This case is about orders, orders that were given to the MPs by military intelligence, other government agencies, and civilian contract intelligence, and it was a persistent and continuing set of orders: Soften up the detainees. Do things to condition them so that we can interrogate them, so that we can interrogate them successfully in support of our mission . . . to the extent that you find that these things were done in accordance with these orders and they're appropriate, then that's called 'justification.' But even if you find that those orders by those intelligence officers of the various agencies were unlawful, it is still an absolute defense in this case that Specialist Graner was acting in accordance with these orders if he really thought and reasonably thought that these were lawful orders, and that a reasonable person [would] under a similar set of circumstances. Those circumstances, and not sitting here on a sunny clear day in Killeen, Texas, but if you were sitting there, going through what they were going through would seem reasonable. Then that's a defense."

Womack insisted that it was pressure on the MI community that had created a climate to soften up the detainees and elicit actionable intelligence. "There was a lot of pressure to [do] that, and for good reason. Our men and women were being killed, were being targeted by the enemy. We had high-value detainees, people we thought had information, at 1A, and, as they say, sometimes when you make an omelet, you have to break some eggs. It may be that, interrogating someone at 1A of Abu Ghraib, you had to be rough. You had to use approaches that you would not want to do with women and children."

The seasoned defense counsel attempted to defuse the infamous photos of his smiling client and cohorts. "Why would you see humor in something like that? It could be dealing with the tension of the moment, gallows humor. That's a way of dealing with the stress that you have in the combat arms. Paramedics, firemen, policemen, reporters that cover grisly stuff. You'll laugh about things that, if it was videotaped, people would say, 'Did you see this Lieutenant Colonel laughing at something? Was that Marine sick or what?' You'd say, 'No, he was just reacting to the stress of the moment.' It could also be that you react that way because it instills confidence in your men. If they see you doing something that is dangerous, which is unpleasant, but you do it with a smile on your face or you do it like, 'Hey, there's some humor in this. We just need to get through this.' That's also a good leader.

"The tragedy here is that this embarrassment . . . those pictures are orphans, and the U.S. government and the chain of command and all of the MIs say, 'Oh, we didn't know anything about it,' and you know that is a lie. Corporal Graner was following orders. He thought they were lawful orders, and we may agree with him. But, certainly, there was no evidence that anyone, that a reasonable person under those circumstances, seeing what he saw over a period of weeks and months, would have thought that this was illegal. It was how it was done at 1A. It didn't matter if you would do it differently in Virginia or in Pennsylvania or somewhere else in a civilian jail. At 1A, at the Baghdad Central Correctional Facility, this was SOP, and MIs who were tasked with knowing this and knowing how to do these things told him to do it and supervised it and did everything. Now, the government would ask a corporal, a young E-4, one of the junior people at 1A, to take a hit for it. It's up to y'all. Thank you."

The jury deliberated for more than five hours. A knock on the jury room's door brought the bailiff to his feet. He opened the door, and the jury filed to their seats. The foreman rose to read the verdict. Guilty on all counts.

✦

In the military justice system, unlike its civilian counterpart, sentencing takes place immediately after the conclusion of a jury trial, and the jury decides the sentence. The judge informs them of the minimum sentence (i.e., no punishment at all) and the maximum sentence. For Graner's crimes, the maximum punishment was fifteen years in prison, a dishonorable discharge, forfeiture of all his military pay, and reduction in rank to the lowest grade, private, E-1. The two sides then have an opportunity to call witnesses. The prosecution can only present evidence of the crime's direct impact on the victims or the Army unit. Sentencing allows the defense, however, to present almost any evidence that will paint a broader picture of the defendant.

So, after a short recess, the court took up the sentencing proceedings the same evening. Prior to trial, Holley and Graveline had decided that the abuses committed by Graner spoke for themselves. Consequently, they presented few witnesses, including a video deposition of one of the Iraqi victims. The defense, in their turn, called two union leaders from the Pennsylvania prison at which Graner worked, two soldiers from the 372d, and family members to speak about Graner's work ethic and good qualities, especially his loyalty and kindness as a friend and loved one.

Given all the witnesses, arguments, and deliberations packed into the weeklong trial, Holley sensed that he had to be succinct if he was going to persuade these ten jurors to follow his recommendation and sentence Graner harshly.

"Mr. President, members of the panel: the hour for Specialist Graner to be responsible is finally here. There are three things that I would ask of you, three things that I would ask you to think about before you propose punishment. First, I'd ask you not to forget the victims. That's been kind of forgotten and passed by the wayside here. There were real men involved. Although their bodies may not have been harmed physically to any great extent, you've seen that, emotionally, in their spirit and their mind, they were wounded deeply. Each of you know that you can take wounds in your mind and wounds in your spirit, and they don't heal quickly.

"Second, I would ask that you consider . . . the potential harm to our Army. Forget, for a moment, the world or even the nation, the nation that we exist to protect. They don't really understand what it takes to maintain this Army. You have to be in the Army to know that we exist on honor. It's what makes our soldiers do what they have to do under difficult circumstances. Honor is our touchstone. When acts are committed like this, it steals the honor from us. We lose the moral high ground. But I would also ask you to think about the harm to the Army in the future and even now. We know that men fight on their will-power, don't they? It's not weapons. It's not equipment. It's the human heart and that drive. The enemy has that, too. The enemy needs rallying points. He needs things that he can use to recruit those to his side, to encourage them in their efforts. You know, the accused has provided them with so much in that regard that I can't begin to tell you, nor can you begin to consider, how much harm that may have caused our soldiers, our Army.

"This conflict that exists now will last some time and there will be conflicts in the future, and we know that our soldiers, at some point, will be held by enemy captors. Our soldiers will be in that reversed position, and when they are, there will be men there who will treat our soldiers well or poorly based on a variety of things: Their religious beliefs, their politics, but they will also have images in their mind about what we are, about who the Americans are. These images will be in their minds. So, to the extent that an American soldier, Marine, sailor, airman is held captive in the future, he or she will be impacted by these events. Please consider that.

"Third, if you want to give Specialist Graner credit for serving as a soldier, do so. A soldier's life is a hard thing. But, members, do not give him credit, do not let him trade upon the honor and sacrifice of your brothers. There have been intimations throughout this trial that this accused did things to protect the life of other soldiers. Each of you knows men and women who have sacrificed limbs, eyesight, and even lives; widows who have nothing but a folded flag because their husbands tried to uphold our honor. So if you want to give him credit for being a soldier and being in difficult circumstances, do so. But do not mention . . . do not let the names of those men who have fallen in honor be mentioned in the same breath as this soldier.

"Members, if the maximum punishment was ever appropriate in a case, it is appropriate in this case. If the maximum punishment was ever appropriate for an accused, it is this accused. If the maximum punishment was ever justly imposed by a panel, you are that panel."

Womack then rose one final time on behalf of Graner. While the verdict had not gone his way, a light sentence could definitely draw much of the sting. He continued to press his view of the evidence.

"Corporal Graner received orders to do things that he thought were reprehensible. We all did. He challenged the orders. He went to his chain of command, and you know how convoluted that was . . . five different lines going up from Corporal Graner. He checked with the MP chain of command, all of the way up to Lieutenant Raeder, his platoon commander, who said, 'The MIs are in charge. Do what they say.' He went the Abu Ghraib chain of command all of the way to Captain Brinson, who said, 'The MIs are in charge. Do what they say.' That's the green side.

"He went to the blue side and challenged them. He talked to Lieutenant Colonel Jordan and he talked to other people there, and they said, 'You know, you're doing a great job, son. You're helping us in the battle in the global war on terrorism. You're helping us in our mission.' The MP side, Captain Brinson, gave him the counseling, 'You're doing a great job.'

"To Corporal Graner, what he was doing, while terrible, had to be done and he had to do it. Now, he also told you that he respects your findings and that you think that a reasonable man shouldn't have done it. But you have to consider the pressures that he was under, the pressures that they were all under, to do the missions, to do the tasks that they were ordered to do. Corporal Graner didn't like it any more than most of us like things that we have done, or parts of it, but it was necessary. We were paid to do it. We wear the uniform because we've sworn to do it.

"People have talked about this case being like a Nuremberg trial because of the idea of the defense of obedience to orders. Well, there's a big difference: In Nuremberg, it was generals who were being prosecuted. It was order-givers who were being prosecuted. We didn't grab sacrificial E-4s and prosecute them at Nuremberg. We were going after the order-givers. Here, the government is going after the order-takers. Corporal Graner, an E-4, was following orders, and there can't be a question like that.

"The question is whether he should have known not to obey those orders, and you've found that he should have known, that a reasonable person would have, and we respect that. But, surely, no one on the panel doubts that he was ordered to do these things and that he made a choice that we wish he hadn't, but for the right reason. The wrong act, but it was for the right reason. He was ordered to do these things. He was ordered to set these conditions. He was rewarded for it by these multiple chains of command and you have some of the evidence [of] that.

"But where are the officers? Where are the senior enlisted people? But it's especially the officers who were giving these orders. There should be more honor than just in being a corporal, and there's no honor in sacrificing the career and the life of a young corporal who was only following orders, however bad the orders were."

Having heard both arguments, the ten jurors now had to decide how egregious Graner's actions had been. Were they, as Holley said, cruelty for cruelty's sake, an affront to the U.S. military's honor? Or were his actions the product of orders that Graner had not been strong enough to reject, as Womack argued?

Neill, Clemens, Sheppard, Holley, Graveline, and Kary had one by one filed into one of the witness waiting rooms to await the jury's decision. The hours seemed to drag by, interminably long. The team sat silent, but the same thoughts ran through their minds: a lenient sentence could mean serious trouble to fellow soldiers in Iraq.

After three hours, the bailiff poked his head in the door: they had a sentence. The ten jurors filed into their seats. The dark green uniform of the jury's foreperson was sharply pressed and filled with ribbons and medals. He looked up from the paper he held in his hand.

The stone-faced senior Army colonel recited, "Specialist Charles A. Graner, this court-martial sentences you to be reduced to the grade of E-1, to forfeit all pay and allowances, to be confined for ten years, and to be discharged from the service with a dishonorable discharge."

13

IT AIN'T OVER 'TIL IT'S OVER

The alarm clock rang. *6:45 already?* Graveline reached over irritably to turn it off. *Why did Mike agree to meet with Davis' defense team this early?*

It was the day after the Graner verdict, Sunday morning, January 16, 2005. Holley and Graveline were supposed to meet Paul Bergrin and Captain Scott Dunn at 7:00 a.m. Several of the defense counsel for the other accused soldiers had watched Graner's trial to see the witnesses firsthand, as well as to see how the prosecutors framed their case and arguments. Within hours of Graner's ten-year sentence, Bergrin was on the phone with Holley to request an immediate meeting. He asked whether Holley thought a plea deal was possible for SGT Javal Davis. Bergrin wanted to meet early Sunday since he was departing Texas later that morning. Holley suggested getting together in the Fort Hood hotel lobby.

Mentally and physically spent, Graveline rolled over in the hotel bed. It didn't help that the trial team was out the night before, celebrating over pizza and drinks. While neither Holley nor Kary drank alcohol, Graveline, Clemens, and the rest had downed enough for their nondrinking friends. *This meeting had better be good.*

Given the testimony and evidence they had discovered, Holley had a good idea how Sergeant Davis fit into the overall context of Abu Ghraib. The burly guard with a quick temper, Davis was essentially a small player. While he had been present at two of the most infamous episodes of abuse (the hooded man on top of the box and the night of the seven rioters), Davis had committed very discreet acts of abuse and then left the situation. He was not, in the prosecution team's estimation, as culpable as some of the others. Consequently, Holley was willing to cut Davis a break, suggesting to Bergrin that if his client would be willing to plead guilty, they would take the six and a half years Davis was facing and cap it at eighteen months. Bergrin and Dunn seemed to like the cap number and said they would take the offer to their client. Yet, they also wanted a jury to decide Davis' sentence, a request not normally granted since one of the main reasons for a guilty plea is to streamline the process as much as possible. Holley said he would take the proposal to Tate, but by the tone of the conversation, it was clear to all that a deal was possible.

✦

While eager to resolve Davis' case, the trial team's more immediate concern was PFC Lynndie England. She was out of Multi-National Corps–Iraq's jurisdiction and her case out of Tate, Holley, Graveline, and Neill's control since she was moved to Fort Bragg because of her pregnancy. A completely different set of prosecutors at Bragg, independent and hundreds of miles away from their Iraq counterparts, had reviewed the evidence, charged her crimes, and held her Article 32 hearing.

From the beginning of their involvement, both Holley and Graveline had not liked this arrangement. It left too much to chance. Without close collaboration between the two prosecution teams, evidence could be discovered but not passed between them, witnesses overwhelmed by the various prosecutors and agents, and differing decisions made on similar defense requests. Graveline had attempted to alleviate those problems by traveling to Fort Bragg in October in order to compare notes and discuss strategy with CPT John Benson, the trial counsel leading England's prosecution. Benson was working at the same time on the death penalty prosecution of Sergeant Akbar. Because of that case, he recognized that he was behind on trial preparation for England even though her trial was scheduled to begin shortly after Graner's trial in January. There was little chance of Benson receiving experienced help since his unit, XVIII Airborne Corps, was deployed to Afghanistan. Even though Graveline initially proposed that he come to Bragg in January to help with England's prosecution, the time lines of the two trials seemed to make that logistically impossible.

After returning to Arlington, Graveline called Holley.

"What do you think about us asking for jurisdiction over England?" he asked his partner.

"I think it would take care of a lot of the problems we've talked about," Holley agreed, "and I believe it would lead to the most just result. Her case is essentially the same one we are handling with the other accused. If we, General Metz, and Colonel Tate take responsibility for England, minimally we can ensure a level of consistency in the decision making between cases. Do you think Bragg will see the wisdom in sending the case to us?"

"I think it's a definite possibility. They're strapped for personnel due to their deployment. I really believe that it would be in everyone's best interest, including England's, for us to get the case." Both attorneys had studied the charges against England and believed that the Fort Bragg prosecutors had overcharged England with a number of indecent act offenses involving sexually themed pictures of England that were apparently taken by Graner at Virginia Beach, Virginia, pre-deployment. Their theory was that these photos demonstrated the soldiers' sexual deviancy prior to their time at Abu Ghraib. Still, these extra charges exposed England to thirty-six years of possible imprisonment, almost double any of her cohorts.

The two JAGs decided that Holley would approach Tate about these considerations. This was one time that Holley could not read his senior officer's reaction. Tate understood the difficulties the split prosecution presented, but taking such a drastic step as working through a transfer of jurisdiction could be problematic. He said that he would think about it, but at this point, he was not comfortable with the idea.

Over the next several months, discussion began in earnest on how best to staff the England prosecution and keep it apace with the others. There was talk about Graveline becoming Benson's cocounsel, flying to Bragg on the eve of trial, and handling any witnesses that he had at Graner's trial. Yet, that plan seemed fraught with uncertainty. Finally, on December 10, 2004, XVIII Airborne Corps decided the best course of action was to request that III Corps take jurisdiction over England since the remainder of the cases were returning to the States. Holley and Graveline were now solely responsible for the case against her. But with Graner's trial preoccupying them during the month of December and the first half of January, they had accomplished little to move the case along. With

Graner's trial complete, their first order of business was dismissing the offenses against England and recharging her, modeling the charges they had brought against Graner, Frederick, and Harman. This move reduced England's potential exposure from thirty-six years to twenty-two.

✦

In the meantime, the prosecutors finished negotiating the plea deal with Javal Davis, with a court date set for February 1, 2005, to take the plea.* Davis pled guilty to dereliction of duty, making a false official statement, and two counts of assault and battery. He admitted to the judge that he had stomped and jumped on top of several detainees the night of November 7, had witnessed his fellow guards further abuse the detainees but failed to stop or report it, and lied under oath to cover up the abuse. It would now be up to the jury to determine his fate. As in the sentencing case Gary Myers put on for Frederick, Bergrin called witnesses who reiterated the difficult prison conditions, psychological experts who testified similarly to Dr. Zimbardo about how conditions will influence a person's actions, and relatives who vouched for his character as a loving family member. After a highly contentious two-day hearing, the jury sentenced Davis to a bad-conduct discharge, six months of imprisonment, and reduction to the lowest rank of private.

Even though Davis had received a lighter sentence than the negotiated agreement, the sergeant was livid. "Six months! Six fuckin' months for stepping on some toes!" Bergrin and Dunn tried to calm their client, but he was enraged. "Six months! You've got to be fuckin' kidding me!"

✦

March 11, 2005. Almost ten months to the day that he was initially told he would be needed for a ninety-day assignment to Iraq, Holley sat quietly in the small passenger area of the Killeen–Fort Hood Regional Airport, ready to go home. *What a wild ride.* After Davis' guilty plea, Holley began entertaining the

---

* Throughout the end of 2004 and early 2005, Sheppard and Holley expended considerable energy reactivating SPC Roman Krol, Cruz's cohort in abuse on the night of October 25, 2003 (the "three rapists" incident). Krol had demobilized and returned to regular civilian life. Sheppard, in particular, navigated the Army bureaucracy to bring Krol back under the military's jurisdiction. On the same day Davis pled guilty, Krol pled guilty at a special court-martial to conspiracy to maltreat and two counts of maltreatment. Judge Pohl sentenced him to ten months of imprisonment, reduction in rank to private, and a bad-conduct discharge.

thought of returning to his position at the JAG school. Only two defendants, Harman and England, remained, their cases well prepared but not scheduled until May due to defense preparations. It had been such a long ten months for Holley given the stresses attendant with being the lead prosecutor on trials of this magnitude. Tate had been immediately supportive of Holley's desire to return to Charlottesville. While he hated to see Holley go, a young man he had grown to trust and depend on, Tate understood what he had sacrificed and was confident that Graveline and Neill could handle the remaining cases.

Holley was so looking forward to seeing Renee and his children. Recalling their smiles he could have sworn he was already home. *And this time, I'll be home for good, no more good-byes.* Nevertheless, his thoughts could not help but run over the events of the last months: Iraq, Colonel Tate, the mortar attacks and loss of his friend, the strong friendships he had formed with his team, Germany, Log Base Seitz, the Graner trial. *Who could have imagined?*

Holley was shaken out of his thoughts when the airline attendant announced that his flight was boarding. As with so many soldiers before him, it was time for Holley to go home. He had fulfilled his duty.

✦

Fort Hood buzzed with media excitement. As the most recognizable soldier implicated in the abuses, England's court appearance drew more television cameras than any of the previous court proceedings, including the heavily covered Graner trial. For all intents and purposes, this petite, young woman from West Virginia had become the embodiment of the failings of U.S. policy in Iraq.

Before Holley departed, he started negotiations toward a guilty plea with England's attorneys, Rick Hernandez and CPT Jonathan Crisp. The two sides had come to a quick agreement that England would plead guilty to two counts of conspiracy to maltreat detainees for her role in the leash incident and the night of the human pyramid; four counts of maltreating detainees for her actions on the same two nights; and one count of committing an indecent act for her posing with a man forced to masturbate the night of November 7. In exchange, the general agreed to limit her sentence to thirty months and, like Davis, allowed a jury to decide her sentence. While the deal called for significantly less time for England than for Graner and Frederick, the prosecutors believed her notoriety and celebrity should not drive her sentence. While she was a willing participant in abuse, no doubt, the fact that she was a follower was equally beyond debate.

It was now May 2, 2005, the day designated for England's guilty plea. With Holley's departure, Neill had taken his spot alongside Graveline in court. Captain Sheppard stepped into Neill's shoes as the media spokesman for the trial team and had his hands full with the throng of reporters in attendance.

In the courtroom, England explained to the judge that she had joined the Army Reserve in December 1999 and was trained as a personnel administrative specialist. She was activated for deployment to Iraq in February 2003 and arrived at Abu Ghraib on October 9. After working a few days in the operations section doing paperwork, she was tasked with helping to in- and out-process detainees from the camp by fingerprinting them and making identification bracelets. She admitted she was not an MP and usually visited the hard-site at night to see her boyfriend, Graner, and other friends. The next step of her plea would not come as easily.

England had no issue stating the basic facts of what had happened the night of the leash incident with Gus: she, Graner, and Ambuhl walked down to the cell, where Graner wrapped the strap around Gus' neck, led the man out of the cell, handed her the strap, and stepped back to snap pictures. But she had a hard time admitting that she knew these actions were wrong at the time. Her responses suggested that she had given little or no thought to having another human being, naked, at the end of a leash. Pohl tried to walk England through a line of questioning to see if she actually knew what she did was wrong.

"Were you there to embarrass and humiliate the detainee by standing there and having your picture be taken?"

"Yes, sir."

"Could you have dropped the leash and walked away?"

"I could've, yes, sir."

"When the camera came out, before any pictures were taken, could you have walked away?"

"Yes, sir."

"Did you choose not to?"

"Yes, sir."

England's nonchalance amazed Graveline. An image that had shocked the world seemed to draw a shrug from the young soldier. "It just is what it is" seemed to be her thinking.

✦

Ever since he arrived at Fort Leavenworth to serve his prison sentence, Graner had been an uncooperative and problematic inmate. Upon an inmate's arrival at Leavenworth, he is kept in solitary confinement for a few weeks to acclimate to being confined and taking guards' directions. Graner, however, had spent almost four full months in solitary because of his refusal to follow any of the guards' directions. As the outward symbol of his defiance, Graner now sported a nearly clean-shaven head, the result of the guards having to hold him down in order to cut his hair. Despite his demonstrated obstinacy, he was wanted as a witness by England's team during her sentencing hearing to explain their relationship and his role in the offenses for which she had pled guilty.

A few days before Graner's scheduled arrival, Sergeant Kary strolled into the large room Neill, Graveline, and Sheppard shared. Clemens was also present, seated at a computer in one corner of the room. "You're not going to believe what I just heard," Kary said with an odd smile.

The four men started guessing at the news by throwing out ridiculous headlines tinged with barbs aimed at each other. Kary just shook his head at their poor attempt at humor. "Not even close . . . Megan Ambuhl is now Megan Ambuhl Graner. They just got married by proxy." The team was speechless, that is, all but Neill who was never at a loss for words.

"Nothing surprises me anymore with these cases . . . of course, you would marry someone with a ten-year prison sentence. It makes perfect sense," Neill cracked.

Because of Graner's propensity to play to the media, the prosecutors decided that the best plan was to bring him through the courthouse's back door instead of parading him through the sea of cameramen in front of the building. Yet, when the tan van carrying Graner drove around to the rear, a number of the reporters and cameramen followed, assuming Graner was inside. Three uniformed MPs stepped out and shuffled the cuffed and shackled Graner toward the entrance. As they approached the back door, Graner hopped close to one of the reporters, slipping the man a folded piece of paper. The reporter unfolded the note and read it to himself:

May 3, 2005

All:

This morning I was asked if I wanted to make a statement. It is my understanding that as a prisoner, I am not allowed to speak with the press. I am however allowed to write to the press. So here you are. Knowing what happened in Iraq, it was very upsetting to see Lynn plead guilty to her charges. I would hope that by doing so she will have a better chance at a good sentence. Since returning to Texas people from all over have wanted me to send her their love and support.

Having said that what is more upsetting to me is knowing that CID Special Agent Ramero [*sic*] is assigned to the CID office at Ft Hood. SA Ramero was the agent who ordered the special treatment of "Gilligan"— the prisoner on the box with the wires. The Government knows all about this. Both Ivan Frederick and I have made sworn statements about his conduct and instructions. In December 2004 SA Ramero failed a polli [*sic*] over this information. To my knowledge the Government has taken no action against this soldier and he remains a law enforcement officer. But that would ruin the whole seven bad apples story.

Respectfully

Charles Graner

✦

After the shaky plea the day before, the defense called Private Graner to the stand. Clad in his dark green Army dress uniform devoid of any rank or ribbons, the soldier walked smartly to the witness stand.

"During the time period of October to December of '03, what was your relationship with Private England?" Hernandez inquired.

"We had a relationship."

"An intimate relationship?"

"Yes, sir."

"During the hours that you were on duty working at the hard-site, would Private England come to visit you?"

"Yes, sir."

Hernandez moved his questioning to the leash incident with Gus. "Tell us about that incident, how it began and how it ended."

"I couldn't tell you the prisoner's Arabic name or his number, but we referred to him as Gus," Graner began. "In the logbook, it had him coming out of the tier at 1400, I believe, which would have been around two o'clock in the afternoon. At shift change, during our pass-on information between myself and Sergeant Joyner, he had told me what had happened with Gus. Gus was out in one of the Ganci yards, which was the main camp, the main prisoner camp from the outside. He had thrown rocks and been assaultive towards the MPs on the camp. The QRF or the IRF, which was the reaction force, needed to extract him from the compound, and they brought him to the hard-site. He'd been stripped down and he was put in the isolation cell . . . he was stating he was going to kill us, meaning the MPs, and he had been naked on the floor."

Hernandez interrupted Graner's long narrative. The defense counsel was already having difficulty controlling the uncontrollable witness. "Could we just start at when you decided to extract him from that cell and why?"

"Somewhere around eight o'clock at night, one of the MI people had come in, and they needed the cell for one of their prisoners. I had already had contact with Gus, and each time I had been in his door, [he'd say] 'I will kill you.' So I needed to move him from his isolation cell to the cell he was actually assigned to on the Bravo side. I opened the door, I told him to get up. Again, he was going to kill me."

"Let me stop you there for a moment. Who else was present when you opened the door and asked him to get up?"

"At that time, it was just me on the floor, and then I believe Specialist England and Specialist Ambuhl were up in the office . . . I felt that I was going to have to fight this prisoner. I had gone up to the office to get help from the other two soldiers, and I was going to attempt to explain the cell extraction, and I had observed my M4 . . . and I had a sling on it. And my intention was, at this point, to just drag him out of the cell before we had a fight. I didn't want to fight him inside the cell. There was urine and feces on the floor. The prisoner had open sores on him. So, I had asked the two soldiers to come follow me down and just, you know, back me up."

"What information did you give Private England before heading down there, if any?"

Graner continued his long-winded answers. "At that point, I didn't give them any information other than, 'Just follow me down and back me up if anything happens with this prisoner.' I had an idea in my head how we could get him out without having to go into the cell. He had been laying with his head towards the door. He was pretty close to the door, and like I said, I didn't want to fight him inside the cell . . . I had wrapped what I called the 'tether' around his shoulders and began to pull him out of the cell, at which point it slid down around his neck. Gus began to crawl out of the cell on his own. Once he got past the door, I had turned around and Specialist England was the first one behind me. I asked her to hold the tether, or the lead, as the prisoner crawled out of the cell. I took three quick pictures of the prisoner. And then once he was fully out of the cell, I took the tether off his neck, snatched him up. I grabbed him by his neck and his arm, and I escorted him to his cell on the B side."

"Were you asking her [to hold the 'tether'] as the NCO in charge of that tier, or were you asking her as a friend or as a fellow soldier?"

"I was asking her as the senior person of that extraction team, I guess you would say, as the NCO."

Graveline and Neill both leaned forward in their chairs. *He just put forward about three different defenses to explain away England's criminal culpability: obedience to orders, self-defense, and lack of conspiracy,* Graveline thought hastily. *He's going to bust this plea.*

Judge Pohl was clearly thinking along the same lines as the prosecutors. "Private Graner, why did you take the pictures?"

"The three pictures I took that night, sir . . . this was going to be a planned use of force, which anything that we did at the prison, since we had no other rules besides from the 800th MP's ROE, I tried to bring what we would have done at Pennsylvania there, and since it was a planned use of force, you document it. We didn't have a video camera. This was the closest way I could document it. Apparently, since we had a lot of information during our case, that's the Army policy for their corrections, that you document planned use of force."

Pohl continued his inquiry. "So, what you're saying is this cell extraction picture was part of a legitimate cell extraction technique with pictures to document what you were doing?"

"I can't say that it was a legitimate . . ."

"Legitimate in the sense that you were doing it to extract him?"

"Yes, sir, it was to me the safest way to get this prisoner out of his cell."

With that answer, Pohl cleared the courtroom of jurors and Graner. He stared across his elevated bench at Hernandez. "Defense, you're now contradicting both the stipulation of fact and your guilty plea. You cannot do that. If you don't want to plead guilty, don't. But you cannot sit here and have this witness come up and say this was a legitimate cell extraction technique. The stipulation of fact that you signed says that he put it around his neck, not his shoulders. You cannot plead guilty and then on sentencing say you're not guilty. Am I missing something here, Mr. Hernandez?"

"I believe what you're missing is the point that he made that he gave no instruction to Private England. She would have not known what an appropriate cell extraction was, and she was not given this information . . . ," Hernandez stammered.

"If Private Graner is doing this in a legitimate cell extraction technique, which, with the evidence which you just presented, how can she be guilty of participating in this?" Pohl paused. "I'm going to take a recess. What I'm telling you right now, also, is that in your stipulation of fact, it says he put it around the person's neck. He comes in and testifies under oath that he put it around the shoulders and it slid to his neck . . ."

Crisp interjected in an attempt to aid his defense partner. "Your Honor, we would request that you instruct the panel to disregard any testimony he gave with . . . "

"What I'm saying is . . . nobody has forced anybody to plead guilty here." Pohl turned toward England who was seated at the defense table. "Private England, I want to talk to you. Yesterday, and more so today, there's evidence being presented by your defense that you're not guilty . . . I'm simply saying, is if Private Graner is to be believed in what he just said, that the cell extraction and the involvement that you had on the tether incident was a legitimate cell extraction technique, therefore, he was not violating any law, which therefore you couldn't be violating any law. Do you understand what I'm saying?"

"Yes, sir," replied England.

"Do you understand the problem I'm having here? Your counsel keep putting on witnesses that are raising defenses, and you can't have it both ways.

I understand the situation you're in. I've been doing this for a long time, and I know it's very difficult sometimes when you're facing the pressure of a trial. But, on the other hand, you only can plead guilty if you believe you are guilty. And if you believe you are guilty, you cannot put evidence on sentencing that says you're not guilty." With those words, Pohl recessed the hearing.

The events sent both sides scurrying. There was a mixture of shock and fury as Graveline, Neill, Sheppard, Kary, Clemens, and Simril regrouped in their boiler room/office. While this development was not totally unexpected, they still could not believe what they had just witnessed.

"I don't see how this guilty plea can go on," Neill stated. "Judge Pohl can't just tell the jury to disregard what they've heard from Graner. It's going to be a mistrial."

"What were they thinking putting that guy on the stand and just letting him ramble?" Clemens added.

"We need to get Colonel Tate on the phone," Graveline concluded. "We've essentially just had one person in a two-person conspiracy testify that he never agreed to any criminal misconduct with the accused."

As Graveline was talking, Neill was already dialing Tate's number. He explained the situation to the senior officer. Tate agreed that it did not look likely that the plea could be saved, but he suggested that they do more research on this particular aspect of conspiracy law. Graveline then called Mulligan back in D.C. and Holley in Charlottesville. Both attorneys saw no way around the mistrial.

Graveline bumped into Crisp in the courthouse hallway. The defense counsel looked at as much of a loss as the prosecutors. Graveline laid out the team's research and conclusions.

"What about a new plea deal?" Crisp asked. "Do you think we can keep the same amount of confinement?"

Graveline was in no mood to even talk about a deal at this point. "Listen, after watching your client for the last two days, I'm not sure that she can ever make it through a guilty plea. She barely made it yesterday. You can talk with Colonel Tate about it, but we're going to need some time to think about it. Let's get back into court."

Pohl agreed with the prosecutors, declaring a mistrial. The deal was off.

As England and her defense team left the courthouse, they were swarmed by dozens of reporters and cameramen. Graveline watched the chaotic scene with some sympathy for the young soldier; she was caught up in a media frenzy beyond her wildest imaginings. He would read later that England, after the mistrial, had turned to Staci Morris, Graner's ex-wife, who had been present at the plea, and said, "Well, he screws up everything, doesn't he?"

✦

Neill and Graveline did not have time to dwell on the England fiasco since Sabrina Harman's court-martial was scheduled to begin the following week on May 11. The youngest of the defendants, Harman had shown no interest in pleading guilty. The evidence and witnesses for this trial were the same as Graner's with a few important exceptions. When CID first opened its investigation back in January 2004, Harman had given four separate statements to investigators. In the first, given to Special Agent James Boerner, Harman confessed to taking pictures the night of the human pyramid and posing with Graner behind it. She stated that she "did not think it was right" when she saw the detainees placed in the simulated fellatio position, so she left. She also told CID about finding out about the detainee who died during an OGA interrogation (whose death had been detailed in the Fay report) in the shower room and posing for pictures over the corpse.

In her second statement given the following day to Special Agent Warren Worth, Harman further detailed her involvement in the abuses leading to the pyramid. This time, she also confessed to her role with the hooded man on the box with wires hanging from his hands. "He is nicknamed 'Gilligan' . . . he was just standing on the MRE box with the sandbag over his head for about an hour. I put the wires on his hand . . . I was joking with him and told him if he fell off he would get electrocuted." Worth questioned why she and Frederick would do this to the man. "Just playing with him," Harman responded. "We were not hurting him," she continued. "It was not anything that bad." Worth concluded by asking if MI had asked her to do this to the detainee. "Not me personally. They were talking to Grainer [sic]. MI wanted to get them to talk. It is Grainer and Fredericks [sic] job to do these things for MI and OGA to get these people to talk. I do not recall anyone from MI or OGA saying this. I do not recall Grainer [sic] or Frederick ever saying that MI or OGA had told them to do this either." So, in addition to calling the main witnesses from the Graner trial, Graveline and Neill also called Agents Boerner and Worth to testify about Harman's confessions.

Despite the fact Harman had been present for several acts of abuse, had devised the plan of putting wires on the man's hands, and had posed in or taken numerous abuse photos, her defense revolved around the premise that Harman had been disgusted about what was going on in the prison and took the photos to document the abuse and expose it later. To lay the foundation for this argument, Harman's attorney, Frank Spinner, called Kelly Bryant, her lesbian partner. Bryant testified that she had received a letter from Harman dated October 20, 2003, that read, in part:

> Kelly, okay, I don't like that anymore. At first it was funny, but these people are going too far. It went too far even I can't handle what's going on. I can't get it out of my head. At first I had to laugh, again, I thought okay that's funny, then it hit me that's a form of molestation, they can't do that. The only reason I want to be there is get the pictures to prove that the U.S. is not what they think, but I don't know if I can take it mentally. What if that was me in their shoes. These people will be our future terrorists. Kelly, it's awful and you know how fucked I am in the head. Both sides of me think it was wrong.

Bryant further stated that Harman had called her on the night of November 7, confirming that she had left the cell block at some point after the human pyramid.

Graveline and Neill were skeptical of this letter from the time they had received it from the defense lawyers. Although it appeared to be Harman's handwriting, how credible were these sentiments? If the letter had been written on October 20 as it purported, Harman would have been at Abu Ghraib for no more than three weeks and possibly even less than a week. Moreover, this letter would have predated her tying wires on the detainee's hands as a joke and her smiling picture behind the human pyramid by two weeks. Additionally, this defense claim that she was only taking pictures to expose the bad behavior was belied by her actions. For instance, when she had been first called in by CID, she had failed to express any relief that she could finally report the abuse or offer the investigators the photos she had taken. Instead, she had not mentioned her involvement with the detainee on the box, the night of the three rapists, or her writing "rapeist" on the detainee. Nor did she turn the photos over to the Army IG or the media when she went home on leave November 11–25, 2003. No, the first time she had mentioned any reference to taking photos to "document" abuse was the first week of February, two weeks and three statements after she had initially been called in. Moreover, how did these thoughts match up with Bryant's testimony that when Harman called her on November 7, a call that immediately followed the pyramid and forced masturbation, Harman did not mention those events or seem upset over the phone?

The jury agreed with the prosecutors, finding her guilty of conspiracy to maltreat, dereliction of duty, and maltreatment for her actions at the prison. However, Spinner and his military cocounsel, CPT Patsy Takemura, succeeded in presenting a compelling sentencing case. Harman, a pizza shop manager back in her home state of Virginia, had befriended a number of young Iraqi children when the 372d was stationed in Al-Hillah. Takemura attempted to replace the photos of Harman mugging over corpses and naked men with numerous photos of her smiling in groups of kids.

Equally compelling was Harman's statement to the jury. Tears ran down her face as she stared fixedly at the statement she had written out. "I would like to end this statement by expressing my sincerest apologies for the decisions I made between mid-October through mid-January at Abu Ghraib, Baghdad, Iraq. I first wish to apologize to any and all detainees I failed to protect from any form of maltreatment that I may have witnessed or had been a part of. As a soldier and a military police officer I failed my duties, I failed my mission to protect and defend. I not only let down the people in Iraq, but I let down every single soldier that serves today. My actions potentially caused an increased hatred and insurgency towards the United States putting soldiers and civilians at greater risk. I take full responsibility for my actions. I do not place blame on my chain of command or others I worked with during this time. The decisions I made were mine and mine alone and I'm truly sorry."

Graveline and Neill both believed the sincere apology and acceptance went a long way to mitigating Harman's sentence in the jury's collective mind: six months of confinement, reduction to the lowest rank of private, forfeiture of all pay, and a bad-conduct discharge.

✦

As the team wrapped up the remaining cases begun in Iraq a year before, Graveline was shifting his attention to the next phase of the investigation. Questions still lingered concerning what action, if any, should be taken against the officers and, in particular, Lieutenant Colonel Jordan, who was now stationed at the Army's Intelligence and Security Command (INSCOM) at Fort Belvoir, Virginia. With Graveline stationed in the area, he became the point of contact for the lawyers reviewing the evidence against Jordan.

Under the Army command structure, INSCOM did not have authority to initiate a general court-martial, meaning that any disciplinary action above an Article 15 would have to be handled by the next higher command, the Military District of Washington (MDW). To give the command the widest range of options, Graveline and Mulligan advised that Jordan be transferred to MDW's jurisdiction. The two JAGs found both INSCOM and MDW's staff judge advocates, COL Richard Pregent and COL Sarah Green, receptive to the idea.

As the rest of the team returned to their normal duty stations, Graveline realized he would not be leaving the Abu Ghraib investigations any time soon; he was in for round two and needed help. After discussing the situation with Mulligan, the senior attorney determined that finding another experienced prosecutor to fill Holley's role would be the best option. Graveline solicited Holley for recommendations. While he had several suggestions, he strongly recommended MAJ Matthew Miller. Holley had known Miller for years and had been impressed with his judgment and courtroom skills. Miller was stationed at Fort Eustis, Virginia, and was working on legal reviews for future Army systems. Mulligan put forward Miller's name to the JAG leadership as the new prosecutor. On April 22, 2005, Miller's participation was approved, and he made preparations to join the team in Arlington, Virginia.

Graveline and CPT Clare O'Shaughnessy, a JAG reservist working for Mulligan at the time, quickly focused on two areas in need of further investigation: Jordan's knowledge of both nakedness and the use of military working dogs as interrogation techniques. The stark images of snarling dogs confronting cowering detainees, coupled with Frederick's, Ambuhl's, and Harman's statements describing games such as the "doggie dance" and a contest to see how many detainees the guards could make urinate on themselves, left Graveline sick to his stomach. *If these were interrogation approaches, we need to find out if the officers knew about them.*

Two Army dog handlers, Sergeants Santos Cardona and Michael Smith, had been identified by the convicted soldiers as those responsible for bringing dogs into Tier 1A. During the spring of 2005, prosecutions were being planned for both of these soldiers, Cardona at Fort Bragg and Smith at Fort Riley. Graveline likened this arrangement to England's case when it had been separated from the others in Iraq in that it opened the door to disparate treatment of the two guards and that making a deal with either soldier to learn if officers had ordered the abuse would be complicated by the split jurisdictions. *The dog handlers are the key to finding out how far up the chain of command some of the abuses go,* Graveline pondered.

He went to Mulligan with his thoughts.

"What if we could get the dog handlers assigned to MDW for jurisdictional purposes," proposed Mulligan.

Graveline smiled, "That might make theses prosecutions easy . . . for once."

14

PUPPY LOVE OR UNLEASH THE DOGS

It was back to square one for Lynndie England. With the failed guilty plea, her defense team seemed to be at a loss about what to do next. The night of the mistrial, Graveline found Crisp walking the halls of III Corps' headquarters.

"It's either going to be me or Rick going forward," Crisp stated grimly, "but not both. I can't work with him anymore. Private England's going to have to decide between the two of us, and I don't think she'll pick me."

To Graveline's surprise, Crisp called the next morning. "Lynndie fired Rick. I'll be her lead counsel from here forward."

While England settled on her defense team, everything else about her case was unsettled. No dates had been set for the now necessary Article 32 proceeding, motion hearings, or probable trial, and it was unclear whether Judge Pohl would stay on as the presiding judge. For the prosecution, Neill was scheduled to transfer permanently from Fort Hood to Fort Riley, Kansas, and Kary was set to return full-time to his job at Fort Bragg. Clemens had already returned to his civilian career, and Tate had recently received word that he had been selected to become a one-star brigadier general. He would be leaving Fort Hood in July. Everything was in flux.

✦

Graveline and Miller hit it off as they began their work on the next round of prosecutions. An athletically built man slightly shorter than Graveline and with closely cropped, speckled gray hair, Miller was a West Point graduate, former

Army helicopter pilot, and an avid soccer player/enthusiast. He was affable and eager to join the team. His energy and vigor were a shot in the arm to Graveline, whose fatigue was beginning to show. The renewed urgency was vital since Mulligan had succeeded in getting the dog handlers, Smith and Cardona, transferred to MDW's jurisdiction, and Graveline, Miller, and O'Shaughnessy had identified more than forty MI personnel they wanted to interview as they evaluated their case against Jordan. These interrogators and analysts had all been stationed at Abu Ghraib but were now spread out over the United States, Europe, and Iraq. Because none of the original defendants had any specific information directly linking Jordan to the abuse, only innuendo and supposition, the attorneys hoped these soldiers could finally confirm if or how Jordan knew about or directed abusive interrogations.

They split the list of names and began the search. Some they interviewed via telephone, others they flew to Washington, D.C. Graveline even flew back to Heidelberg, Germany, to interview others. Their questions were specific. What was Jordan's role in approving interrogation plans? Did he ever suggest any techniques? Did he order detainees stripped as a form of humiliation? How prevalent was the nakedness on Tier 1A? Was nakedness being used as a way to further interrogations? Did Jordan know about the nakedness in the prison? What was his role in the Iraqi police roundup? Was he present the entire night? What abuses did each individual witness the night of the roundup? Did Jordan order any of the abuse that night?

They had spoken with only a few of the witnesses when they recognized similar responses and reactions. When asked about Jordan's role in formulating interrogation plans, a slight smirk would come over the soldier's face. Although military intelligence by training, Jordan had little or no experience in interrogations and rarely gave any input in the process. He busied himself with welfare issues for the soldiers at the prison, trying to improve their living conditions. In fact, many of the witnesses referred to him as the "mayor of Abu Ghraib." But not a single person identified Jordan as being involved in dictating interrogation plans or approaches. Instead, they stated that CPT Carolyn Wood and CWO Jon Graham had been the officers reviewing interrogation plans and proposed techniques. Yet, not one interrogator described an incident where Wood or Graham approved nakedness or an abusive technique, although Wood freely admitted that her interrogators used stress positions and sleep adjustment as part of interrogation plans at Abu Ghraib.

The interrogators downplayed the nakedness in the tiers, stating that while they saw a naked detainee periodically, they never ordered stripping or removal of clothes. Regarding the IP roundup, all of the soldiers stated Jordan was present in the cell block that night. However, almost to a person, none of them could say with any certainty exactly what Jordan was doing since they had been busy interrogating the Iraqi guards to find out if there were any other weapons in the prison. The three prosecutors also noted that several of these same witnesses, who had characterized in previous statements the scene as chaotic, now remembered it as more subdued. No one denied the Iraqi guards were stripped, but they were only down to their underwear as opposed to complete nudity. Voices were raised in the excitement but not in an uncontrollable fashion. In their hindsight, the situation had never spun totally out of control. Graveline and Miller could not tell if the slight change in tone was a case of revisionist history, fading memory, or actual recollection of the events. Whatever the reason, Graveline and Miller both knew that these vague and muted reminiscences were not the kind that made for successful prosecutions.

As Graveline sat across from interrogator after interrogator, he realized a prosecution based primarily on their testimony would be next to impossible. *You can see it in their eyes during the entire interview. They're constantly gauging which interview "approach" I'm "trying" on them and attempting to counteract it, calibrating their every word. The only problem with that is I'm not trying any fancy approach. I'm only asking questions to get to the bottom of this!*

✦

After months of delay, England's trial began on September 22, 2005. The team reassembled from around the country, with Neill, Graveline, Clemens, and Kary flying in the week prior to trial. Similar to Harman's trial, the prosecution evidence and witnesses mirrored those who had testified against Graner and were coupled with admissions England made to CID during the early days of the investigation. Specifically, in a statement from January 15, 2004, England admitted all of the defendants' actions on the night of the seven rioters and added that "everyone would laugh at the things we would have them do," describing the soldiers' overall mood that night.*

In her defense, Crisp conceded to the jury that his client had committed the acts captured in the photographs of abuse. But he argued that England had developed an overly compliant personality because of lifelong learning disabilities, leaving her particularly susceptible to following authority figures, particularly the authority figure for her at Abu Ghraib, Charles Graner. The defense contended that England's love for the older, more charismatic Graner had hindered her ability to enter into an agreement to harm detainees. The defense was not arguing legal insanity, but rather Crisp was attacking whether England's psychological makeup allowed her to form the specific intent necessary to enter into a conspiracy.

To further their case, the defense relied on two expert witnesses, Dr. Thomas Denne, England's school psychologist from her earliest days in West Virginia's Mineral County public schools, and Dr. Xavier Amador, a New York psychologist who had interviewed her after the events. Denne testified that from the age of four, when he first met England, she had possessed a complex language processing base dysfunction, in effect being electively mute, which meant that she was uncomfortable speaking in almost all environments to almost anyone. The psychologist, a tall, older man with an abundant crop of gray hair, described England as a young girl who failed to interact with any of her classmates, choosing instead to interact with only one particular adult in the school setting. While Denne conceded England was not mentally impaired and had tested above average in visual comprehension, her difficulties stemmed from language comprehension. Crisp then asked Denne to link her educational difficulties with any behavioral patterns.

---

* On January 14, 2004, England gave a much more complete statement describing several incidents of abuse, including the leash incident ("Graner had suggested he take a picture of me with Gus pretending to drag him on a leash type thing . . . Graner then got out a tie-down strap and went downstairs to solitare [sic] . . . Graner had Gus lay down on the floor and he made a big loop in the tie-down strap . . . then placed the tie-down strap loosely around Gus' head and neck. He gave me the end of the strap and took a picture"). In pretrial hearings held in July, Judge Pohl, after hearing expert psychological testimony about England's learning disabilities, ruled that England had not voluntarily waived her rights to remain silent given the overall circumstances that surrounded that statement. These circumstances included England's difficulties grasping language-based concepts, her surprise at CID agents and a quick reaction force coming into her room in the middle of the night, and her lack of sleep before she gave this statement.

"When confronted with social situations, and all I mean by social situations . . . if there is more than one person there, and if in fact she perceives that person to be an authority figure, she complies," Denne explained. "She almost automatically reflexively complies . . . within the school environment, Lynndie England was not a problem. Within the school environment, when the teacher asked Lynndie England to do something, Lynndie England did what the teacher asked. When Lynndie was asked to complete assignments, Lynndie worked her best to complete assignments. When Lynndie was asked to do something by teachers, Lynndie did it."

Graveline listened intently to Denne. He had spoken with him on numerous occasions and had come to respect him as a good man who truly cared for England's well-being. Graveline could also sense a touch of remorse in the doctor who had worked so diligently with England as a child and knew her as a loving person, not the one-sided character she had been reduced to by the abuse photos. However, there was also more to England than what the defense wanted to portray her as. She was not a barely mentally functioning individual whom Graner led around by the nose.

"Now, you mentioned her compliant personality, correct?" Graveline asked.

"I mentioned, sir, that she was compliant when in a situation where she perceives authority. I didn't mention compliant personality, per se, sir."

"So, when she's in a structured setting, she obeys?" Denne agreed, so Graveline continued. "She obeys teachers, correct?"

"Yes, sir."

"In your experience as you tracked her through her educational process, did she ever have any behavioral problems in the school setting?"

"None, sir, other than those behavioral difficulties that I had alluded to in the earlier years in terms of the elective mutism and so forth. But, in terms of behavior problems of noncompliance, none, sir. In contrast, sir, the assistant principals who were in charge of discipline said that she would do her best to avoid putting herself into situations where others were misbehaving."

Graveline then turned to England's educational difficulties with Denne, confirming that England had been mainstreamed into the normal high school environment.

"And the reason for that is she did a lot of hard work during elementary and middle school, correct?" Graveline inquired.

"Absolutely, sir," Denne firmly responded.

"She worked very hard in overcoming these language-based processing disorders, correct?"

"Thank you for asking me, sir, yes, sir."

"In fact, you were very happy in eighth grade by the amount of progress she had made from kindergarten up to eighth grade . . . ," Graveline started before Denne cut him off.

"Very happy is an understatement, sir."

"So, then she was mainstreamed into high school and she performed well in high school, correct?" Denne concurred. "In fact, she graduated with a 3.0 from high school?"

"That is accurate, sir," Denne testified. He then confirmed that she had graduated in the middle of her class academically and that her learning difficulties would not prevent her from holding down a variety of jobs, making decisions for herself and a family, and essentially leading a normal life. *Apparently, England is not the completely helpless person her counsel is making her out to be,* Graveline thought as he ended his examination of the doctor.

Xavier Amador followed Dr. Denne on the witness stand. A clinical psychologist, Amador testified that, based on his interviews of the young clerk, in addition to her language-based processing deficits, he believed that at the time of the abuses England suffered from clinical depression and symptoms of post-traumatic stress disorder. Separate and distinct from these issues, Amador also diagnosed England as having an overly developed compliant personality trait that allowed Graner to influence her to such a degree that she was not able to enter into a true conspiracy with him. While Amador's theory seemed convoluted to the prosecutors, Amador summed up that she overly relied on individuals, singling out somebody to be her social and moral compass in questionable situations—a person who would tell her when to laugh, what was right or wrong. Unfortunately, at Abu Ghraib, that person was Charles Graner, Amador stated. When in the presence of an authority figure, he continued, England would exhibit no critical thinking.

"There's no reflecting on her internal values about this or anything. It's like a child in that way. It really is like a child," Amador concluded.

While there was no doubt in his mind that England was a follower, Neill found Amador's sweeping conclusions to be inconsistent with facts that the prosecutors had discovered. Neill began his cross-examination by delving into Amador's propensity for appearing in high-profile trials and testifying for the defense every time. He then ran the doctor through England's school history, which showed good grades and some advanced placement courses, and her work history where she had held several jobs, including working at a chicken packing plant before quitting.

"Can you tell the panel why she quit?" Neill asked.

"The belt was moving very, very fast. She was in a situation where she and other coworkers were ending up having to put bad chicken on a good belt and was really angry about the whole situation and angry about the bad chicken going on there."

"What happened the first time she reported the bad chicken to the manager?"

"She went with coworkers, and the management essentially minimized her concerns and said they'll deal with it, but nothing changed."

"Did she eventually quit that job?"

Amador admitted that she did quit, but that she had also returned to the chicken packing plant at a later point based on the assurances from management that the problem had been resolved. She quit again when she found out that nothing had changed.

"So, at least in that context, she had the ability to make a decision to leave her job. Is that right?" Neill continued

"In the social context, being supported as she was by her coworkers, yes."

"So, in your opinion, she only left the job because she had the support of coworkers. Is that right?"

"Yes, I don't think she would have . . . certainly would not have talked to her manager on her own," Amador offered.

This last answer typified the prosecutors' angst about every psychologist who had testified during the trials. The attorneys did not doubt that environment could play a role in shaping a person's actions or that some of the soldiers were leaders and others followers. However, the doctors portrayed these soldiers as having no control over their own actions, as if they were some sort of automatons. When presented with evidence to the contrary, they attempted to shoehorn the facts into their theories.

Neill continued to press Amador on his response that England could seemingly only act right when bolstered by friends or coworkers. He pointed out that other soldiers had left Tier 1A the night of the seven rioters but that England had not.

"I'm not sure that she wanted to leave, but . . . is there a reason she would not have viewed it as an opportunity to leave? No, I think she felt she could leave," Amador stated.

"So, she chose to stay on the tier that night?"

"Yes, because it was her birthday and she was spending it with Charles Graner."

Neill asked if there were any limits to Graner's "control" over England. "For example, if Corporal Graner had ordered PFC England to kill a detainee, would she have done it?"

"I don't believe she would have. I think the criminality and wrongfulness of that act would be so crystal clear, that it's so extreme and outside of her experience that I think that would have overcome a compliant personality in that instance."

Yeah, because holding a naked man on a leash and laughing and smiling at Arab men being forced to masturbate are not that extreme, Graveline thought to himself sarcastically.

Amador concluded the defense's case, and then it was time for each side to sum up its views of England's culpability. Crisp summed up England's defense. "She's a follower. She's an individual who was smitten with Corporal Graner, who just did whatever he asked her to, who complied with authority in the presence of her perceived authority figure, whether it was Graner, whether it was Frederick, whether it was an MP. And, compounding all of this is her depression, her fear, her anxiety, not a normal person in the context of what you know . . . she is not guilty of these offenses."

Having the last word, Graveline focused on England's own social and moral compass as exemplified in her decision to quit her previous job when she saw unsanitary conditions. "She can quit over bad chicken, but she can't understand that making men masturbate is wrong? This is the same person? That's what the defense wants you to believe. No, she knows what's right and wrong. She chooses not to do what's right. She chose because she thought it was funny. Not because Graner thought it was funny, not because Harman thought it was funny, but because she thought it was funny."

The prosecutor then took on the argument that she should be exonerated because of her role as a follower. "The defense wants you to put all the blame on Corporal Graner, and the government will be the first one to tell you Corporal Graner led the abuse that night. There's no doubt about it. You are not innocent because you were a follower and not the leader. Being a follower, that's a mitigation thing. That's not an 'avoid criminal culpability' thing."

The jury found England not guilty of conspiring with Graner to maltreat Gus, but she was guilty of four charges of maltreating detainees, to include posing with Gus on the end of the leash; one charge of conspiracy to maltreat detainees on the night of the seven rioters; and one charge of indecent acts for her role in the forced masturbation. For her crimes, the jury sentenced her to three years of confinement, reduction to the lowest enlisted rank of private, and a dishonorable discharge. Graveline and Neill watched silently as her MP escorts waited patiently as England said her good-byes to her one-year-old child, the son she had borne with Graner.

✦

By summer's end, 2005, Graveline had been giving much thought to Colonel Jordan. Neither he nor Miller believed they had a case against him. After talking with MI personnel, they knew Jordan had rarely been involved in planning specific interrogations. Consequently, the most Jordan could arguably be responsible for as leader of the Joint Interrogation Debriefing Center was dereliction of duty for failure of oversight, or possibly setting overall conditions that opened the door for abuse. *Nakedness had been clearly used in some degree by MI in that cell block to manipulate detainees. But none of the interrogators state they, or anyone they know, used it as part of an interrogation plan and say they only saw a naked detainee very sporadically, if at all. The MPs can't identify any MI personnel who told them to strip a detainee. And forget about ordering, we're going to have a hard time proving beyond a reasonable doubt that Jordan even knew about the nakedness. We only have Captain Reese, the 372d commander, who positively states that Jordan saw naked detainees, and he has his own credibility issues.*

Their investigation also failed to uncover any evidence that Jordan ordered the presence of dogs for any interrogations. With these thoughts, Graveline went down the hallway and sat in Miller's office. "This case is going nowhere," he evaluated.

Miller could not help but agree with his partner. "You can't win a case against someone of Jordan's rank, given the inherent credibility that an officer accrues over a long career, with testimony like 'he must have seen that' or 'he had to have known this.' That's the very definition of reasonable doubt. On top of that, dereliction could be viewed as a stretch given Jordan had little or no background in interrogation before being assigned out at Abu Ghraib. Plus, there's going to be multiple witnesses coming in to say that he wasn't just sitting around doing nothing. He did do a good job at what he did know, making the living conditions better at Abu Ghraib for soldiers stationed there."

"Even our most solid charges," Graveline picked up where Miller left off, "are hampered by the fact that apparently Taguba and Fay did not read Jordan his rights before taking his statement." Both lawyers believed they could prove that Jordan had not been completely truthful to these two investigators. However, there was a major problem. Jordan's statement to Taguba would never be allowed into evidence since it was clear from the verbatim transcript of the interview that the general had never read Jordan his rights. Similarly, with the statement taken by Fay, the two prosecutors could find no evidence that the colonel had been read his rights.*

Still, had Jordan been more vigilant as the officer in charge of the interrogation center, Miller and Graveline believed he could have prevented the abuse stemming from MI misconduct. Furthermore, they had reliable information that (1) Jordan disobeyed a direct order given by Fay not to discuss the investigation, and (2) after Jordan left Abu Ghraib, but while still in Iraq, he filed false payment vouchers.

---

* In the military justice system, anyone investigating potential misconduct, once he or she suspects the soldier being interviewed of committing a crime, that person must read the soldier, regardless of rank, the equivalent of his or her Miranda rights. In Jordan's statement to Taguba, it became apparent early on that the general suspected Jordan of lying to him, reminding him that he was under oath. For Fay, he should have suspected Jordan of potential misconduct given that Taguba's report had identified Jordan as being "directly or indirectly" responsible for abuses at the prison.

Miller and Graveline concluded that while Jordan was a deficient leader, lied on multiple occasions, and no longer deserved to be in the Army, his misconduct did not warrant a full court-martial. The two JAGs decided the best course of action was to recommend Article 15 punishment and ensure Jordan leave the Army either through voluntary retirement or punishment that would end his Army career. They presented their assessment to the staff judge advocate supervising Jordan's case, Colonel Green. An experienced officer with a kindly yet firm disposition, Green had given Miller and Graveline strong support throughout the summer and had been eagerly awaiting their assessment of the evidence against Jordan. She listened intently as they summarized the case's strengths and weaknesses. She agreed that the Article 15 was the way to proceed, as long as Jordan also submitted his retirement paperwork simultaneously. Jordan and his attorney, CPT Sam Spitzberg, were receptive to the idea and offered to plead guilty to this nonjudicial punishment and then retire. After Graveline returned from England's court-martial, the prosecutors put the finishing touches on the charges Jordan would plead to at the Article 15 proceeding: negligent dereliction of duty for not properly supervising the interrogators, a false official statement to Fay for stating that he never witnessed interrogations occurring in the actual prison, failure to obey Fay's order not to communicate with other witnesses, and three other charges resulting from the false vouchers he had filed after leaving Abu Ghraib. After the plea, Jordan would accept whatever punishment the general meted out and retire immediately.

In late August, Miller, Graveline, and Green presented the resolution to the MDW's commanding general. The general quizzed the prosecutors on their investigation and seemed amenable to their recommendation. However, in October, a few hours before Jordan was to resolve his Article 15, Green received word that the general had concluded that an Article 15 was not sufficient for the misconduct and that the investigation should be returned to his subordinate commanders for further inquiry and recommendations. Caught by surprise by this decision, and after serious reflection and discussion, both Graveline and Miller suggested that Green reassign Jordan's case since they did not believe the evidence warranted a court-martial. Green reluctantly agreed, and a senior reserve JAG officer, LTC John Tracy, was put on the case.

Eventually, in April 2006, Jordan was charged with disobeying lawful orders from both Taguba and Fay by discussing the ongoing investigations, negligent dereliction of duty for failure to supervise interrogations at Abu Ghraib, two counts of willfully disobeying Sanchez's order about obtaining his permission prior to using military working dogs during interrogations on the night of the IP roundup, maltreating detainees by use of forced nudity and military working dogs, false official statements to both Taguba and Fay, two counts for filing a false claim, and obstruction of justice regarding the false claim.

The charges pertaining to Jordan's false statement to Taguba were dismissed early on when the military judge found that the general had not read the officer his rights. The charges based on Jordan's false statement to Fay were dismissed after Fay, who originally testified that he had notified Jordan of his rights, contacted the prosecutors on the eve of trial and admitted that, after reviewing his notes, he had failed to do so. By the time the case finally reached trial in 2007, the original twelve counts had been reduced to four, and the scope of Jordan's alleged misconduct was essentially reduced to the night of the IP roundup. A military jury acquitted Jordan of all charges involving detainee maltreatment and found him guilty only of disobeying Fay's order not to communicate with other witnesses on August 29, 2007. It delivered a sentence of a reprimand, one of the lightest punishments possible.[*]

✦

In juxtaposition to Jordan's case, the more Miller, Graveline, and O'Shaughnessy learned about the dog handlers, the more they became convinced that serious misconduct had occurred. Five military working dog teams, three Navy and two Army, arrived at the prison facility November 18–23, 2003. They were assigned to the 320th MP Battalion to provide force protection (i.e., security walks around the perimeter of the tent camps and outer walls, presence at the gates as a show of force, and the quelling of any potential prisoner outbursts or riots). However, the prosecution team soon noticed that the Army dog handlers, Smith and Cardona, began to spend more and more time in the hardsite during December. It was during this month that the startling photographs of the snarling dogs in the tiers were taken.

By coupling the photos with statements from Frederick, Harman, Ambuhl, and several interrogators describing abusive treatment of detainees by the han-

---

* In 2008, a new commanding general of MDW, in his role as convening authority, disapproved the guilty verdict and sentence and filed only a written administrative reprimand in Jordan's file.

dlers, the team recommended a litany of charges against Smith and Cardona. The charges revolved around particularized misconduct: conspiring to use their dogs to see who could make the most detainees urinate or defecate on themselves; using their unmuzzled dogs to threaten and scare Ashraf Al-Juhayshi (the man nicknamed al Qaeda, or AQ); using their unmuzzled dogs in a cell search of Mohammed Bollendia, resulting in Bollendia being bitten; and scaring other detainees with their dogs. The charges involving AQ were of particular importance in Graveline's mind. They represented the first time MP soldiers were charged for actions taken at the request of MI. Multiple witnesses had identified a civilian interrogator, Steve Stefanowicz, as having Smith and Cardona use their dogs to intimidate AQ prior to interrogations. *We've drawn a line at charging MPs if there was even a hint of MI involvement that may have led to confusion about how detainees should be treated. But this conduct is so egregious. Smith and Cardona should have known better.*

The MDW extends from Fort Belvoir, outside of Alexandria, Virginia, to Fort Meade, just south of Baltimore, Maryland. Colonel Green determined that the only courtroom in the district capable of handling the media and spectators was at Fort Meade. Moving away from Fort Hood also meant a new military judge. To remove any perception of conflict of interest, the head of the Army judiciary requested that the Navy judiciary assign a judge. U.S. Marine LTC Paul McConnell received the call. With the logistics in place, Smith's trial, the first of the two, was set for March 13, 2006.

Composed of two military defense counsel, CPT Mary McCarthy and CPT Jason Duncan, Smith's defense team echoed the same arguments as the counsel before them. "Sergeant Smith . . . at the time that he was in Abu Ghraib, was twenty-two-years old, fresh out of military working dog handling school, following the orders he was given, doing his job defending freedom doing what he thought needed to be done, and what he was told by his superiors needed to be done to control the prison population at Abu Ghraib," Duncan stated, framing the defense's position in his opening statement.

The prosecution countered Duncan's arguments by presenting testimony about the training Smith received as a military dog handler. An instructor from Lackland Air Force Base, where all military dog handlers are trained, explained the tremendous emphasis placed on keeping the dogs at a safe distance, at least fifteen feet, from other people to avoid accidental bites. This testimony was reiterated by two of the Navy dog handlers also stationed at Abu Ghraib. After witnessing the IP roundup, Chief Petty Officer William Kimbro, the senior Navy dog handler on the scene, forbade his fellow naval dog handlers to enter the hard-site because of the difficulty in keeping positive control of their dogs. To round out this point, the prosecution called CPT Darren Hampton, the officer in charge of force protection at Abu Ghraib. Hampton testified that he had set up a rotating schedule to occupy the dog teams with patrolling and working on gate security and quick reaction force details. Cardona and Smith had refused, however, to integrate into the work schedule and worked their own agenda instead.

This testimony did not go unchallenged. The defense had both the instructor and the Navy dog handlers admit that while a fifteen-foot radius around a military dog is the correct textbook answer, oftentimes in operational environments, especially a prison situation, that radius is simply unavailable. Hampton also admitted that Cardona's refusal to integrate with the work schedule, at least in part, arose from a disagreement about whether using the Army dogs, trained to detect narcotics, would be useful on gate security operations.

✦

After establishing the context of Smith's training, responsibilities, and attitude at the prison,* the prosecution turned to the actual incidents of misconduct by calling PVT Ivan Frederick. Since pleading guilty, Frederick had become a key witness against the remaining defendants, although he never lost his propensity for minimizing his own role. Frederick testified that he had been on duty the night of December 12, 2003, when Graner called him to report that a detainee had pushed the plywood out of his cell window on Tier 1A. He explained that all the cells on the bottom tier had plywood over their windows to preclude any contraband or weapons being smuggled in. He continued that he had called the dog handlers down to assist in a cell search for any firearms or explosives. "We [Graner and Frederick] pulled him out and put him, the detainee . . . in the middle of floor standing up and tried to make him lay down. And then the dogs came in to . . . assist with the search."

* Evidence was also presented in support of a charge of indecent acts for an incident where Smith used his military working dog to lick peanut butter off of another male soldier's genitals and a female soldier's breasts.

"How did Mr. Bollendia react when he saw the dog?" Graveline asked.

"When the dog started barking, he got a little shaken up and a little scared and nervous, and he jumped up." Frederick related that Graner and an interpreter began telling the man, Mohammed Bollendia, to get down on the floor in a prone position. To Frederick, Bollendia appeared to be scared of the dogs. There were numerous photos of Bollendia, stripped naked and cowering from the dogs, and others depicting the snarling, leaping, unmuzzled dogs pinning the screaming man against the wall.

Graveline turned Frederick's attention to a picture that showed Frederick walking away from this scene with a smirk on his face. "Why are you walking away at that point?"

"Because I was afraid I was going to get bit by the dog. I didn't want to make no sudden movement. And so, I was walking away so I wouldn't get bit," the guard answered. Frederick testified that as this scene played out, the detainee ran across the floor, jumped on Graner, and smacked him on the side of the head. "That's when Sergeant Cardona told him . . . told Corporal Graner to push him away, that he was going to drop the leash and let the dog go. And Corporal Graner pushed him away and Sergeant Cardona dropped the leash and the dog nipped the detainee on the left leg." He finished his narrative by describing how Bollendia ran across the hallway again and jumped on Graner. Cardona released his dog again, and the dog bit Bollendia on his right leg this time.

Graveline emphasized the threat disparity between the detainee and the guards to blunt any self-defense claims. "Mr. Bollendia, how tall is he?"

"Approximately five foot, eight inches . . . five foot, nine inches."

"How much did he weigh?"

"Approximately 150 pounds."

"Corporal Graner, how big of a man is he?"

"About five foot, ten inches, approximately 200 to 210 pounds." Frederick also stated that in addition to Graner, the dog handlers and two other MPs were present.

"When Mr. Bollendia ran across the hallway, do you believe you could have physically restrained him at that point?" Graveline inquired.

"Yes, sir."

"Without the use of the dog?"

286 ♦ THE SECRETS OF ABU GHRAIB REVEALED

"Yes, sir." The guard went on to admit that the dogs had escalated the situation "a little bit more" that night.

Graveline next asked Frederick about a picture of a detainee, dressed in an orange jumpsuit, with Smith standing a few feet away, his unmuzzled dog directly in the man's face. Frederick identified the detainee as AQ and that the photo was taken in Tier 1A. The picture Graveline had originally shown Frederick was part of a series of photos, one of which showed a sandbag on AQ's head. Frederick stated that Smith had his dog bark at the detainee and then pull the sandbag from the man's head.

"How did this particular detainee react to dogs?" Graveline asked.

"He was kind of scared of the dog." Graveline followed up by asking if the detainee had been yelling, screaming, and apparently terrified. "Yes, sir," came the response.

"Who was this detainee's interrogator?"

"Big Steve." The guard said he knew that the interrogator's last name began with an *S*, but had a difficult time pronouncing it. He then described Big Steve as being "six foot, six inches tall, 250 to 260 pounds."

"Was he present when those dogs—when these photographs were taken?"

"Yes, sir, he was standing, observing from the top tier."

"Did he actually go in and interrogate al Qaeda after this occurred?"

"Yes, sir. He would instruct us to stop, and we would stop, and he would say put the inmate back in the little holding cell there that didn't have no windows and anything. And then he would come down the steps and go in and talk to him . . . shut the door behind him."

"Did you witness Sergeant Cardona do something with his dog in the isolation cell?"

Frederick began to explain. "The leash was approximately six or eight feet long and he allowed the dog to go in, and he shut the door to where it couldn't reach the inmate. He was several feet from the detainee, and he would tell the dog just to watch the detainee."

Graveline continued to explore this incident. "So, Sergeant Cardona's standing outside in the hallway of the tier?" Frederick agreed. "The dog's in the cell? And the door is shut?"

"Yes, sir."

"Steve Stefanowicz, when does he come down and interrogate?"

"He would come down in between, like when we pulled the dog off, he would come down in between and go in the room and talk to him."

Frederick related that these incidents were not the first time he had seen dogs used during interrogations. The night that Saddam Hussein was captured, the thirteenth of December 2003, three people were brought in with him. "We was down in the hallway, and I had the bite sleeve on to allow the dog to bite me.* Staff Sergeant [Christopher] Aston from the military intelligence section was observing also, and after we got done and he came up and approached us, asked if they were interested in using the dogs during interrogations. And Sergeant Smith and Sergeant Cardona said, 'Yeah, get permission from Colonel Pappas first.'" According to Frederick, Smith, Cardona, and Aston then went and spoke to Pappas. "When I came back out of the interrogation booth, I seen them standing there, and they were done talking with Colonel Pappas and I asked them if they were going to use the dogs and they said yes. They said it was all right. Colonel Pappas authorized the use of dogs as long as there was muzzles [*sic*] involved."

Frederick explained how he watched the interrogation behind a one-way mirror. The interrogators had the detainee sit in a chair next to the door while the dogs barked behind the closed door. After further interrogating the man, they opened the door and let the detainee see the dogs up close, but the dogs were never allowed inside the interrogation booth.

Finally, Graveline asked Frederick to detail a conversation he had with Cardona about a game between the dog handlers. The guard stated that Cardona had told him that he and Smith were having a contest to see how many detainees they could get "to piss on themselves." Frederick also related how he and Graner would identify "problem" detainees for Smith and Cardona by handcuffing these detainees' hands high on the cell doors. Smith and Cardona would position the dogs outside the doors, barking and snarling within a few inches of the detainees, to threaten the men.

---

* Frederick had previously testified how he and Graner would put a bite sleeve on their arms and allow Smith's and Cardona's dogs to practice attacking them.

288 THE SECRETS OF ABU GHRAIB REVEALED

On cross-examination, Duncan tried to defuse the Bollendia incident as a legitimate defense of Graner. Frederick agreed that the detainee had run toward and hit Graner prior to the handlers releasing their dogs. The focus of the questioning, however, quickly shifted to AQ.

"Did you tell Sergeant Smith and Sergeant Cardona why that detainee was there?" Duncan asked.

"I was told by his interrogator, Big Steve, that he was a member of al Qaeda."

"Big Steve told you that he had permission to use the dogs in the interrogation, didn't he?"

"Yes, sir."

"He told you to tell the dog handler, Sergeant Smith, to come down for the interrogation, didn't he?"

"Yes, sir. He said, 'Any chance you get, put the dogs on this guy, AQ.'"

"You in turn relayed that order to Specialist Smith at the time?" Frederick agreed. "You told him to use the dogs so that Steve could interrogate this guy?"

"Yes, sir."

◆

A number of witnesses, both interrogators and fellow guards, supported Frederick's testimony. Sabrina Harman described the Bollendia dog-bite incident the same as Frederick had, a cell search because of a broken-out window, with some important additions. Harman stated that the MPs had already conducted the cell search, prior to the dogs arriving on the tier. She also related how Bollendia complied with Graner's order to get on the ground, but as the dogs came closer, the scared man stood back up, eventually running at Graner.

"From your perspective, what was the man doing?" Miller asked.

"He looked like he was trying to get away from the dogs," Harman responded.

The day shift guards, SSG Christopher Ward and SGT Hydrue Joyner, related to the jury that no cell search would be conducted without the detainee restrained by handcuffs and away from the cell. They both also stated that they rarely saw the two dog handlers during their day shift. Additionally, several MI personnel testified to witnessing dog handlers threatening detainees in the tiers for no apparent reason. Steven Pescatore, a civilian contract interrogator, testified that he witnessed an MP with a black dog walking cell to cell in Tier 1A and having his dog bark at each prisoner inside. When he confronted the soldier, the

MP replied that he was simply scaring the detainees. Pescatore told him to stop it. SGT John Ketzer, a military interrogator, testified how he had seen Smith pinning two screaming juvenile detainees, one shielding the other behind him, in a cell with his dog. When Ketzer asked Smith what he was doing, the handler replied, "My buddy and I are having a contest to see if we can get them to shit themselves, because we already had some piss themselves."*

The defense began their case with SSG Christopher Aston, the interrogator who had sought and gained Colonel Pappas' approval for using the military working dogs to frighten the detainees caught the same night as Hussein. Aston told the jury that Pappas had approved the use of dogs but insisted that the dogs be muzzled if they were in the actual interrogation booth with the detainee. Aston said he and his team kept the unmuzzled dogs outside the booth but in the line of sight of the detainee inside. He stated that they did not find it to be an effective technique and never requested it again.

Aston's testimony laid the framework for Colonel Pappas to take the stand. Since they began working for Sergeant Smith in June of the previous year, Captains McCarthy and Duncan targeted Colonel Pappas as a key witness in their client's defense. McCarthy and Duncan wanted to exploit the fact that Pappas had authorized the use of dogs the night Hussein was captured and to further establish the confusion surrounding authorized interrogation techniques at Abu Ghraib.

Pappas had not escaped punishment for his role at Abu Ghraib, and Graveline had followed his case closely. The colonel had redeployed back to Germany by the time Holley, Graveline, and Tate arrived in Iraq. Consequently, Pappas fell under the jurisdiction of his home unit, 21st Theater Support Command. Holley and Graveline forwarded information to that JAG office to keep its staff abreast of any developments. In April 2005, the commanding general decided that the former commander would not be court-martialed but that he had been negligent in two ways: in not adequately training and supervising his personnel in proper interrogation techniques and in failing to obtain Lieutenant General

---

* Ketzer was also the interrogator responsible for Bollendia. He testified that he had never requested the dogs be used on him and that after suffering the dog bites Bollendia had become inconsolable.

Sanchez's permission prior to authorizing the use of military working dogs in an interrogation. The general punished Pappas for his derelictions with an Article 15, ordered a forfeiture of $8,000 of his pay over a two-month period, and issued a written reprimand for his official file. Pappas had already been relieved of his command.

Graveline was skeptical of MI personnel, especially the commanders, claiming confusion about Sanchez's policy. *Isn't that your job—to know the policy? It's awfully convenient now to say that you didn't know you had to get Sanchez's approval to use some of the "harsher" interrogation techniques.* Also unexplained were the unsigned requests for use of dogs in interrogation plans and interrogation notes for AQ on the Abu Ghraib computer server that stated Pappas had approved dogs during late December/early January. Had Pappas actually seen these requests or approved them verbally? Pappas denied seeing them; but these denials had not cleared all the doubts lingering in the prosecutors' minds. Still, the Article 15 was no slap on the wrist, either. *I wonder if all the people who are critical of Pappas receiving this punishment and not being court-martialed would think they were being let off easy if their boss brought them into his office, told them that they weren't going to get $8,000 of their paycheck, that their career was essentially over, and they were never going to be promoted again for something that the boss thought they had been negligent on.* Still, neither Miller nor Graveline was interested in seeking immunity for Pappas should more information come to light during the dog handlers' trials.

But the defense counsel pursued immunity for Pappas from the MDW commander, and with punishment already meted out by his command and no new information positively tying Pappas to the use of dogs beyond that one night, the prosecutors were in no position to argue. The MDW general granted the colonel immunity. An incredibly thin and diminutive man, Pappas took the stand under questioning by McCarthy. She directed his attention to the September visit of MG Geoffrey Miller, the general in charge of Guantanamo Bay.

"General Miller made recommendations for a change in task organization, for centralizing interrogations at one location, and the implementation of more holistic methodologies for conducting interrogations," Pappas explained. "CJTF-7 published a set of instructions, a policy memorandum on interrogations and counter-resistance policy, that became our governing document." Pappas identified Miller's team as the first people to suggest dogs as an effective tool in the execution of interrogations, especially since many Arab people were afraid of dogs.

"Exactly what impact did General Miller's visit have on your decision to use the dogs?" McCarthy asked.

"On my decision to use the dogs, it really didn't. Certainly, they got put onto our organizational chart; because of that visit, it became part of the request for forces. But it was really the CJTF-7 interrogation policy, the second one, that influenced my decision."

McCarthy began to show him four sets of interrogation notes that discussed how dogs were used on AQ with Pappas' authorization. "Sir, how do you explain that?"

"I can't."

"Sir, what guidance, if any, did you give interrogators as to how the dogs should be used during interrogations?"

"The only guidance that I gave was orally to Sergeant Aston on the one that, I believe, I approved." Pappas further admitted that he provided no training about the use of dogs during interrogations for either the dog handlers or interrogators.

As he stood to begin his cross-examination, Miller did not know exactly what to make of Pappas' testimony. As he and Graveline had discussed many times before, the senior officer's explanation of being confused about his authority to approve the use of dogs did not make sense. Nor did they know how to evaluate Pappas' statement that he never saw the interrogator's notes from the database concerning use of dogs with AQ. Still, Miller knew Pappas could clear up certain misunderstandings that had swirled around the Abu Ghraib cases from the beginning.

First, he walked Pappas through General Miller's visit. Pappas explained that General Miller's ten-day visit had improved intelligence collection by suggesting ways to improve staff organization: having analysts paired with interrogators and designating a layer of staff responsible for fusing any collected intelligence with more strategic considerations.

"You also mentioned this phrase, 'setting the conditions for interrogations,' right?" Miller asked.

"Yes."

"That phrase can be taken a lot of different ways, correct?"

"Yes, it certainly can."

"That could be as little as making sure a guard doesn't give cigarettes to a detainee that doesn't deserve cigarettes, right?"

"Yes, absolutely."

"It may mean you simply have your biggest security guards around certain detainees, right?"

"It certainly could."

"In essence, security needs to keep an eye on, be integrated with, the interrogation process, right?"

"Yes. Certainly, there's nothing necessarily bad about that phrase. What we're talking about is trying to, like in any military operation, ensure that we had a synchronized, functioning mission, working towards a singular objective." Pappas pointed out that he and his team were clear the Geneva Conventions applied in Iraq and strove to inform his personnel of these requirements with blocks of instruction and posted rules. However, he was at a loss when attempting to explain how he could authorize the use of dogs when there was a large poster prominently displayed in the interrogation center stating that "use of military working dogs—CG approval." He also admitted that his unit initially believed the detainee known as AQ was an al Qaeda member. It was later determined that he was not, and he was released.

After a flurry of questions from the jury and the lawyers following Pappas' initial questioning, Judge McConnell succinctly summed up the colonel's testimony before he left the stand. "So, the use of dogs, in your mind, would've been illegal for interrogation purposes, unless they'd come to you for approval, is that accurate?" Pappas concurred, so McConnell continued. "You only approved of the one?"

"Yes."

"Therefore, any others would've been, in your view, illegal?"

"Yes."

"You're not aware of any other use of these dogs, other than the one that you approved, is that correct, sir?"

"Except, as has been presented to me, as part of preparation for this hearing, the only one that I was aware of was the one that I personally approved for Sergeant Aston," Pappas answered.

✦

Graveline rose to address the jury for his closing argument. "This case is not a case about lack of instruction or guidance. It's a situation where a soldier consciously decided to use his military working dog, his partner and his weapon, as a toy: a toy to harass detainees, a toy to get laughs from his fellow soldiers, a toy that would menace the detainees in the hard-site at Abu Ghraib." As he moved through his argument, Graveline turned to the defense's claim that Smith was being prosecuted for simply having his dog bark. "It's not just barking; it's offering a bite . . . if it was just a dog barking, we've all heard dogs barking. But when you're jogging along, you're riding your bike, and the dog comes sprinting out of the backyard up to that fence, it's a lot different than if you just hear the dog barking, isn't it? Because the concern is I'm going to get bit, not that the dog is barking. It's about threatening them; it's about harassing them with his toy." He also addressed the question of Smith following orders from MI, specifically Big Steve's, to use his dog in interrogating AQ. Graveline attacked Smith's actions of putting his unmuzzled dog in the man's face as being patently unreasonable, pointing out the only time he had seen Colonel Pappas authorize the use of a dog, the colonel had insisted on having his dog muzzled when in the vicinity of a detainee. When viewed in the context of Smith's actions, the prosecutor argued Smith's use of his unmuzzled dog against AQ was yet one more manifestation of the amusement he got out of threatening the defenseless prisoners.

He ended his argument with one last plea to the jury. "The accused stopped being a disciplined, professional soldier. He started using his dog in whatever manner he thought it should be used. He was on his own mission at Abu Ghraib: one of fun, one of games. Do not let him cloak his abuse, his cruelty, his maltreatment in duty, in love of country, in 'I was just doing what I was told.' No, the real label we put on this is 'criminal.'"

McCarthy delivered the closing argument in Smith's defense. She attacked the government's witnesses by pointing out that Frederick and Harman were testifying under immunity and had reason to help the prosecution in order to receive sentence reductions. She also emphasized the confusion that seemed to permeate the entire Abu Ghraib prison and that left her client unaware of the correct rules and procedures. "The government wants you to believe that Sergeant Smith was part of this rogue band of soldiers who went about Abu Ghraib prison tormenting detainees for their pleasure, for their leisure. Sergeant Smith is not a criminal. Sergeant Smith is a kid from Florida who raised his right hand and took an oath to defend this country. Sergeant Smith is a son who left his family to fight for freedom. Sergeant Smith is a soldier who saved the lives of others so that they could go back to their units and to their families. Most of all, Sergeant Smith is not guilty."

The jury retired to begin its deliberations around noon on Friday, March 17. It stayed until 7 p.m. that night, all day Monday until 8 p.m., and for two more hours on Tuesday without a resolution. Bailiffs sitting in the courtroom down the hallway from the jury deliberation room reported loud shouting and arguing. During those twenty hours of deliberation, the court received word of a revote on two different occasions.

Finally, on Tuesday morning, the jury reached a split verdict, finding Smith guilty of two counts of maltreating detainees, specifically AQ and the general count of unnamed detainees, but not guilty of three other maltreatment counts, including the one dealing with Bollendia. They also found him guilty of conspiring with Cardona to scare detainees in an attempt to make them urinate and defecate, dereliction of duty, assaulting AQ with his military dog, and committing the indecent acts with the peanut butter. The jury decided Smith was not guilty of the remaining assault charges and conspiring with Graner and Frederick to harass detainees. Demonstrating the obvious intense feelings inside the jury room, the strong sentencing case presented by the defense, and the compromising necessary to reach its verdict, the jury sentenced Smith to only 179 days of imprisonment, forfeiture of $750 a month for three months, reduction to the lowest enlisted rank of private, and a bad-conduct discharge.

✦

Cardona's trial started May 22, 2006, with essentially the same evidence as Smith's, save one key witness, MG Geoffrey Miller, the former commander of the Guantanamo Bay Detention Center and the officer whose visit in September of 2003 had sparked a great deal of speculation by the defense counsel since the investigation's inception. Just as the other generals interviewed by defense counsel during the summer of 2004, Major General Miller had insisted that neither he nor his team directed or instructed anyone to abuse detainees. However, based on his answers during that interview, the defense counsel for the soldiers initially charged had decided not to call Miller to the witness stand.

In a surprising move in January 2006, when asked to submit to another interview with Smith's and Cardona's defense counsel, the general invoked his right to remain silent. According to his counsel, Miller was invoking because he had already given multiple interviews and testimony before Congress, enough to answer all possible questions about his involvement. After his invocation made the national news, Miller finally agreed to the interview with Cardona's attorneys, Harvey Volzer and CPT Kirsten Mayer. Volzer had previously represented Megan Ambuhl and was well acquainted with the personalities and facts involved in the case. Despite the other counsel's assessment of Miller's value as a witness, he wanted Miller on the witness stand.

Volzer began by establishing Miller's position as the joint task force commander of Guantanamo Bay and the general's mission to Iraq in September 2003. "We received a tasking from the Joint Chiefs of Staff through the Southern Command [SOUTHCOM] to JTF Guantanamo to provide an assistance team to go to assist CJTF-7 in Iraq, to look at intelligence, interrogation, and detention operations," Miller stated. He went on to relate that he had brought a seventeen-member team to help with this task.

"How many days were you at Abu Ghraib?" Volzer inquired.

"I believe two days."

"And I assume they took you on a tour of the prison?"

"Yes, the prison at Abu Ghraib had been attacked and ransacked, and so it was fairly in shambles, to be frank with you. And the CJTF-7 was starting to establish temporary facilities out there for the detention of the detainees and starting to put together an interrogation capability; but it was very new at that time, and they just had a couple tents, to be frank with you. And so it was just starting to do this transition from their main base at Camp Cropper at the Baghdad International Airport out to Abu Ghraib."

Volzer continued by confirming that Miller had met with Brigadier General Karpinski, Colonel Pappas, and Lieutenant Colonel Phillabaum. "When did you first broach the subject of interrogation . . . effective interrogation techniques with anyone?" the defense counsel asked.

"With General Sanchez, when we did the entrance, I told him I thought one of the most important things was to have interrogation authorities outlined in a document so that all the levels of units would have the baselines on what they could interrogate, and that the commander should promulgate those and sign them out so that every unit would understand."

"And then did you subsequently discuss that with General Karpinski?"

Miller shook his head. "No, with General Fast. General Karpinski was a military policeman and was not in the interrogation chain or had responsibility for interrogation other than custody and control." The witness then stated that his staff lawyer had also sat down with the CJTF-7's attorneys in order to work out a framework for establishing a written set of interrogation authorities that Sanchez could promulgate.

Volzer asked Miller for his assessment of the CJTF-7 MI personnel he had seen during his visit. "The interrogators at Abu Ghraib . . . were effective at the tactical level and doing very well, but they needed . . . they would need additional resources and help to work at the strategic level."

"Would you please tell the members of the panel and me, frankly, the distinction between a tactical interrogation and a strategic interrogation?"

"A tactical interrogation is a recently captured combatant or detainee who would have knowledge of local unit operations or ambushes that had . . . very localized information. It's normally only fresh for seventy-two to ninety-six hours, and so it's imperative that it's done very quickly. It's normally done by the capturing unit . . . the strategic interrogation was more focused at, for example, how is an insurgency organized? How is it recruited? So it's the next level of intelligence data that would be critical to the . . . the larger operation to ensure that we had intelligence to be able to defeat the enemy."

After some more discussion of intelligence gathering and structure, Volzer moved to the role of military police in the overall operation. "What was the role that you perceived military policemen should be doing at Abu Ghraib?"

"They should first be able to effectively conduct custody and control operations of the detainees to secure them in a detention center, and then to provide assistance to the intelligence function for transportation, for example, back and forth to the interrogation booths, and to provide passive intelligence that they would find out from the detainees," Miller answered. "By 'passive intelligence,' what I mean is what the detainees were doing each day, who they were talking to, those kind of things that would assist . . . they first assist in custody and control. Our recommendation was that they pass that information on to the military intelligence personnel to be able to assist them to know the tenor of the detainee that they would interrogate, to know who his friends in the camp were, what's his disciplinary record, those kind of things that would be, I think . . . I thought were very valuable in assisting an effective interrogation."

"We've heard the term 'setting the conditions.' What does that term mean?"

"'Setting the conditions' was exactly what we talked about. That's the passive intelligence gathering in the custody and control operations that the military police would do. Their first priority was custody and control, to ensure a safe and secure environment for the detainees that they were responsible for. And their secondary mission was to do the recommendations that we made in the development of passive intelligence, to assist in updating the military intelligence or the interrogation effort."

Volzer turned his attention to linking Miller's visit more closely with leaders in Washington, D.C. "After you left Iraq, you had a briefing at the Pentagon, correct?"

"No. After I returned to JTF Guantanamo, I forwarded the report that we had done to SOUTHCOM for their awareness, and then they forwarded it up to the Joint Chiefs of Staff. In late October or November, I was requested to come to the Pentagon to give a briefing on the assessment visit that we had conducted. It was a slide briefing to the deputy secretary of defense that outlined the recommendations . . . the assessments and recommendations."

The defense counsel ended his direct examination of Miller by asking how military working dogs were used at Guantanamo. The witness responded by saying that the dogs were not used during interrogations but only for custody and control purposes.

Miller's testimony had been consistent with what he had related during his interview with the defense counsel. Despite defense counsel's efforts, the concept of MPs "setting the conditions" clearly took on a more commonsense meaning when explained by both Miller and Pappas. Consequently, Graveline saw little use for any extensive cross-examination given the general's responses to Volzer's inquiries. Still, there were some differences between the general's and Colonel

Pappas' testimony. A few pointed questions needed to be asked.

"Did you have any conversations with Colonel Pappas about military working dogs at Abu Ghraib?"

"I did. We had a discussion about the use of military working dogs for custody and control operations."

"At any point did you talk to Colonel Pappas about using military working dogs as part of an interrogation method at Abu Ghraib?"

"No," was Miller's response. While this response differed from Pappas' testimony that it had been Miller who first suggested dogs be used in conjunction with interrogation, the prosecutors did not believe that it was a crucial point given Pappas' further testimony that he had only approved the use of dogs once and that any other use of them during interrogations would have been illegal.

✦

Even with Miller's presence, as in Smith's court-martial, the jury engaged in another round of lengthy deliberations. Finally, after hours of arguing, the military jury found Cardona only guilty of dereliction of duty and assault for placing his unmuzzled dog in a detainee's face. He was acquitted of the other more serious charges. The jury then sentenced him to a relatively light sentence, ninety days of hard labor and reduction of one rank to specialist.

As Graveline drove away from Fort Meade for the last time, he reflected on his long journey through the cases and the evidence that the team had sifted through. *Quite a winding and convoluted road. If one thing is clear from the entire mess that was Abu Ghraib, it's that neither the theory of a few bad apples nor that it was all ordered from the administration is correct . . . as always, the truth lies somewhere in between.*

Epilogue

Throughout this book, we have tried to present the facts, in the witnesses' own words, with as little commentary as possible to allow the reader to draw his or her own conclusions. However, as we traveled throughout the course of our investigation and in the years following, many people have engaged us in conversation about what happened at Abu Ghraib and, more specifically, who is to blame. Typically, most views are divided into two very divergent, and oftentimes, mutually exclusive, camps: one believes that the Bush administration, Donald Rumsfeld, or one of his aides directly ordered all of the abuse at the prison while the other holds that all of the culpability of the abuse lies completely at the feet of "seven bad apples." Many people have said that the terrorists only got what they deserved and that the soldiers' acts paled in comparison to beheadings committed by the insurgents. As you have seen in the details of the events, and is most times the case, the truth is far more complex than either extreme allows.

It is on the continuum between these two opinions that the truth about what occurred at Abu Ghraib falls. Based on our investigation, we believe that criminal culpability falls closer on the continuum to the enlisted soldiers working the night shift who were identified and prosecuted. The vast majority, and most notorious, photographs of abuse had absolutely nothing to do with intelligence collection. Many of the victims, plain and simple, were not terrorists or ever interrogated. As the evidence revealed:

Gus (the mentally impaired man on the end of the leash): held for simple assault, only identified with a magistrate number, never interrogated
the seven men in the human pyramid: held on charges ranging from rape to
burglary, all seven only identified with magistrate numbers, none were ever
interrogated
Noor Kareem (woman photographed exposing her breasts): held on prostitution
charge, only identified with a magistrate number, never interrogated, held at
Abu Ghraib for three days
Said Mohammed (photograph and video of mentally impaired man hitting his
head into the metal door and photos of him naked and covered in mud or
feces): held on charge of home invasion, only identified with a magistrate
number, never interrogated

Whether being stacked in a pyramid, photographed in sexual positions, or
threatened with snarling dogs to make them soil themselves, the detainees became, for lack of better terms, props or playthings for the night shift's amusement. One of the more illuminating aspects of this scandal is how well the day
shift soldiers performed and how well regarded they were by the detainees. MP
Staff Sergeant Ward and Sergeant Joyner admirably performed the same mission
and under the same difficult circumstances that the night shift faced.

Even with this assessment, many have questioned the criminal culpability
for these soldiers' chain of command. We did not find any orders, explicit or im-
plicit, given to these soldiers to stack naked men in a pyramid, to force detainees
to masturbate, or to lead them by a leash around the neck. Consequently, the
trial team drew a line for prosecution at individuals who actually participated or
had knowledge that these actions occurred.

Without a doubt, these abuses were made easier to accomplish by the lack
of manpower at the prison and lax supervision by the officers of the 372d MP
Company, the 320th MP Battalion, and the 205th MI Brigade. There truly
was a lack of command leadership at Abu Ghraib. We are well aware that many
would have preferred that these leaders be held to a criminal standard to account for their negligence. However, based on our investigation, we believed
that the better course of action was to take administrative action to discipline
these officers.

The conclusion that the bulk of the criminal actions lie with the soldiers of the night shift does not deny or minimize that real abuses occurred during interrogations at Abu Ghraib. As shown throughout the trials and detailed in both the Taguba and Fay reports, these abuses included stripping detainees of their clothes, putting detainees in stress positions for indeterminate time periods, assaulting detainees physically, and using unmuzzled dogs to strike the fear of possible death into AQ and others. It has been well documented that many of these abuses were perversions of techniques that were outside of the Army field manual for interrogations and had found their way to Iraq via individual soldiers and units that had previously served in Afghanistan, Miller's visit from Guantanamo, or interrogators from other governmental agencies.

In answer to the question of the Bush administration's criminal culpability for the abuses at Abu Ghraib, we did not find any direct link such as an order to a guard or an interrogator at Abu Ghraib or higher up the chain of command to treat a particular detainee one way or another. Once again, this conclusion does not ignore the fact that there were clear failures in interrogation policy throughout the DoD beginning in 2002 or possible abuses in other theaters of the global war on terror. Some of the proposed interrogation techniques were unnecessarily vague and innocuous, calling for military discipline and restraint to remain legitimate. However, policymakers forgot who would be implementing their policy changes and the military's need for bright line rules of action. Most military interrogators and intelligence analysts are very young (oftentimes between twenty- and twenty-five-years old) and inexperienced. Asking these young men and women, or MP soldiers in the case of sleep management programs, to implement techniques they were not trained to do placed too much discretion in the hands of people ill equipped to make such decisions.

With that being said, however, in terms of how those policies were implemented in Iraq, since all of the command recognized the Geneva Conventions applied to interrogations conducted in that country, the breakdown in the interrogation ranks occurred much closer to the on-ground level with a lack of oversight and clear demarcation of what was authorized. The poor training and vigilance fall squarely on the MI officers. Still, we could not prove any officer had actual knowledge of the individual abuses that occurred during certain interrogations at Abu Ghraib. Consequently, it was determined that administrative action was the appropriate way to address their negligence.

Going forward, it is important to recognize that precise, clear interrogation rules be promulgated in order to avoid the exploitation of the vague techniques that were in effect at the time of the Abu Ghraib abuses. Many concrete efforts have already been taken, especially by the military, to tighten the ambiguity of permissible interrogation techniques. The best way to ensure that detainees are treated humanely is to set clear interrogation plans, have military officer supervision, and have senior leaders throughout the federal government who will insist that legal obligations are followed.

Acknowledgments

This project has taken us several years to complete, and we owe numerous people our sincerest gratitude in helping us along the way. Any attempt to name each person singly would fill a dozen more pages and run the risk of accidental omission. However, there are certain people who have contributed to such a large degree that we would be remiss if we did not give special recognition to them.

First, this book could never have been completed without the input, editing, and guidance of Mike Holley. His memory of events and insight into his thoughts were critical in writing the narrative. From our front-row seat, neither of us has met a prosecutor or officer with the skill and heart of Mike. He was, and is, a true credit to his chosen professions, military service, and the law.

The behind-the-scenes work of getting a book published is time consuming and often overlooked. We owe a debt of gratitude to Lou Aronica for his input and editing early in the process. Many thanks to Mary Jo Malone for her many hours spent editing our spelling and grammar. We also would like to thank MAJ David Goodwin of the Missouri National Guard for allowing us to use his personal photograph on the cover of this book. More than any other person, Hilary Claggett has stood by the project, guiding it to completion with generous doses of patience and persistence.

Mike would like to thank his many friends and colleagues who offered their input and continual support. Many thanks to Paul, Rick, Gordon, and Mel. More thanks to his mentor Ed, Faith, Nate, Andy, and Casey. A special thank you to SSG Richard Russell for all of his contributions and support of this book. A significant acknowledgment goes to Mike's parents, Jeff and Shirley, for instilling in him the values and beliefs that the truth must always be told.

Finally, as at the time of this investigation and trials, the two people who have contributed the most are our spouses, Jennifer and Colleen. They have shown incredible belief in us and the project. Even after our return home, they endured countless days and nights with us "away" at the computer. They have been, at one time or another throughout this project, our counselors, sounding boards, editors, and cheerleaders. Thank you for your never-wavering energy and support.

Personnel Update

ABU GHRAIB COURTS-MARTIAL

SPC Megan Ambuhl pleaded guilty to dereliction of duty at a summary court-martial on October 30, 2004, and her sentence included a reduction in rank to private (E-1) and loss of a half month's pay. She was administratively discharged out of the Army and testified in the Graner and Harman courts-martial. Ambuhl later married Charles Graner while he was confined in prison.

SGT Santos Cardona was convicted of dereliction of duty and aggravated assault at a general court-martial on June 1, 2006. He was sentenced to ninety days of hard labor at Fort Bragg, North Carolina; his rank was reduced to specialist (E-4); and he lost $600 of pay per month for twelve months. He was subsequently transferred to a new unit and repromoted to sergeant. In 2009 he was killed in an IED attack in Afghanistan, where he was working as a U.S. civilian contractor.

SPC Armin Cruz pleaded guilty to conspiracy to maltreat and maltreatment of detainees at a special court-martial on September 11, 2004. His sentence included eight months' confinement, a reduction in rank to private (E-1), and a bad-conduct discharge. He testified in the Graner and Harman courts-martial.

SGT Javal Davis pleaded guilty to assault, dereliction of duty, and false official statement at a general court-martial on February 1, 2005, and his sentence included six months' confinement, a reduction in rank to private (E-1), and a bad-conduct discharge.

PFC Lynndie England was convicted of conspiracy to maltreat, maltreatment of detainees, and committing an indecent act at a general court-martial on

September 26, 2005. She was acquitted on a second conspiracy count. England's sentence included three years' confinement, forfeiture of all pay and allowances, a reduction in rank to private (E-1), and a dishonorable discharge.

SSG Ivan Frederick pleaded guilty to conspiracy, dereliction of duty, maltreatment of detainees, assault, and committing an indecent act at a general court-martial on October 20, 2004. His sentence included eight years' confinement (reduced from ten years due to his plea agreement), forfeiture of pay, a reduction in rank to private (E-1), and a dishonorable discharge. He testified in the courts-martial of Graner, Harman, England, M. Smith, Jordan, and Cardona. He was paroled in 2007.

CPL Charles Graner was convicted of conspiracy to maltreat detainees, dereliction of duty, assault, maltreatment of detainees, and committing an indecent act with detainees at a general court-martial on January 14, 2005. His sentence included ten years' confinement, forfeiture of all pay and allowances, a reduction in rank to private (E-1), and a dishonorable discharge. He is still incarcerated at Fort Leavenworth, Kansas.

SPC Sabrina Harman was convicted of conspiracy to maltreat detainees, dereliction of duty, and maltreatment of detainees on May 17, 2005. She was acquitted of one count of maltreatment. Her sentence included six months' confinement, a reduction in rank to private (E-1), and a bad-conduct discharge.

LTC Steven Jordan was the highest-ranking Army officer to have charges brought against him in connection with the Abu Ghraib abuse. Prior to his court-martial, eight of twelve charges against him were dismissed. On August 28, 2007, Jordan was acquitted of all charges related to prisoner mistreatment and received a reprimand for disobeying an order not to discuss his statements to Major General Fay during Fay's investigation into the abuse allegations with others. The commanding general of the Military District of Washington subsequently dismissed both the conviction and sentence in 2008.

SPC Roman Krol pleaded guilty to conspiracy and maltreatment of detainees at a special court-martial on February 1, 2005. His sentence included ten months' confinement, a reduction in rank to private (E-1), and a bad-conduct discharge.

SPC Jeremy Sivits pleaded guilty to conspiracy to maltreat, maltreatment of detainees, and dereliction of duty at a special court-martial on May 19, 2004. His sentence included the maximum one year in prison, a reduction in rank to private (E-1), and a bad-conduct discharge. He testified in the courts-martial of Graner, Harman, and England.

SGT Michael Smith was convicted of prisoner maltreatment, assault, conspiracy to maltreat, dereliction of duty, and committing an indecent act at a general court-martial on March 21, 2006. His sentence included 179 days in prison, a fine of $2,250, a reduction to private (E-1), and a bad-conduct discharge.

OTHER INDIVIDUALS ASSOCIATED WITH
THE EVENTS AT ABU GHRAIB IN 2003

CPT Christopher Brinson received a reprimand from the Army in January 2005 for his actions at Abu Ghraib. He left active duty and continued working for Congressman Mike Rogers (R-AL) as deputy chief of staff.

SGT Joseph Darby received notoriety as the "whistleblower" of the Abu Ghraib scandal. He was profiled as the "Person of the Week" on May 7, 2004, on ABC's *World News Tonight*. He received a John F. Kennedy Profile in Courage Award on May 16, 2005, in recognition of his bravery in exposing the abuses at Abu Ghraib.

BG Janis Karpinski became commanding general of the 800th Military Police Brigade, with soldiers stretching from Kuwait to northern Iraq, beginning in the summer of 2003. She was relieved of her command on April 8, 2005, and demoted to colonel on May 5, 2005, based upon allegations of dereliction of duty and shoplifting.

1SG Brian Lipinski was initially suspended from his duties with the 372nd Military Police Company on January 17, 2004, but returned to his same position on April 30, 2004.

MG Geoffrey Miller was the two-star commander of Guantanamo detention facility during 2003–2004. He and his team toured the Abu Ghraib facility in September 2003 to give their recommendations on detention and intelligence operations. He served as commanding general of detainee operations in Iraq during 2004 (after the photos were published). He retired from the Army as a two-star general after testifying in *United States v. Sergeant Santos Cardona* in 2006.

Adel Nakla, the civilian contract interpreter, was later sued along with his former employer, L-3, and CACI International, Inc., for his actions at Abu Ghraib.

COL Thomas Pappas was relieved of his command of the 205th Military Intelligence Brigade on May 13, 2005, after he received nonjudicial punishment for dereliction of duty for his actions at Abu Ghraib. His punishment included a fine of $8,000 and an official memorandum of reprimand.

LTC Jerry Phillabaum was issued a general officer memorandum of reprimand by LTG Ricardo Sanchez, who also relieved him of command of the 320th Military Police Battalion for failing to prevent the detainee abuse at Abu Ghraib. Phillabaum has retired from military service.

CPT Donald Reese was initially suspended from his duties with the 372nd Military Police Company on January 17, 2004, but he returned to command on April 30, 2004. He was promoted from captain to major and remains in the Army Reserve with the 300th Military Police Brigade of Inkster, Michigan.

Secretary of Defense Donald Rumsfeld stated in subsequent interviews that in the immediate aftermath of the publication of the abuse photos, he twice made an offer to President George W. Bush to resign the office of secretary of defense. Both of these offers were declined, but he did resign after the 2006 midterm congressional elections.

LTG Ricardo Sanchez was the three-star commander of U.S. forces in Iraq during 2003–2004. He was widely considered to be on the fast track for promotion and his fourth star, but he retired prior to any such promotion. He wrote a book about his experiences in Iraq, *Wiser in Battle: A Soldier's Story*, in 2008.

Steven Stefanowicz, the civilian contract interrogator, was later sued along with his former employer, CACI International, Inc., for his actions at Abu Ghraib.

INDIVIDUALS ASSOCIATED WITH THE ABU GHRAIB TRIALS

Paul Bergrin is currently under federal indictment on charges of racketeering (including drug trafficking, prostitution, and money laundering allegations), witness tampering, mortgage fraud, and murdering a federal witness.

MSG Michael Clemens retired from the Army Reserve after twenty-two years and has returned to work as a federal agent in Wisconsin.

CPT Christopher Graveline was promoted to the rank of major in 2005. He has left the Army and now works as an assistant U.S. attorney in Michigan.

MAJ Michael Holley left the Army in 2006 and has returned to Texas to work in a law firm.

SGT Jared Kary earned his master of business administration while still serving on active duty. He left the Army in 2007 and is now a special agent with the Federal Bureau of Investigation.

MAJ Matthew Miller was promoted to the rank of lieutenant colonel and serves as the deputy chief, U.S. Army Defense Appellate Division.

LTC Michael Mulligan was promoted to the rank of colonel. He is currently serving as the chief, U.S. Army Government Appellate Division, and is overseeing the prosecution of *United States v. Major Nidal Hasan* (the Fort Hood shooting suspect).

Gary Myers continues to practice military criminal defense law and has represented clients in multiple other high-profile cases from Iraq.

CPT Steven Charles "Chuck" Neill was promoted to the rank of major and serves an instructor in military criminal law at the U.S. Army Judge Advocate General's Legal Center and School.

COL James Pohl remains a military judge. In 2009 he was also appointed as the chief presiding officer for the Military Commissions at Guantanamo. Shortly after this appointment, he denied a request from the Obama administration to delay certain proceedings for 120 days. He stated that the commissions rules vested sole authority to delay proceedings to the appointed judges and that the requested delay was not reasonable and would not serve the interests of justice.

SSG Richard Russell completed his work for the Davis defense team and his third deployment since 9/11 and then returned to his home in Wisconsin. He left the Army Reserve in 2005 and decided to return to college.

CWO (Special Agent) Art Simril was promoted on active duty and later left the Army. He now works as a civilian investigator for the Department of Defense.

Frank Spinner continues to practice military criminal defense law and has represented clients in multiple other high-profile cases from Iraq.

COL Clyde "Butch" Tate was promoted to brigadier general in 2006 and again to major general in 2010. He now serves as the deputy judge advocate general of the U.S. Army.

Harvey Volzer continues to practice law in the Virginia/D.C. area.

Guy Womack continues to practice criminal defense law, both civilian and military, from his offices in Texas. He has represented clients in multiple other high-profile overseas military cases.

Authors' Notes

This book is primarily an exposition of the authors' investigative efforts and the trials of the soldiers accused of abuse. We have attempted to be as accurate as possible in relating the words of others. The in-court quotations are the participants' actual words. The conversations related in the book's narrative reflect the authors' best collective memories, assisted with notes where available, and should not be viewed as a verbatim transcript. In addition to these two sources, reference to outside material was necessary to present the most complete picture of the events possible. The specific additional sources used were:

Pages ix, 8–9: The quotes from the *60 Minutes II* episode came from the official CBS News transcript, "Court Martial in Iraq," as reported by Dan Rather, *60 Minutes II*, 6, no. 27, April 28, 2004.

Page 9: The *Boston Globe* ran the first headline on its editorial page on May 7, 2004. That same day the *New York Times* ran the second headline over its lead editorial. Abd-el Bari Atwan, the editor of *Al-Quds Al-Arabi*, an Arabic-language newspaper published in London, England, provided the quote we used as representative of international reaction to Samia Nakhoul, Reuters, Dubai, April 30, 2004. Finally, President Bush's statement came from an interview he gave Al Arabiya, an Arabic television network, on May 5, 2004.

Pages 10–11: The quoted questions, answers, and statements are from the May 7, 2004, Senate Armed Services Committee Hearing as reported at http://www.washingtonpost.com/wp-dyn/articles/A8575-2004May7.html.

Page 33: The article referred to in this passage was written by Christian Daven-
port and Michael Amon, "3 to Be Arraigned in Prison Abuse," *Washington
Post*, May 19, 2004.

Pages 51–52: The *Houston Chronicle* article Neill showed Graveline ran on June
22, 2004, under an Associated Press byline.

Page 54: Some of BG Antonio Taguba's biographical details were gleaned from
articles written by Laura Sullivan and David L. Greene, "Taguba Is Called
a straight arrow," *Baltimore Sun*, May 6, 2004; and Bert Eljera, "Army Ap-
points Its Second Fil-Am General," *AsianWeek*, August 1–7, 1997.

Page 137: Frederick's and Myers' statements came from an article written by
Daniel Williams, "Second Soldier to Plead Guilty to Prison Abuse," *Washington Post*, August 24, 2004.

Page 152: The details the authors knew about the court-martial of Navy LT Andrew Ledford's court-martial were supplemented by articles written by T. R.
Reid, "Trial Starts in Abu Ghraib Death," *Washington Post*, May 25, 2005;
and "SEAL Acquitted in Beating of Iraqi Prisoner Who Died," *Washington
Post*, May 28, 2005.

Pages 199–200: The block quote is from Leann Junker, "Memories of Atrocities
in Iraq Invade Mind of Monessen Man," *Pittsburgh Tribune Review*, August
29, 2004.

Page 265: England's quote about Graner comes from Kate Zernike's article, "Behind Failed Abu Ghraib Plea, a Tangle of Bonds and Betrayals," *New York
Times*, May 10, 2005.

Pages 279–82: Details of Lieutenant Colonel Jordan's court-martial, which oc-
curred after both authors left active duty, were found in several news articles
including: Josh White, "Army Drops More Charges in Officer's Abu Ghraib
Case," *Washington Post*, August 21, 2007; Dana Milbank, "Humiliation at
Abu Ghraib, and Then at the Prosecution Table," *Washington Post*, August
24, 2007; Adam Zagorin, "The Abu Ghraib Cases: Not Over Yet," *Time*,
August 29, 2007; and Josh White, "Reprimand Is Sentence for Officer at
Abu Ghraib," *Washington Post*, August 30, 2007.

Page 295: General Miller's defense counsel, MAJ Michelle Crawford, attempted
to explain the general's invocation during an interview with Josh White,
"General Asserts Right on Self-Incrimination in Iraq Abuse Cases," *Washington Post*, January 12, 2006.

Index

About the Authors

Christopher Graveline was the Army prosecutor involved in major criminal prosecutions stemming from the Abu Ghraib scandal and was the lead prosecutor of Lynndie England. Previously, he served as a prosecutor with the 101st Airborne Division; the appellate division in Washington, D.C., and V Corps; and on deployments to Kosovo and Iraq. Graveline now works for the U.S. Department of Justice, where in 2008 he was one of the attorneys responsible for the successful human rights prosecution of Chuckie Taylor, the son of the former Liberian dictator, Charles Taylor, for torture.

Michael Clemens served as a military policeman and investigator in the U.S. Army Reserve for twenty-two years, deploying to and conducting criminal investigations in Bosnia, Croatia, Hungary, Kuwait, and Iraq. As a civilian, he has worked as a vice and organized crime detective, a deputy U.S. Marshal, and a federal agent. He served as the noncommissioned officer in charge of MP operations and Iraqi police training in Mosul before becoming the Abu Ghraib prosecution team's special investigator. For his work related to the Abu Ghraib investigations, Clemens received the Meritorious Service Medal and the Legion of Merit, the nation's sixth-highest award.